乞力马扎罗山的雪

海明威短篇小说精选

名家导读有声版

英汉对照·插图版

[美]海明威 著
朱振武 主编
杨鸿雁 任慧芝 副主编

華東理工大學出版社
EAST CHINA UNIVERSITY OF SCIENCE AND TECHNOLOGY PRESS
·上海·

图书在版编目(CIP)数据

乞力马扎罗山的雪：海明威短篇小说精选：英汉对照·名家导读有声版 / 朱振武主编. —上海：华东理工大学出版社，2019.2
（经典短篇双语阅读）
ISBN 978-7-5628-5468-5

Ⅰ.①乞…　Ⅱ.①朱…　Ⅲ.①英语—汉语—对照读物 ②短篇小说—小说集—美国—现代　Ⅳ.①H319.4：I

中国版本图书馆CIP数据核字(2018)第093323号

策划编辑 / 信　艳
责任编辑 / 芮建芬
装帧设计 / 风信子
插　　画 / 李　丹
出版发行 / 华东理工大学出版社有限公司
地址：上海市梅陇路130号，200237
电话：021-64250306
网址：www.ecustpress.cn
邮箱：zongbianban@ecustpress.cn
印　　刷 / 上海盛通时代印刷有限公司
开　　本 / 890mm × 1240mm　1/32
印　　张 / 9.375
字　　数 / 217千字
版　　次 / 2019年2月第1版
印　　次 / 2019年2月第1次
定　　价 / 39.80元

扫一扫，听有声导读

走进上海师范大学

博士生导师朱振武教授的

文学课堂

聆听该音频，你可以获知：

1. 海明威的传奇人生及其写作风格。
2.《杀手》精彩导读。
3. 什么时候阅读经典。

经典阅读的当下意义

朱振武

有个学生要考我的研究生，我回信给她说，考我的研究生，要能够静下心来读书，不枉过三年，不要只顾蝇头微利，不要陷入琐碎，不要流于肤浅，立足在眼前，但立志要高远，至少要做一个文化人，而不是个只顾眼前利益的小市民，渐次达到人生较高的境界。这个学生很坚决，她回信说，读研的目的不仅是学习更多的知识，更重要的是充实人生，完善人格，提高自己的精神境界。回答得很好，正是我要的答案，后来她得偿所愿，心无旁骛地读起书来，再后来表现出很强的后劲。

要否读书，读书重要与否，重要到什么程度，这些在不久前被看作是只有白痴才会问的问题在当下还真成了问题。我们的孔老夫子曾说，不读诗，无以言。十七世纪英国哲人弗朗西斯·培根说得好，读书使人充实，不常读书者须欺世有术，始能无知而显有知。人之才智但有滞碍，无不可读适当之书使之顺畅。读书，首要的是读什么书呢？当然是读经典著作。什么是经典？常念为经，常数为典，是为经典。经典就是经得起反复重复的文本，其之所以得以如此就在于其丰厚的文化蕴含，就在于我们每次对之重温都能从中开掘出熏染和涤荡我们灵魂的东西。

同样一篇文章或一个理论，能经得起人反复咀嚼。经典还具有不可超越性，更不是我们眼前这些急功近利的东西所能替代的。著名电视导演张纪中说：“经典是不能超越的。你可以在他旁边再垒一座山，却无法超越这座山。”经典就是这样的一些作品，常读常新，且不会过时或落伍。历史文化学者易中天说得好，经典就是最有价值、最有意义的著作。他还引用中国那句老话教育大家，“取法其上，得乎其中。取法其中，得乎其下。”“取法其上”，对于我们读书人来说，当然就是阅读经典。

有个读者在网上留帖子说，没有读意大利的伊塔洛·卡尔维诺的《为什么读经典》，那是旷世奇憾。旷世不旷世不敢说，遗憾是肯定有的。卡尔维诺对经典的阐发却是深刻，他认为，经典作品是一些产生某种特殊影响的书，他们要么本身以难忘的方式给我们的想象力打下印记，要么乔装成个人或集体的无意识隐藏在深层记忆中，经典作品是一本不会耗尽它要向你说的一切东西的书。他还认为，经典作品是这样的一些书，它们带着先前解释的气息走向我们，背后拖着它们经过文化或多种文化（或只是多种语言和风俗）时留下的足迹。这些话说得真是深刻，我曾经在一次关于经典阅读的讲座上稍事夸张地说：经典文学是这样的书：

它是使没有头脑的人变得有头脑，没有文化的人变得有文化的书，是使肤浅之徒变得稳重、呆板之人变得诙谐、迟滞之人变得睿智、短视之人变得远见、丑陋之人变得俊拔、狭隘之人变得宽容、妒忌变得羡慕、贪婪变得节制、吝啬变得慷慨、苛刻变得宽容、卑微变得高贵、猥琐变得雍容、空虚变得充实、奢靡变得简朴、情调低俗变得品位高雅、百无聊赖变得丰富多彩的书，是那些让你得到调整、使你得到憩息、能够与你沟通、可以帮你排遣郁闷的书，是能够为你提供生活坐标的书，是可以让你放松身心、宣泄激愤的书，是使你保持坦荡荡免于常戚戚的书，是使你高出只掌握某种一般技能的人的书，是使你摆脱生存尴尬、尽享人生乐趣的书，是使你懂得一个人为什么要活着的书，是使高级动物有别于其他动物的书。

有个听众问我什么时候读经典，我戏谑地回答说："当你神情抑郁、兴趣寡淡的时候，当你情场失意、官场失落的时候，当你挫败连连、股市大跌的时候，当你参透人生、看破红尘的时候，当你失业下岗的时候，当你屡试不中的时候，当你穷得只剩下钱的时候，当你辗转反侧、夜不成寐、茶饭不思、百无聊赖的时候，当你不知道人为什么而活着的时候，当你不知道你到底有什么用处的时候，当你在充满喧哗与骚动的都市里无处逃逸的时候，不要想入非非，不要萌生他想，尽情享受经典阅读带给你的乐趣吧！"

为什么要读经典？易中天说得好，就是因为能从经典中读人生，读智慧，读社会。我颇以为然，所以，每天没有不看书的时候，没有不接触经典的时候，否则就觉得怅然若失，缺少了根基，没了底气，丢了自信。

这套四卷本的"美国名家短篇小说精选"所收作家作品就是前面所说的那样的经典之作，很具代表性，基本上让我们看到了美国短篇小说的整体面貌，而且这些作品仍与当下有着很强的意义关联，因此，其读者群也比较宽广。画龙点睛般的导读、简练严谨的注释和紧扣源语的译文为读者体会作品主旨意蕴、创作技巧和学习、欣赏原文文本提供了很大便利。

这套书的撰译者都是在高校里专门从事英美文学教学和研究的人员，主编是上海师范大学的朱振武，副主编是上海师范大学的冯德河、蓝云春，山东大学的高静，三峡大学的陈月红、杨鸿雁、黎智林、任慧芝，以及上海大学外国语学院的张惠英。大家在多年的教研实践中达成一个共识：一个不读经典作品的人是不完整的人，没有一定的英美文学经典作品的阅读量，一个人的英语水平是不可能达到较高层次的，他在这个方面的整体文化素养肯定是有缺陷的。因此，我们向各位读者奉上这套“美国名家短篇小说精选”。

关于欧内斯特·海明威

杨鸿雁

欧内斯特·米勒·海明威（Ernest Miller Hemingway, 1899—1961）是美国现代主义作家、新闻记者，海明威式英雄在现实生活中的形象代言人。海明威于1953年获得普利策奖，并于1954年获得诺贝尔奖，成为荣获诺贝尔文学奖的第五个美国人。海明威的形象与美国现代文学史上几个重要的意象联系在一起：放逐于巴黎的美国侨民，迷惘的一代的代言人，打不败的海明威式英雄（硬汉形象），冰山创作原理等等。这几个意象并非只是简单的堆砌，它们的有机组合建构出海明威传奇般的生活经历以及起伏跌宕的思想轨迹和创作历程。海明威一生的足迹遍布世界各地，喜欢户外生活的天性以及后来多年的记者生涯使得他的作品有着广阔的社会生活背景，并涵盖了他个人惊险刺激的生活方式。两条并行的主线始终贯穿于海明威的文学创作以及现实生涯。一条主线是海明威个人的战争和游历经历，另一条主线是他的数次艳遇和婚史。海明威个人的生活方式和经历在一定程度上是他文学创作生涯的有力注脚。

海明威出生于美国芝加哥郊外的橡树园。父亲是一位酷爱野外运动的医生，母亲是一名虔诚的新教徒。他与当医生的父亲一起行医、狩猎及打鱼的经历，构成了之后尼克·亚当斯故事系列的重要素材。从1913年到1917年，海明威就读于当地的中学。在学校期间，他不仅体育天赋非常突出，而且文学天赋初显，是其所在中学的校报编辑。海明威高中毕业后，没有选择继续进大学深造，而是通过一位亲戚的介绍来到了堪萨斯州，成为《堪萨斯明星报》的一名记者。

在海明威中学尚未毕业的时候，1914年第一次世界大战爆发。1918年5月，海明威作为红十字会的司机，开赴意大利前线。不久他于7月在前线身负重伤。海明威作为在意大利受伤的第一个美国人，得到了意大利政府所授予的十字军功勋章和银质勇敢勋章。海明威受伤后住在意大利米兰的一所医院里，他爱上了来自美国华盛顿年长他七岁的护士库洛斯基（Agnes Von Kurowsky）。这段浪漫史以库洛斯基钟情于一位意大利军官而告幻灭。

一战结束后海明威回到美国，成了他家乡橡树园的战斗英雄。当英雄的光环散尽，海明威发现自己无所事事，荒废时日，与母亲的观念冲突也日益凸现。海明威离家前往芝加哥，想通过写作来谋生。在芝加哥期间，海明威遇到了他的婚姻生涯以及文学生涯中的两个重要人物：一个是"高个子红色短发女孩"哈德莱·理查逊（Hadley Richardson，1891—1979），他们于1921年秋结为伉俪。另一个是海明威文学生涯中的第一位贵人：舍伍德·安德森（Sherwood Anderson，1876—1941）。安德森在扶持文学新人方面几乎是不遗余力，海明威、福克纳等都受到过他慷慨的扶持。他热心地推荐海明威到巴黎去游历。

在巴黎，海明威成为侨居在巴黎的众多美国文学艺术家中的一员。通过安德森的书信引荐，海明威走进了位于巴黎花园街27号斯坦因（Gertrude Stein,1874—1946）的文学艺术沙龙，并在那里以其专注的眼睛、四射的青春活力以及文学青年对文学事业的热望而受到热忱的接待和衷心的欢迎，继而成为那里的常客。

1925年4月底，海明威在法国遇到了与自己年纪相仿但却已是美国畅销书作家的F. S. 菲茨杰拉德（F. Scott Fitzgerald,1896—

1940)，并与他一见如故。菲茨杰拉德给予海明威不少帮助。海明威认为菲茨杰拉德的才能“像一只粉蝶翅膀上的粉末构成的图案那样地自然”，但在其短篇小说《乞力马扎罗山的雪》里，他把菲茨杰拉德称作是被对富人莫名的敬畏给毁了的年轻人。

1925年海明威迎来了文学生涯的一个重要转折点。同年10月，海明威在美国纽约首次发行处女作《在我们的时代里》(*In Our Time*)。

1926年海明威的文学生涯开始走向辉煌。这年10月，《太阳照常升起》(*The Sun Also Rises*) 发表。这本书是海明威的第一部长篇小说，带有半自传性质。《太阳照常升起》被认为是美国迷惘的一代的代表作。“迷惘的一代”这一个词语道出了战后一代年轻人的心态：战争使传统的精神信仰之柱坍塌，现下纸醉金迷的生活所掩盖的是他们精神世界的极度空虚以及梦醒后无路可走的悲凉。这部小说发表后，受到批评界和读者的一致欢迎，小说中主人公的生活方式被现实中的年轻人竞相效仿，“迷惘的一代”成为当时一张时髦的个性标签。

同年，海明威创作了《春潮》(*The Torrents of Spring*)。

1927年，《没有女人的男人》(*Men Without Women*) 发表。在这些小说中，少年尼克的形象渐趋清晰和完整。尼克的形象无疑有着海明威少年生活、记者生涯和战争生活中的痕迹。

1929年长篇小说《永别了，武器》(*A Farewell to Arms*)的发表使得海明威名利双收。小说以弗雷德里克·亨利(Frederic Henry)与凯瑟琳·巴克利 (Katherine Barkley) 的爱情故事为主线，揭示了战争对于个人幸福的摧残以及对普通人的理想和激情的愚弄，带有明显的反战情绪。《永别了，武器》出版时正值美国的经济危机时期，但小说却久居畅销书榜首。这部长篇小说的出版将海明威推向了文学大师的宝座，而此时的海明威刚至而立之年。

三十年代初期，海明威发表的作品比较少，除了通讯报道外，主要有《死在午后》(*Death in the Afternoon*, 1932) 和《非洲的青山》(*Green Hills of Africa*, 1935)。《非洲的青山》是描写狩猎的纪实性作品。《死在午后》是部关于斗牛的专著，反映了海明威丰富的斗牛知识。他的小说《打不败的人》和《太阳照常升起》中斗牛士 (matador) 所展现的压力下的优雅，体现了海明威式的硬汉形象。在《死在午后》中，海明威阐述了自己的创作体会，他把创作原理比喻成冰山："一座冰山的仪态之所以庄严，是因为它只有八分之一露出水面。"[1] 从非洲狩猎回来，海明威于1936年发表了两篇较长的以狩猎为背景的短篇小说《乞力马扎罗山的雪》(*The Snows of Kilimanjaro*) 和《弗朗西斯·麦康伯短促的幸福生活》(*The Short Happy Life of Francis Macomber*)。这两部小说获得了巨大的成功，其主题仍旧是死亡与救赎。

1937年2月，海明威作为北美报业联盟的战地记者与玛莎在欧洲会合，共赴西班牙报道西班牙内战，并于同年在巴塞罗那共度圣诞。西班牙内战期间，海明威发表了《有钱人和没钱人》(*To Have and Have Not*, 1937)，剧本《第五纵队》以及《首辑四十九篇》合集 (*The Fifth Column and the First Forty-Nine Stories*, 1938)。《首辑四十九篇》包括了海明威在其他小说集里所发表的很多著名的短篇小说。西班牙内战结束后不久，1940年10月，海明威以西班牙内战为背景的长篇小说《丧钟为谁而鸣》(*For Whom the Bell Tolls*) 出版。这是一部反法西斯小说。主人公罗伯特·乔丹 (Robert Jordan) 是美国一位在大学教西班牙语的教师，他自愿来到西班牙参加国际纵队。这部作品的叙事以同心圆方式展开，同心圆的中心人物是乔丹，中心事件是炸桥。圆圈依次荡开，反映了内战中各种势力的纷繁纠纷。主人公乔丹最后身负重伤，生死未卜。这部小说是欧美现

1 海明威：《死在午后》，金绍禹译，上海：上海译文出版社，2004年，第193页。

代文学中反映西班牙内战的优秀作品，也在一定程度上反映了海明威的左派思想和理想主义色彩。

1950年海明威发表了《过河入林》(*Across the River and into the Trees*)，评论界对之反应冷淡。但两年后出版的《老人与海》(*The Old Man and the Sea*, 1952)却被认为是海明威创作生涯的巅峰之作。《老人与海》篇幅较短，故事情节简单。故事写古巴老渔夫圣地亚哥(Sandiago)已经有84天没打到鱼了，第85天出海时有一条1500磅左右的马林鱼上钩。这条鱼将圣地亚哥的船拖到深海，经过艰苦的搏斗，圣地亚哥终于制服了马林鱼，但在返航途中却遭到鲨鱼群的袭击，靠岸时，这条马林鱼只剩下一根长长的白骨。圣地亚哥被认为是海明威式的英雄即硬汉形象的提炼和升华。小说通过圣地亚哥所驾驶的挂着破帆的孤舟在沧海深处的历险，展现了苍年老人圣地亚哥在必败的命运前所显示的非凡的勇气和优雅的风范。“人不是为失败而生的。一个人可以被毁灭，但不能给打败。”[1]圣地亚哥在战胜第一条鲨鱼后所说的这句话成为用来概括海明威式英雄的经典名言。《老人与海》发表后受到评论界和读者的高度认可，1953年这部小说获得普利策奖。1954年海明威获得诺贝尔奖时，《老人与海》在颁奖词中被认为是海明威“叙事技巧的典范”。[2]

《老人与海》的发表为海明威赢得了国际声誉，但此时他的身体却是每况愈下。

1961年7月2日，海明威在爱达荷州(Idaho)的凯特丘姆(Kethum)用一把双管猎枪决绝地结束了自己的生命。海明威的自尽，到底是“迷惘的一代”情结的延续，还是“海明威式英雄”的不愿意屈从于既定命运的写照，这个疑问一直伴随着所有喜爱海明威的读者。

1　海明威：《海明威文集·春潮·老人与海》，吴劳译，上海：上海译文出版社，2004年，第204页。

2　建钢等编译：《诺贝尔文学奖颁奖/获奖演说全集》，北京：中国广播电视出版社，1993年，第409页。

目　　录

Ernest Miller Hemingway

1899 – 1961

Ernest Miller Hemingway was an American journalist, novelist, and short-story writer, who won the Nobel Prize in Literature in 1954. His style—the iceberg theory—had a strong influence on 20th-century fiction, while his adventurous lifestyle and his public image brought him admiration from later generations.

Hills Like White Elephants[1]
白象似的群山

① white elephant：“白象”用来指代无用而累赘的东西、沉重的包袱。女孩几次说到群山像白象，而远处山体朦胧的轮廓很像女人怀孕的肚子，可见她对怀孕生子是非常憧憬的；但是对于男主人公来说，群山像不像白象与他无关，他只想自私地让女孩去做那个所谓的“简单”的小手术，这样一来，女孩肚子里的小生命成了他沉重的包袱与累赘。作者用“白象”来形容群山，赋予题目极大的理解空间。

《白象似的群山》(*Hills Like White Elephants,* 1927)堪称海明威写作风格的经典体现，讲述一个美国男人和姑娘在一个西班牙小站等火车期间发生的事。本篇小说并没有过多的主观或背景上的描写，而只是将这一幕幕场景如实地呈现在读者面前，然而开放式的开头却给我们提供了不少信息。从某种角度来看，女孩吉格年纪不大，不会说西班牙语，一直处于男主人公也就是那个美国人的男性权势之下，对他的依赖很大，缺乏抗争到底的勇气。而那个美国人却会说西班牙语，有着绝对的主导权和决定权。虽然小说从头到尾并没有直接说明他们所谈论的到底是个什么手术，但是凭着我们的生活阅历和小说中两个人的对话，我们可以肯定那就是堕胎手术。于是小说中的神秘面纱消失了，男主人公的自私本性和女孩的软弱与无奈也得到了进一步体现。但是本篇小说又绝非道德小说那么简单。因而，小说的结尾也就是什克洛夫斯基[①]所说的“消极”结尾或“零度”结尾 (“negative” or “degree zero” endings)，即结尾似乎没有严格意义上的封闭。因此，我们只知道火车五分钟之后到，女主角在等男主人公，也在等火车，至于她有没有去做堕胎手术以及和男主人公的关系，小说结尾处并没有交代清楚，给了读者很大的想象空间。至此，海明威那电报式简洁明了的语言以及冰山创作理论得到了充分的体现。

---

① 什克洛夫斯基：Viktor Shklovsky(1893—1984)，苏联时期的批评家、作家和宣传家，也是苏联文学理论中形式主义的发起人之一。

The hills across the valley of the Ebro[1] were long and white. On this side there was no shade and no trees and the station was between two lines of rails in the sun. Close against the side of the station there was the warm shadow of the building and a curtain, made of strings of bamboo beads, hung across the open door into the bar, to keep out flies. The American and the girl with him sat at a table in the shade, outside the building. It was very hot and the express from Barcelona[2] would come in forty minutes. It stopped at this junction for two minutes and went on to Madrid.

"What should we drink?" the girl asked. She had taken off her hat and put it on the table.

"It's pretty hot," the man said.

"Let's drink beer."

"*Dos cervezas*[3]," the man said into the curtain.

"Big ones?" a woman asked from the doorway.

"Yes. Two big ones."

The woman brought two glasses of beer and two felt pads. She put the felt pads and the beer glasses on the table and looked at the man and the girl. The girl was looking off at the line of hills. They were white in the sun and the country was brown and dry.

"They look like white elephants," she said.

"I've never seen one," the man drank his beer.

"No, you wouldn't have."

"I might have," the man said. "Just because you say I wouldn't have doesn't prove anything."

---

① 埃布罗河，位于西班牙东北部，东南流向，是西班牙最长和最大的河流。
② 巴塞罗那，位于西班牙东北部地中海沿岸，是西班牙第二大城市、第一大工商城和港口。
③ Dos cervezas：西班牙语，"cerveza"指的是"啤酒"，在西班牙语中属于阴性名词；而"dos"为量词，意为"两(杯或者瓶等)"。

埃布罗河河谷的彼岸，绵延着白色的群山。而这一边却无处成荫，一棵树也没有。阳光下，车站就在两条铁路线的中间。靠车站的一边，一栋房屋投下了暖烘烘的影子，竹珠子编成的门帘挂在酒吧间进门处挡苍蝇。一个美国人和跟他一起的那个女孩坐在那所房屋外面阴凉处的一张桌子旁边。天气十分炎热，从巴塞罗那来的快车40分钟后才到站。列车在此站只停靠两分钟，然后继续开往马德里。

“我们喝什么呢？”女孩问。她已经摘下了帽子，放在了桌子上。

“天气真热，”男人说。

“我们喝啤酒吧。”

“两杯啤酒，”男人冲着门帘里的人喊道。

“大杯的吗？”一个女人站在门口问道。

“对。两大杯。”

那女人端来两大杯啤酒和两个毡制杯垫。她把杯垫和啤酒放在桌子上，看了看那个男人和那个女孩。女孩正眺望着远方群山的轮廓。阳光下，山都是白色的，而乡野却是一片灰褐色，显得干巴巴的。

“它们看起来像一群白象，”她说。

“我从未看到过大象，”男人喝着啤酒。

“对，你不会看到的。”

“我也许看到过，”男人说，“就你说我不会看到，并不能说明什么。”

The girl looked at the bead curtain. "They've painted something on it," she said. "What does it say?"

"Anis del Toro[①]. It's a drink."

"Could we try it?"

The man called "Listen" through the curtain. The woman came out from the bar.

"Four reales[②]. "

"We want two Anis del Toro."

"With water?"

"Do you want it with water?"

"I don't know," the girl said. "Is it good with water?"

"It's all right."

"You want them with water?" asked the woman.

"Yes, with water."

"It tastes like licorice," the girl said and put the glass down.

"That's the way with everything."

"Yes," said the girl. "Everything tastes of licorice. Especially all the things you've waited so long for, like absinthe[③] .

"Oh, cut it out."

"You started it," the girl said. "I was being amused. I was having a fine time."

"Well, let's try and have a fine time."

"All right. I was trying. I said the mountains looked like white elephants. Wasn't that bright[④]?"

---

① Anis del Toro：西班牙语，一种茴香酒，无色的酒精饮料。
② reale：一种银币，旧时在西班牙和拉丁美洲国家通用的货币单位，1 雷阿尔等于 1/8 比索。
③ absinthe：苦艾酒，一种带有茴芹味的高酒精度蒸馏酒。
④ bright：在这里指"聪明的，机灵的；(显示出)头脑灵活的"。

女孩看着珠帘。“他们在上面画了些东西，”她说，“那上面写的是什么？”

“托罗茴香酒。一种饮料。”

“我们也能尝尝吗？”

男人隔着珠帘喊了一声“喂”。那女人从酒吧间走了出来。

“四雷阿尔。”

“我们要两杯托罗茴香酒。”

“兑水吗？”

“你想兑水到里面吗？”

“我不知道，”女孩说，“兑了水好喝吗？”

“好喝。”

“你们要兑水吗？”女人问。

“好，要兑了水的。”

“这种酒喝起来味道像甘草一样，”女孩说完，放下了酒杯。

“一切皆如此。”

“是的，”女孩说，“一切事物都有甘草一样的味道。尤其是你盼望已久的东西，就跟苦艾酒一样。”

“哦，别再说了。”

“你先开始的，”女孩说，“我刚才一直觉得挺有意思的。我一直开心着呢。”

“嗯。让我们想办法开心点。”

“好啊。我一直在努力。我说那些山看起来像一群白象。难道那么说不妙吗？”

"That was bright."

"I wanted to try this new drink: That's all we do, isn't it — look at things and try new drinks?"

"I guess so."

The girl looked across at the hills.

"They're lovely hills," she said. "They don't really like white elephants. I just meant the coloring of their skin through the trees."

"Should we have another drink?"

"All right."

The warm wind blew the bead curtain against the table.

"The beer's nice and cool," the man said.

"It's lovely," the girl said.

"It's really an awfully simple operation, Jig," the man said. "It's not really an operation at all."

The girl looked at the ground the table legs rested on.

"I know you wouldn't mind it, Jig. It's really not anything. It's just to let the air in."

The girl did not say anything.

"I'll go with you and I'll stay with you all the time. They just let the air in and then it's all perfectly natural."

"Then what will we do afterward?"

"We'll be fine afterward. Just like we were before."

"What makes you think so?"

"That's the only thing that bothers us. It's the only thing that's made us unhappy."

The girl looked at the bead curtain, put her hand out and took hold of two of the strings of beads.

"妙极了！"

"我想尝尝这种没喝过的饮料：那就是我们所做的一切，不是吗——看看风景，尝尝没喝过的饮料？"

"我想是这样的。"

女孩遥望着远处的群山。

"这些山多么秀丽啊，"她说，"它们并不真的看上去像一群白象。我只是在说，透过那些树林，山体的颜色。"

"我们再喝一杯？"

"行啊。"

温暖的风将珠帘吹得拂过桌子。

"这啤酒不赖，也爽口，"男人说。

"棒极了，"女孩说。

"那真的只是一种很简单的手术，吉格，"男人说，"或者连手术也谈不上。"

女孩盯着桌腿下的地面。

"我知道你不会介意的，吉格。真的没什么。只要吸进去一点空气就行了。"

女孩什么也没说。

"我会跟你一起去，一直陪着你。他们只是注入空气，然后一切就恢复自然啦。"

"那么我们以后呢？"

"我们以后会很好啊，就跟我们以前一样。"

"你为什么会这么想？"

"因为那是唯一烦扰我们的事情，也是唯一让我们不开心的事情。"

女孩又看着珠帘，伸手抓起两串珠子。

"And you think then we'll be all right and be happy."

"I know we will. You don't have to be afraid. I've known lots of people that have done it."

"So have I," said the girl. "And afterward they were all so happy."

"Well," the man said, "if you don't want to you don't have to. I wouldn't have you do it if you didn't want to. But I know it's perfectly simple[①]. "

"And you really want to?"

"I think it's the best thing to do. But I don't want you to do it if you don't really want to."

"And if I do it you'll be happy and things will be like they were and you'll love me?"

"I love you now. You know I love you."

"I know. But if I do it, then it will be nice again if I say things are like white elephants, and you'll like it?"

"I'll love it. I love it now but I just can't think about it .You know how I get when I worry."

"If I do it you won't ever worry?"

"I won't worry about that because it's perfectly simple."

"Then I'll do it. Because I don't care about me."

"What do you mean?"

"I don't care about me."

"Well, I care about you."

① simple：这个单词在小说中出现了很多次，而且大多数都是出现在那个美国人的话语中。他越是想向女孩说明那个手术很简单，他自私的本性就显露得越明显。

"你还觉得从那以后我们就会没事了，开开心心的。"

"我知道我们会的。你没必要怕。我认识许多做过这种手术的人。"

"我也认识不少，"女孩说，"手术以后他们都过得那么开心。"

"好吧，"男人说，"如果你不想做手术那就不必去做。如果你不愿意，我不会勉强你。但是我知道那相当简单。"

"你真的希望我做吗？"

"在我看来，那是最好的办法。但如果你真的不想做，我不想你去做。"

"如果我做，你会开开心心的，一切就跟原来一样，而你还会爱着我？"

"我现在就爱着你。你知道我是爱你的。"

"我知道。但是如果我做了，那么情况就又会好起来，倘若我说什么东西像白象，你会喜欢？"

"我会喜欢的。我现在就喜欢，只是我没办法想那些。你知道我心烦的时候就会是怎样的。"

"如果我去做手术，你就不会心烦？"

"我不会心烦了，因为那确实很简单。"

"那我决定做。因为我不在乎自己。"

"你这话是什么意思？"

"我不在乎自己。"

"喔！我在乎你啊！"

"Oh, yes. But I don't care about me. And I'll do it and then everything will be fine."

"I don't want you to do it if you feel that way."

The girl stood up and walked to the end of the station. Across, on the other side, were fields of grain and trees along the banks of the Ebro. Far away, beyond the river, were mountains. The shadow of a cloud moved across the field of grain and she saw the river through the trees.

"And we could have all this," she said. "And we could have everything and every day we make it more impossible."

"What did you say?"

"I said we could have everything."

"We can have everything."

"No, we can't."

"We can have the whole world."

"No, we can't."

"We can go everywhere."

"No, we can't. It isn't ours any more."

"It's ours."

"No, it isn't. And once they take it away, you never get it back."

"But they haven't taken it away."

"We'll wait and see."

"Come on back in the shade," he said. "You mustn't feel that way."

"I don't feel any way," the girl said. "I just know things."

"I don't want you to do anything that you don't want to do—"

"Nor that isn't good for me," she said. "I know. Could we

“噢，是的。但是我对自己却不是那么的在乎。而且我去做那手术，一切都会好起来。”

“如果你是那样想的话，我可不愿让你去做手术。”

女孩站起身来，走到车站的另一头。铁路对面，另一边，埃布罗河的两岸都是粮田和树木。远处，河的那边，是起伏的山峦。一片云影掠过粮田；透过树林，她看到了河流。

“我们原本可以拥有这一切，”她说，“我们原本可以拥有一切，但每过一天，我们只能让它变得越来越不可能。”

“你刚才说了什么？”

“我说我们原本可以拥有一切的。”

“我们可以的。”

“不，我们不能。”

“我们可以拥有整个世界。”

“不，我们不能。”

“我们可以去任何地方。”

“不，我们不能。这已经不再是我们的了。”

“是我们的。”

“不，不是的。一旦他们拿走了，你便永远不可能再收回。”

“但他们并没有拿走。”

“我们等着瞧吧。”

“回到阴凉处来吧，”他说，“你千万不要再那么想了。”

“我并没有胡思乱想，”女孩说，“我只知道事实。”

“我不想你去做任何你不想做的事情——”

“或者对我不怎么好的事，”她说，“我知道。我们再来杯啤

have another beer?"

"All right. But you've got to realize—"

"I realize," the girl said. "Can't we maybe stop talking?"

They sat down at the table and the girl looked across at the hills on the dry side of the valley and the man looked at her and at the table.

"You've got to realize," he said, "that I don't want you to do it if you don't want to. I'm perfectly willing to go through with it if it means anything to you."

"Doesn't it mean anything to you? We could get along."

"Of course it does. But I don't want anybody but you. I don't want any one else. And I know it's perfectly simple."

"Yes, you know it's perfectly simple."

"It's all right for you to say that, but I do know it."

"Would you do something for me now?"

"I'd do anything for you."

"Would you please please please please please please please stop talking?"

He did not say anything but looked at the bags against the wall of the station. There were labels on them from all the hotels where they had spent nights.

"But I don't want you to," he said, "I don't care anything about it."

"I'll scream," the girl said.

The woman came out through the curtains with two glasses of beer and put them down on the damp felt pads. "The train comes in five minutes," she said.

酒好吗？”

“好的。但你必须明白——”

“我明白，”女孩说。“我们能不能不要再谈下去了？”

他们在桌边坐了下来。女孩又遥望着对面河谷干涸的那侧的群山，男人则看了看女孩，又看了看桌子。

“你必须明白，”他说，“如果你不想做，我不会非要你去做。我非常乐意去承受这一切，如果这对你很重要的话。”

“这难道对你不重要吗？我们还得继续走下去啊。”

“这对我当然也重要。但我只想要你一个人。我不想再要别的什么人。再说，我知道这手术相当简单。”

“对，你就知道那相当简单。”

“随你怎么说，但我真的知道。”

“你现在能为我做点事吗？”

“我愿为你做任何事情。”

“那就拜托你，拜托你，拜托你，拜托你，拜托你，拜托你，拜托你，不要再说了，好吗？”

他没吭声，只是望着那堆靠在车站墙边的旅行包。上面贴着所有他们曾经过夜的旅馆的标签。

“但我并不希望你去做手术，”他说，“我一点也不在意。”

“你再说，我会尖叫的，”女孩说。

那女人端着两杯啤酒穿过珠帘，走了出来，把酒放在已经湿了的杯垫上。“火车还有五分钟就到站了，”她说。

"What did she say?" asked the girl.

"That the train is coming in five minutes."

The girl smiled brightly at the woman, to thank her.

"I'd better take the bags over to the other side of the station," the man said. She smiled at him.

"All right. Then come back and we'll finish the beer."

He picked up the two heavy bags and carried them around the station to the other tracks. He looked up the tracks but could not see the train. Coming back, he walked through the barroom, where people waiting for the train were drinking. He drank an Anis at the bar and looked at the people. They were all waiting reasonably for the train. He went out through the bead curtain. She was sitting at the table and smiled at him.

"Do you feel better?" he asked.

"I feel fine," she said. "There's nothing wrong with me. I feel fine."

“她刚刚说的是什么？”女孩问。

“她说火车还有五分钟就到站。”

女孩朝那女人灿烂一笑，以示感谢。

“我还是去把旅行包放到车站那边去吧，”男人说。女孩对他笑了笑。

“行。然后马上回来，我们一起喝光啤酒。”

他拎起两只挺沉的旅行包，绕过车站把它们送到另一条路轨处。他又顺着铁轨望去，却没看见火车。回来的时候，他穿过酒吧间，候车的人们都在这里喝酒。他在柜台上喝着茴香酒，看着这些人群。他们都在心平气和地等火车的到来。他穿过珠帘，走了出来。她正坐在桌旁，冲他微笑着。

“你觉得好些了吧？”他问。

“我感觉很好啊，”她说，“我没事。我感觉很好啊。”

Cat in the Rain
雨中的猫

旅店里人来人往，其中只有两个美国人。这两个美国人并非素昧平生，而是一对夫妻。在异域他乡客居，他俩是该我行我素、各自为政，还是应卿卿我我、如影随形？海明威在《雨中的猫》(*Cat in the Rain,* 1925) 里给读者留下了永久的悬念和无尽的话语阐释空间。但这篇小说关注的主题却是明确的，即婚姻中两性关系的定位。

故事聚焦于女主人公视域里异域他乡的三个充满着隐喻的象征符号“猫”“雨”“镜”，围绕着两条线性叙事时间，展现了看似平淡的一场雨中这对夫妻生活里的惊涛骇浪。这两条线性的叙事时间分别为女主人公的见猫——寻猫——失猫以及照镜自怜——向丈夫寻求交流及认可——希望落空。“猫”的形象是女主人公内心的自我及欲望在外部世界的投射，“雨”是笼罩在这对夫妻生活天空中的情感氛围，而“镜”则展示了女主人公的交流欲望落空后的自恋与自怜。在这篇篇幅很小的小说里，海明威通过“猫”这一外部媒介展现了这对夫妻生活中的身份认同危机、交流危机和信任危机等等。由于女主人公对心理身份的认同摇摆不定，也使得她与丈夫的交流出现了困难，以至于小说的最后她与乔治的对话实际上已经变成了她自己的喃喃梦呓。作者海明威在这篇叙事中采取了零度介入，把悬念都留给了读者自己来解答。

There were only two Americans stopping at the hotel. They did not know any of the people they passed on the stairs on their way to and from their room. Their room was on the second floor facing the sea. It also faced the public garden and the war monument. There were big palms and green benches in the public garden. In the good weather there was always an artist with his easel. Artists liked the way the palms grew and the bright colors of the hotels facing the gardens and the sea. Italians came from a long way off to look up at the war monument. It was made of bronze and glistened in the rain. It was raining. The rain dripped from the palm trees. Water stood in pools on the gravel paths. The sea broke in a long line in the rain and slipped back down the beach to come up and break again in a long line in the rain. The motor cars were gone from the square by the war monument. Across the square in the doorway of the cafe a waiter stood looking out at the empty square.

The American wife stood at the window looking out. Outside right under their window a cat was crouched under one of the dripping green tables. The cat was trying to make herself so compact that she would not be dripped on.

"I'm going down and get that kitty," the American wife said.

"I'll do it,"her husband offered from the bed.

"No, I'll get it. The poor kitty out trying to keep dry under a table."

The husband went on reading , lying propped up with the two pillows at the foot of the bed.

"Don't get wet," he said.

留宿在旅馆里的只有两个美国人。他们进出房间时，在楼梯上遇到的人，他们一个也不认识。他们的房间在二楼，面向大海。房间也面向公园和战争纪念碑。公园里有高大的棕榈树和绿色的长条椅。每当天气好的时候，总可以看到个把带着画架的画家。艺术家们喜欢棕榈树的这种长势以及面向公园和大海的那几家旅馆明快的色彩。有意大利人不辞长旅，赶来瞻仰这座纪念碑。它是由青铜铸就的，在雨中闪闪发亮。天正在下雨。雨水不断地从棕榈树上滴落下来。石径上有一潭潭的积水。海水挟着雨势沿着长长的海岸线涌了上来，又顺着海滩溜了回去，然后又挟着雨势沿着长长的海岸线涌上来。停在战争纪念碑广场上的汽车都不在了。在广场的那头，在小餐馆的门口，一个侍者站在那里，朝空荡荡的广场张望。

那位美国太太站在窗边，朝外张望。外边，就在他们的窗子下面，几张绿色的桌子淅沥沥地淌着雨水，有一只猫蜷伏在其中的一张桌子下面。那只猫尽力缩紧身子，不让雨水滴到身上。

"我下去把那只小猫咪抱来，"美国太太说。

"我去吧，"她的丈夫在床上应道。

"不，我去。外面那只可怜的小猫咪竟然想在桌子底下避雨呢！"

丈夫继续看书。他身下高高地垫着床尾的两个枕头。

"别淋湿了，"他说。

The wife went downstairs and the hotel owner stood up and bowed to her as she passed the office. His desk was at the far end of the office. He was an old man and very tall.

"*Il piove*[①]," the wife said. She liked the hotel-keeper.

"*Si si, Signora, brutto tempo*. It is very bad weather."

He stood behind his desk in the far end of the dim room. The wife liked him. She liked the deadly serious way he received any complaints. She liked his dignity. She liked the way he wanted to serve her. She liked the way he felt about being a hotel-keeper. She liked his old, heavy[②] face and big hands.

Liking him she opened the door and looked out. It was raining harder. A man in a rubber cape was crossing the empty square to the cafe. The cat would be around to the right. Perhaps she could go along under the eaves. As she stood in the doorway an umbrella opened behind her. It was the maid who looked after their room.

"You must not get wet," she smiled, speaking Italian. Of course, the hotel-keeper had sent her.

With the maid holding the umbrella over her, she walked along the gravel path until she was under their window. The table was there, washed bright green in the rain, but the cat was gone. She was suddenly disappointed. The maid looked up at her.

"*Ha perduto qualque cosa, Signora*?"

"There was a cat ," said the American girl.

"A cat?"

---

① 本短篇小说《雨中的猫》英文部分的斜体字，原文为意大利语。本篇参考了曹庸先生翻译的《雨里的猫》中对意大利语的翻译，见上海译文出版社2004年版《海明威文集短篇小说全集》。
② heavy：指面部线条粗犷。

太太下了楼。当她走过办公室时，旅馆主人站起来，向她鞠了一躬。他的办公桌在办公室的那一头。他是个老头，个子高高的。

"下雨啦，"太太说。她喜欢这个旅店管理者。

"是的，是的，夫人。坏天气。天气太糟了。"

他站在光线朦胧的房间那一头的办公桌后面。这个太太喜欢他。她喜欢他那种当人朝他诉苦时他认真以待的态度；她喜欢他体面的举止；她喜欢他那种乐于为她效劳的模样；她喜欢他那种以旅店管理者身份自居的神态；她喜欢他那不再年轻、线条粗犷的面容以及他那一双大手。

真的喜欢他。她打开门，向外张望。雨下得更大了。有个穿着短橡胶雨披的男人正穿过空荡荡的广场，向小餐馆走去。猫大概就在这一带的右边。也许她可以沿着屋檐底下走过去。当她站在门口时，一把伞在她身后撑开来。是整理他们房间的那位女侍者。

"您千万别淋湿了啊。"她笑着用意大利语说。不用说，是旅店管理者派她来的。

由女侍者给她打着伞，她沿着石径走过去，一直走到他们的窗户下面。桌子还在那儿，在雨中被冲刷得绿意盎然，那只猫却不见了。失望之情油然而生。女侍者抬头望着她。

"您丢了什么东西了吗，夫人？"

"刚才有只猫在这儿，"美国女孩说道。

"一只猫？"

"*Si, il gatto*."

"A cat?" the maid laughed. "A cat in the rain?"

"Yeah," she said, "under the table." Then, "Oh, I wanted it so much. I wanted a kitty."

When she talked English the maid's face tightened.

"Come, *Signora*," she said. "We must get back inside. You will be wet."

"I suppose so ," said the American girl.

They went back along the gravel path and passed in the door. The maid stayed outside to close the umbrella. As the American girl passed the office, the padrone bowed from his desk. Something felt very small and tight inside the girl. The padrone made her feel very small and at the same time really important. She had a momentary feeling of being of supreme importance. She went on up the stairs. She opened the door of the room. George was on the bed, reading.

"Did you get the cat?" he asked, putting the book down.

"It was gone."

"Wonder where it went to," he said, resting his eyes from reading.

She sat down on the bed.

"I wanted it so much," she said. "I don't know why I wanted it so much. I wanted that poor kitty. It isn't any fun to be a poor kitty out in the rain."

George was reading again.

She went over and sat in front of the mirror of the dressing table looking at herself with the hand glass. She studied her profile,

“是的，一只猫。”

“一只猫啊？”女侍者笑了，“雨中的猫？”

“是啊，”她说，“在这桌子底下。”顿了顿又说：“哦，我刚才太想要它了。我曾经想要一只小猫咪来着。”

她用英语说话的时候，女侍者面无表情。

“来吧，夫人，”她说，“我们该进去了。您会被淋湿的。”

“我想也是，”美国女孩说道。

她们沿着石径走了回去，穿过了门。女侍者待在外面收伞。美国女孩经过办公室时，这家客栈主人从办公桌那儿向她鞠了一下躬。女孩感到无比卑微，却又无尽陶醉。客栈主人让她感觉到很卑微又很重要。有那么一会儿她感到重要得不得了。她继续走上楼梯。乔治在床上看书。

“弄到那只猫啦？”他问道，放下了手中的书。

“它不见了。”

“不晓得它会跑到哪里去，”他说着，就势休息一下一直在看书的眼睛。

她在床上坐下。

“我曾经是那么地想要它，”她说，“我不知道我怎么会那么想要它。我曾经想要那只可怜的小猫咪来着。做一只待在外面雨地里的可怜的小猫咪可不是什么乐事啊！”

乔治又在看书了。

她走过去，坐在梳妆台镜子前，从手镜里打量自己。她端详自己的侧面像，先看看这一侧，再看看那一侧。接着，她又端详

first one side and then the other. Then she studied the back of her head and her neck.

"Don't you think it would be a good idea if I let my hair grow out?" she asked, looking at her profile again.

George looked up and saw the back of her neck clipped close like a boy's.

"I like it the way it is."

"I get so tired of it," she said. "I get so tired of looking like a boy."

George shifted his position in the bed. He hadn't looked away from her since she started to speak.

"You look pretty darn nice ," he said.

She laid the mirror down on the dresser and went over to the window and looked out. It was getting dark.

"I want to pull my hair back tight and smooth and make a big knot at the back that I can feel," she said. " I want to have a kitty to sit on my lap and purr when I stroke her."

"Yeah?" George said from the bed.

"And I want to eat at a table with my own silver and I want candles. And I want it to be spring and I want to brush my hair out in front of a mirror and I want a kitty and I want some new clothes."

"Oh, shut up and get something to read," ① George said. He was reading again.

His wife was looking out of the window. It was quite dark

① "shut up and get something to read"这句话表明乔治对其妻子的一系列浪漫幻想根本不感兴趣。

起自己的后脑勺和脖子来。

“你不觉得我把头发蓄起来是个好主意吗？”她问道，又端详起自己的侧面像来。

乔治抬起头，看到她后面的脖子。头发剪得很短，像个男孩的头发。

“我喜欢你现在的发型。”

“我可烦透它了，”她说，“看起来像男孩子，我真是烦透了。”

乔治在床上换了个姿势。从她开口说话以来他的目光就没有从她身上移开过。

“你就这个样子蛮好。”他说道。

她把镜子放到梳妆台上，向窗子走过去，朝外张望。天渐渐黑了。

“我要把头发往后梳得又紧又滑，在后脑勺打个我能感觉到的大髻儿，”她说道，“我要有只小猫咪坐在我的腿上，我抚摸它的时候，它就高兴得发出呼噜声。”

“嗯哼？”乔治在床上说。

“我还要用我自己的银餐具来就餐，而且还要一根根蜡烛。我还要现在是春天，我还要在镜子前梳理我的长发，我还要一只小猫咪，我还要些新衣裳。”

“哦，别说了。找点书来看看吧。”乔治说道。他又在看书了。

他的太太看着窗外。现在天已经很黑了。棕榈树上，雨仍然拍打不停。

now and still raining in the palm trees.

"Anyway, I want a cat," she said, "I want a cat. I want a cat now. If I can't have long hair or any fun I can have a cat."

George was not listening. He was reading his book. His wife looked out of the window where the light had come on in the square.

Someone knocked at the door.

"*Avanti*," George said. He looked up from his book.

In the doorway stood the maid. She held a big tortoise-shell cat pressed tight against her and swung down against her body.

"Excuse me," she said, "the padrone asked me to bring this for the *Signora*."

“反正我想要只猫，”她说道，“我想要只猫。我现在就想要只猫。如果我不能留长发或有别的乐子，我有只猫总可以吧？”

乔治并没有听。他在读他的书。他的太太朝窗外望去。广场里的灯光透了进来。

有人敲门。

“请进，”乔治说道。他从他的书上抬起眼睛来。

门口站着女侍者。一只大大的玳瑁猫被她紧紧抱着，又腾地被她从身上扔了下来。

“打搅了，”她说道，“客栈主人要我把这送给夫人。”

A Day's Wait
一天的等待

《一天的等待》(*A Day's Wait,* 1933) 向我们讲述了一个简单的小故事：在一个冬日的早晨，一个九岁的小男孩患上了流感，但是由于他不知道华氏度和摄氏度的区别，而误以为发烧至 102 度（华氏）的自己快要死了，于是便躺在床上不言不语，等待死亡。

小说由小男孩的父亲以第一人称的口吻向我们娓娓道来，其中还穿插了两段他给儿子吃完药后到户外打猎时的场景描写。在这部分场景描写中，作者运用动静结合的手法，将冬日之美淋漓尽致地表现了出来。在这篇描写小男孩等死的小说中，通篇未见关于他等死时孤独与无助的心情的描写，反而加入了一段美好生活的场景描写。由此，读者不难发现，作者旨在以生活的美好来与死亡的可怕形成强烈的对比，从而反映出小男孩在等死时的矛盾心理：勇敢面对的同时却又痛苦绝望。因此，正是这部分凸显冬日之美的场景描写为作品之美增添了亮丽的一笔。

He came into the room to shut the windows while we were still in bed and I saw he looked ill. He was shivering, his face was white, and he walked slowly as though it ached to move.

"What's the matter, Schatz[①]?"

"I've got a headache."

"You better go back to bed."

"No. I'm all right."

"You go to bed. I'll see you when I'm dressed."

But when I came downstairs he was dressed, sitting by the fire, looking a very sick and miserable boy of nine years. When I put my hand on his forehead I knew he had a fever.

"You go up to bed," I said, "you're sick."

"I'm all right," he said.

When the doctor came he took the boy's temperature.

"What is it?" I asked him.

"One hundred and two."

Downstairs, the doctor left three different medicines in different colored capsules with instructions for giving them. One was to bring down the fever, another a purgative, the third to overcome an acid condition. The germs of influenza can only exist in an acid condition, he explained. He seemed to know all about influenza and said there was nothing to worry about if the fever did not go above one hundred and four degrees. This was a light epidemic of flu and there was no danger if you avoided pneumonia.

Back in the room I wrote the boy's temperature down and made a note of the time to give the various capsules.

① Schatz：德语词"亲爱的宝贝"，与英语中的"darling"一词意思相同。

他进屋来关窗户时，我们还在床上，但我注意到他看上去像是生病了。他浑身发抖，脸色苍白，走起路来慢吞吞的，好像动一下都会痛一样。

"怎么了，宝贝儿？"

"我头痛。"

"你还是回床上去吧。"

"不用。我没事儿。"

"你到床上去吧。我穿好衣服就去看你。"

但是我到楼下时，他已经穿好衣服，坐在火炉旁，一副病得厉害、难受痛苦的九岁男孩的样子。我把手往他的额头上一放，便知道他发烧了。

"你上去睡觉吧，"我说，"你病了。"

"我没事，"他说。

医生来后，给儿子量了量体温。

"多少度？"我问他。

"102度。"

楼下，医生留下三种装在不同颜色胶囊里的药，并交代了服用方法。一种是退烧药，另一种是泻药，第三种是抑酸药。他解释说，流行性感冒的病菌只能存在于酸性状态中。他像是对流行性感冒无所不知一样，还说只要体温不高过104度就不用担心。这是轻度流感，只要防止肺炎的并发就没有危险。

回到房间后，我写下儿子的体温，并记下服用各种胶囊的时间。

"Do you want me to read to you?"

"All right. If you want to," said the boy. His face was very white and there were dark areas under his eyes. He lay still in the bed and seemed very detached from what was going on.

I read aloud from Howard Pyle's [1] *Book of Pirates*; but I could see he was not following what I was reading.

"How do you feel, Schatz?" I asked him.

"Just the same, so far," he said.

I sat at the foot of the bed and read to myself while I waited for it to be time to give another capsule. It would have been natural for him to go to sleep, but when I looked up he was looking at the foot of the bed, looking very strangely.

"Why don't you try to go to sleep? I'll wake you up for the medicine."

"I'd rather stay awake."

After a while he said to me, "You don't have to stay in here with me, Papa, if it bothers you."

"It doesn't bother me."

"No, I mean you don't have to stay if it's going to bother you."

I thought perhaps he was a little lightheaded and after giving him the prescribed capsules at eleven o'clock I went out for a while.

It was a bright, cold day, the ground covered with a sleet that had frozen so that it seemed as if all the bare trees, the bushes, the

① Howard Pyle：霍华德·派尔(1853—1911)，美国著名的插画家、作家。其作品大多取材于中世纪的神话或殖民地时期的历史。他创作的《海盗集》(*Book of Pirates*) 被奉为欧洲最经典的海盗题材巨作。电影《加勒比海盗》便是由此书改编而成的。

“你要我读书给你听吗？”

“好吧。你想读就读吧，”儿子说。他脸色煞白，眼睛下面还有黑眼圈。他一动不动地躺在床上，好像对接下来的事情漠不关心一样。

我大声地读着霍华德·派尔的《海盗集》，但我看得出来他并没有听我读。

“你觉得怎么样，宝贝儿？”我问他。

“到现在为止，还是老样子，”他说。

我一边坐在床脚看书，一边等着到时间后他吃另一种胶囊。对他而言，睡着本来是件很容易的事，但是我抬眼一看，他正表情非常古怪地看着床脚。

“你怎么不试着睡会儿？吃药时我会叫醒你的。”

“我宁愿醒着。”

过了一会儿，他对我说：“你不用待在这儿陪我，爸爸，要是这让你心烦的话。”

“没让我心烦。”

“不，我的意思是说如果会让你心烦的话，你就不用待在这儿。”

我想他可能有些头晕，到了11点，我给他吃了医生开的胶囊后就去了外面一会儿。

那天晴朗而寒冷，覆盖在地面上的一层雨雪已经结成冰了，因此，所有光秃秃的树木、小灌木、修剪过的灌木林以及所有的

cut brush and all the grass and the bare ground had been varnished with ice. I took the young Irish setter for a little walk up the road and along a frozen creek, but it was difficult to stand or walk on the glassy surface and the red dog slipped and slithered and I fell twice, hard, once dropping my gun and having it slide away over the ice.

We flushed a covey of quail under a high clay bank with overhanging brush and I killed two as they went out of sight over the top of the bank. Some of the covey lit in trees, but most of them scattered into brush piles and it was necessary to jump on the ice-coated mounds of brush several times before they would flush. Coming out while you were poised unsteadily on the icy, springy brush they made difficult shooting and I killed two, missed five, and started back pleased to have found a covey close to the house and happy there were so many left to find on another day.

At the house they said the boy had refused to let any one come into the room.

"You can't come in," he said. "You mustn't get what I have."

I went up to him and found him in exactly the position I had left him, white-faced, but with the tops of his cheeks flushed by the fever, staring still, as he had stared, at the foot of the bed.

I took his temperature.

"What is it?"

"Something like a hundred," I said. It was one hundred and two and four tenths.

"It was a hundred and two," he said.

"Who said so?"

草地和空地看起来都像是用冰漆过了一样。我领着一条幼小的爱尔兰长毛猎犬走上那条路，沿着结冰的小溪散步，但是在这玻璃般光滑的路面上站立或行走是件费力的事，那条红毛狗就滑倒滑了出去，我也狠狠地摔了两跤，有一次我的枪都掉了，在冰面上滑了好远。

我们惊飞了一群鹌鹑，它们正躲在悬垂着灌木枝的高高的土堤下面，它们从土堤顶上飞走时，我打死了两只。鹌鹑中有些栖息在树上，但是大多数都分散在灌木枝堆里，在惊飞它们之前，必须在结冰的灌木枝堆上跳几下。然而，当你还在覆盖着冰的、松软的灌木枝堆上左右摇摆寻求身体平衡时，它们就飞走了，因此要打中它们并不容易，我就只打中了两只，打空了五只，但是当我动身回去时，发现房子附近还有一群鹌鹑，心里便很是高兴，日后还能找到这么多可真幸运。

到家后，家人说儿子不让任何人进他的房间。

“你们不能进来，”他说，“你们千万不能染上我的病。”

我上楼去看他，发现他仍然保持着我离开时的那个姿势，脸色苍白，不过脸颊因为发烧而绯红，他像之前那样盯着床脚看。

我给他量了体温。

“多少度？”

“大约100度，”我说。实际上是102度4分。

“是102度，”他说。

“谁说的？”

"The doctor."

"Your temperature is all right," I said. "It's nothing to worry about."

"I don't worry," he said, "but I can't keep from thinking."

"Don't think," I said. "Just take it easy."

"I'm taking it easy," he said and looked straight ahead. He was evidently holding tight onto himself about something.

"Take this with water."

"Do you think it will do any good?"

"Of course it will."

I sat down and opened the *Pirate* book and commenced to read, but I could see he was not following, so I stooped.

"About what time do you think I'm going to die?" he asked.

"What?"

"About how long will it be before I die?"

"You aren't going to die. What's the matter with you? "

"Oh, yes, I am, I heard him say a hundred and two."

"People don't die with a fever of one hundred and two. That's a silly way to talk."

"I know they do. At school in France the boys told me you can't live with forty-four degrees. I've got a hundred and two."

He had been waiting to die all day, ever since nine o'clock in the morning.

"You poor Schatz," I said. "Poor old Schatz. It's like miles and kilometers. You aren't going to die. That's a different thermometer. On that thermometer thirty-seven is normal. On this kind it's

"医生。"

"你的体温还好，"我说，"不用担心。"

"我不担心，"他说，"不过我不能不想。"

"别想了，"我说，"放轻松。"

"我现在很轻松，"他说着，眼睛一直看着前方。显而易见，他在竭力隐藏什么事情。

"就着水把这药吃了吧。"

"你认为吃了会有用吗？"

"当然会。"

我坐下，翻开那本《海盗集》开始读，但我看得出来他并没有听，于是我停了下来。

"你认为我什么时候会死？"他问。

"什么？"

"还有多久我就要死了？"

"你不会死的。你怎么了？"

"哦，是的，我快死了，我听他说是102度。"

"人烧到102度是不会死的。你这么说可真傻。"

"我知道会死的。在法国的学校时，同学告诉过我，烧到44度你就活不成了。可我已经烧到102度了。"

原来从早上9点到现在，他这一整天都在等死。

"你这可怜的宝贝儿，"我说，"可怜的小宝贝儿，这跟英里和公里一样。你不会死的。那是一种不同的体温计。那种体温计上37度算正常。而这种要98度。"

ninety-eight."[1]

"Are you sure?"

"Absolutely," I said, "It's like miles and kilometers. You know, like how many kilometers we make when we do seventy miles in the car?"

"Oh," he said.

But his gaze at the foot of the bed relaxed slowly. The hold over himself relaxed too, finally, and the next day it was very slack and he cried very easily at little things that were of no importance.

① 华氏度 (Fahrenheit) 和摄氏度 (Centigrade) 是两种计量单位，二者的转换公式为：华氏度＝ 32 ＋摄氏度 ×1.8。因此人的正常体温为 37 摄氏度，大约 98.6 华氏度。包括我国在内的世界上许多国家都使用摄氏度，而美国和其他一些英语国家则使用华氏度。

“你确定吗？”

“当然，”我说，“这就像是英里和公里。你要知道，我们开车时车速70英里是多少公里吗？”

“哦，”他说。

不过他盯着床脚的目光慢慢地涣散了。他因竭力克制而绷紧的心弦也终于松弛了，第二天便完全松了下来，为了无关紧要的小事，他动不动就哭起来。

A Clean, Well-Lighted Place
一个干净明亮的地方

《一个干净明亮的地方》(*A Clean, Well-Lighted Place,* 1926) 向我们讲述了一个深夜里发生在一家咖啡馆的小故事。小说情节简单无奇：两名服务员针对唯一的顾客——一位迟迟不肯离开的老人，展开了一番对话；最终，年轻的服务员因急于回家而赶走了老人，年长的服务员则在打烊后去了另一家酒吧喝酒。

一般而言，小说情节的发展总是以事件本身的发展顺序为准，遵循着“线性结构”的发展模式。然而，本篇小说采用了“回环式结构”的叙事模式，从不同角度对同一人或事进行描述。老人是这篇小说的聚焦人物，他是一个双耳失聪的有钱人，没有家室，曾经因为孤独和空虚而企图上吊自杀。老人是对生活完全绝望的老年人的代表，以他为中心，两名服务员通过对话发表了各自不同的见解。年轻的服务员是充满幻想的青年人的代表，他因急于回家同妻子相聚，便欺骗老人说没酒供应而赶走了老人；年长的服务员是希望破灭的中年人的代表，因为深感生活的空虚乏味而理解并同情老人，于是便三番两次地规劝同伴不要着急。两人对待老人的不同态度分别影射出了他们对待生活的态度：一个热衷于享乐快活；一个则对生活丧失了激情。围绕老人这一中心，两名服务员不同的看法和态度分别构成了一个绝妙的回环。

It was late and every one had left the café except an old man who sat in the shadow the leaves of the tree made against the electric light. In the day time the street was dusty, but at night the dew settled the dust and the old man liked to sit late because he was deaf and now at night it was quiet and he felt the difference. The two waiters inside the caf knew that the old man was a little drunk, and while he was a good client they knew that if he became too drunk he would leave without paying, so they kept watch on him.

"Last week he tried to commit suicide," one waiter said.

"Why?"

"He was in despair."

"What about?"

"Nothing."

"How do you know it was nothing?"

"He has plenty of money."

They sat together at a table that was close against the wall near the door of the café and looked at the terrace where the tables were all empty except where the old man sat in the shadow of the leaves of the tree that moved slightly in the wind. A girl and a soldier went by in the street. The street light shone on the brass number on his collar. The girl wore no head covering and hurried beside him.

"The guard will pick him up," one waiter said.

"What does it matter if he gets what he's after?"

"He had better get off the street now. The guard will get him. They went by five minutes ago."

天色晚了，其他人都已离开咖啡馆，只剩下一位老人，他坐在被树叶遮住了灯光的阴影里。白天，街上灰尘弥漫，但是到了晚上，露水便让灰尘落了下去，这位老人喜欢坐到很晚，因为他双耳失聪，夜晚这个时候非常寂静，他可以感觉出与白天的不同。咖啡馆里面的两名服务员知道这位老人有点醉了，尽管他是位好顾客，但是他们知道如果他喝得太醉了，就会不付账便走，所以他们一直留意着他。

“他上周想自杀。”一名服务员说。

“为什么？”

“他绝望了。”

“为了什么？”

“没什么。”

“你怎么知道没什么？”

“他有很多钱。”

他们一起坐在咖啡馆大门靠墙的桌子前，看着露台，除了老人坐的那张桌子，其他桌子都空荡荡的，老人坐在树叶的阴影里，那些树叶随风轻轻地拂动。一个女孩和一个士兵从街上走过。路灯把士兵衣领上的黄铜编号照得闪闪发光。那个女孩没戴帽子，匆忙地走在他的旁边。

“警卫员会把他带走的，”一名服务员说。

“如果他得到了他想要的，又有什么关系呢？”

“他最好赶快从街上离开。警卫员会抓住他的。他们五分钟前刚从这里经过。”

The old man sitting in the shadow rapped on his saucer with his glass. The younger waiter went over to him.

"What do you want?"

The old man looked at him. "Another brandy," he said.

"You'll be drunk," the waiter said. The old man looked at him. The waiter went away.

"He'll stay all night," he said to his colleague. "I'm sleepy now. I never get into bed before three o'clock. He should have killed himself last week."

The waiter took the brandy bottle and another saucer [①] from the counter inside the café and marched out to the old man's table. He put down the saucer and poured the glass full of brandy.

"You should have killed yourself last week," he said to the deaf man. The old man motioned with his finger. "A little more," he said. The waiter poured on into the glass so that the brandy slopped over and ran down the stem into the top saucer of the pile. "Thank you," the old man said. The waiter took the bottle back inside the café. He sat down at the table with his colleague again.

"He's drunk now," he said.

"He's drunk every night."

"What did he want to kill himself for?"

"How should I know."

"How did he do it?"

"He hung himself with a rope."

"Who cut him down?"

"His niece."

---

① another saucer：一只茶托代表一杯酒，顾客结账时以茶托的数量为准。

坐在阴影里的老人用他的杯子敲了敲茶托。年轻的服务员朝他走了过去。

“你想要什么？”

老人看了看他。“再来杯白兰地，”他说。

“你会喝醉的。”服务员说。老人看了看他。服务员便走开了。

“他会通宵待在这儿，”他对他的同事说，“我现在困了。我从来都没在三点以前上过床。他该在上周自杀然后死掉的。”

服务员从咖啡馆的柜台里拿出白兰地酒瓶和另外一只茶托，快步走了出去，来到老人的桌边。他放下茶托，往杯中倒满了白兰地。

“你该在上周自杀死掉的，”他对着那个失聪的老人说。老人用手指比画了一下。“再加一点儿，”他说。服务员便又往杯中倒白兰地，以至于酒溢了出来，顺着酒杯的柄脚淌进了最上面的一只茶托里，它的下面还有一叠茶托。“谢谢你，”老人说。服务员把酒瓶拿回咖啡馆。他又和他的同事一起坐在了桌边。

“他这会儿醉了，”他说。

“他每晚都会醉。”

“他为什么要自杀？”

“我怎么知道。”

“他怎么自杀的？”

“他用一根绳子上吊。”

“谁把他放下来的？”

“他侄女。”

"Why did they do it?"

"Fear for his soul."

"How much money has he got?"

"He's got plenty."

"He must be eighty years old."

"Anyway I should say he was eighty."

"I wish he would go home. I never get to bed before three o'clock. What kind of hour is that to go to bed?"

"He stays up because he likes it."

"He's lonely. I'm not lonely. I have a wife waiting in bed for me."

"He had a wife once too."

"A wife would be no good to him now."

"You can't tell. He might be better with a wife."

"His niece looks after him. You said she cut him down."

"I know."

"I wouldn't want to be that old. An old man is a nasty thing."

"Not always. This old man is clean. He drinks without spilling. Even now, drunk. Look at him."

"I don't want to look at him. I wish he would go home. He has no regard for those who must work."

The old man looked from his glass across the square, then over at the waiters.

"Another brandy," he said, pointing to his glass. The waiter who was in a hurry came over.

"Finished," he said, speaking with that omission of syntax stupid people employ when talking to drunken people or

"他们为什么要这么做?"

"为他的灵魂担忧。"

"他有多少钱?"

"他有很多。"

"他一定有80岁了。"

"反正我猜他有80岁了。"

"我真希望他回家去。我从来都没在三点以前上过床。那是个什么样的上床时间啊?"

"他不睡觉因为他喜欢这样。"

"他孤单一人。可我并不孤单。我有个老婆在床上等着我呢。"

"他也有过老婆。"

"现在老婆对他就没什么用了。"

"谁知道呢。不过有个老婆的话,他可能会好些。"

"他侄女在照顾他。你刚才说是她把他放下来的。"

"我知道。"

"我可不想活那么老。老人都是邋遢鬼。"

"不一定都是的。这个老人就干干净净的。他喝酒时没有把酒洒出来。即便是现在喝醉了。你看他。"

"我才不想看他。我只希望他回家去。他一点儿也不考虑那些必须工作的人。"

老人的目光离开酒杯,越过空地,然后落在了两名服务员身上。

"再来杯白兰地,"他指着杯子说。那位着急的服务员走了过去。

"完了,"他的话里省略了句法结构,一般而言,蠢汉对醉汉或外国人就是这么说的,"今晚没了,打烊了。"

foreigners. "No more tonight. Close now."

"Another," said the old man.

"No. Finished." The waiter wiped the edge of the table with a towel and shook his head.

The old man stood up, slowly counted the saucers, took a leather coin purse from his pocket and paid for the drinks, leaving half a peseta① tip.

The waiter watched him go down the street, a very old man walking unsteadily but with dignity.

"Why didn't you let him stay and drink?" the unhurried waiter asked. They were putting up the shutters②. "It is not half-past two."

"I want to go home to bed."

"What is an hour?"

"More to me than to him."

"An hour is the same."

"You talk like an old man yourself. He can buy a bottle and drink at home."

"It's not the same."

"No, it is not," agreed the waiter with a wife. He did not wish to be unjust. He was only in a hurry.

"And you? You have no fear of going home before your usual hour?"③

"Are you trying to insult me?"

"No, *hombre,* only to make a joke."

---

① peseta：比塞塔西班牙的货币单位。

② put up the shutters："(临时性或永久性地)停止营业"的意思，在文中也可指"关店、打烊"。

③ 这句话是年长的服务员说的。他暗示说，如果年轻的服务员提早回家的话，可能会发现他的老婆正在跟其他男人偷情。

“再来一杯，”老人说。

“不行。没酒了。”服务员一边拿块毛巾擦着桌沿，一边摇了摇头。

老人站起身，慢慢地数着茶托，然后从口袋里拿出一个装硬币的皮钱包，付了酒钱，并留下半个比塞塔作小费。

服务员看着他沿街走去，那位上了年纪的老头儿走起路来不是很稳，但是却不失体面。

“你怎么不让他留下来喝酒？”那个不着急的服务员问。他们正在关百叶窗。“还没到两点半呢。”

“我要回家睡觉了。”

“一个钟头算什么？”

“对他不算什么，对我就很重要了。”

“都是一个钟头啊。”

“你说得跟你自己也是个老头儿似的。他可以买瓶酒回家喝啊。”

“那不一样。”

“是啊，那是不一样，”有老婆的服务员赞同地说。他不希望说得不合理，他只是有些着急。

“你呢？没到平常的时间就回家，你不担心吗？”

“你想羞辱我？”

“不，老兄，只是开个玩笑。”

"No," the waiter who was in a hurry said, rising from pulling down the metal shutters. "I have confidence. I am all confidence."

"You have youth, confidence, and a job," the older waiter said. "You have everything."

"And what do you lack?"

"Everything but work."

"You have everything I have."

"No. I have never had confidence and I am not young."

"Come on. Stop talking nonsense and lock up."

"I am of those who like to stay late at the caf ," the older waiter said. "With all those who do not want to go to bed. With all those who need a light for the night."

"I want to go home and into bed."

"We are of two different kinds," the older waiter said. He was now dressed to go home. "It is not only a question of youth and confidence although those things are very beautiful. Each night I am reluctant to close up because there may be some one who needs the café."

"*Hombre,* there are *bodegas* open all night long."

"You do not understand. This is a clean and pleasant café. It is well lighted. The light is very good and also, now, there are shadows of the leaves."

"Good night," said the younger waiter.

"Good night," the other said. Turning off the electric light he continued the conversation with himself. It is the light of course but it is necessary that the place be clean and pleasant. You do not want music. Certainly you do not want music. Nor can you stand

"不会的，"着急的服务员说，他关上金属百叶窗后站了起来，"我有信心。我非常有信心。"

"你有青春，有信心，还有工作，"年长的服务员说，"你什么都有。"

"那你缺什么？"

"除了工作什么都缺。"

"我有的你都有啊。"

"不，我从没有自信过，而且也不再年轻了。"

"得了。别说废话了，把门锁上吧。"

"我是那种喜欢在咖啡馆里待到很晚的人，"年长的服务员说，"和所有不想上床睡觉的人一样。和所有在夜晚需要亮光的人一样。"

"我要回家睡觉了。"

"我们是两种人，"年长的服务员说。他现在穿好衣服要回家了。"这不仅仅是青春和信心的问题，尽管那些东西都非常美好。每晚，我都不愿意打烊，因为可能有人需要这咖啡馆。"

"老兄，有通宵营业的酒铺。"

"你不懂。这是一家干净舒适的咖啡馆。地方明亮。灯光很棒，而且现在还有树叶的阴影。"

"晚安，"年轻的服务员说。

"晚安，"另一个说。他关掉电灯，继续自言自语。灯光当然重要，但是地方也必须干净舒适。你不需要音乐。你当然不需

before a bar with dignity although that is all that is provided for these hours. What did he fear? It was not fear or dread. It was a nothing that he knew too well. It was all a nothing and a man was nothing too. It was only that and light was all it needed and a certain cleanness and order. Some lived in it and never felt it but he knew it all was *nada y pues nada y nada y pues nada*. Our *nada* who art in *nada, nada* be thy name thy kingdom *nada* thy will be *nada* in *nada* as it is in *nada*. Give us this *nada* our daily *nada* and *nada* us our *nada* as we *nada* our *nadas* and *nada* us not into *nada* but deliver us from *nada; pues nada*.① Hail nothing full of nothing, nothing is with thee. He smiled and stood before a bar with a shining steam pressure coffee machine.

"What's yours?" asked the barman.

"*Nada*."

"*Otro loco más*②," said the barman and turned away.

"A little cup," said the waiter.

The barman poured it for him.

"The light is very bright and pleasant but the bar is unpolished," the waiter said.

The barman looked at him but did not answer. It was too late at night for conversation.

"You want another *copita*③?" the barman asked.

"No, thank you," said the waiter and went out. He disliked

① nada：西班牙语，"没有什么"的意思，同英语中的"nothing"。本段自"our nada who art in nada"起至"pues nada"，作者模仿了《圣经·路加福音》第11章中耶稣教门徒祷告的内容，并将其中大量的词都替换成了"nada"。

② Otro loco más：西班牙语，意思是"又是个疯子"。

③ copita：指"(郁金香形状的)雪利酒杯"。雪利酒是西班牙的保护品牌。葡萄酒雪利酒杯主要用于盛装雪利酒。

要音乐。你也无法怀着尊严站在吧台前，尽管那份尊严就是为这个时间准备的。他害怕什么？那不是害怕，也不是恐惧。那是他深深体会到的一种虚无的感觉。一切都是虚无，一个男人也是虚无。仅此而已，所需要的只是灯光，还有一点儿干净和整齐。有些人活在其中，却从来都不曾感觉到，但是他知道一切都是虚无，因此虚无和虚无，因此虚无。我们在虚无的虚无，愿人都尊你的名为虚无，愿你的国虚无，愿你虚无在虚无如同行在虚无。我们日用的虚无，虚无赐给我们，虚无我们的虚无，因为我们虚无我们的虚无，不虚无我们遇见虚无，救我们脱离虚无；因而是虚无。向充满虚无的虚无欢呼，虚无与你同在。他笑着站在一个吧台前，上面放着一架闪亮的气压煮咖啡机。

“你要什么？”酒吧招待问。

“虚无。”

“又是个疯子，”酒吧招待说完便转过头去。

“来一小杯，”那个服务员说。

酒吧招待给他倒了一杯。

“灯光很亮，也很舒适，但是吧台没有擦亮。”

酒吧招待看了看他，没有吱声。夜太深了，不是谈话的时候。

“你要再来一杯雪利酒吗？”酒吧招待问。

“不用了，谢谢你，”服务员说完便走了出去。他讨厌酒吧和酒铺。而一个干净明亮的咖啡馆就是另外一回事了。现在，他

bars and *bodegas*. A clean, well-lighted café was a very different thing. Now, without thinking further, he would go home to his room. He would lie in the bed and finally, with daylight, he would go to sleep. After all, he said to himself, it is probably only insomnia. Many must have it.

不再多想什么了，他要回家到他的房间去。他要躺在床上，最后，黎明到来时，他会睡着的。终究，他自言自语地说，有可能只是失眠。许多人肯定都这样。

Cross-Country Snow
越野滑雪

《越野滑雪》(*Cross-Country Snow,* 1925) 是海明威描写滑雪运动的经典之作。20 世纪 20 年代海明威曾几次去瑞士为报社收集相关资料。这些都为后来他的小说创作积累了大量的构思与素材。小说中对滑雪运动的细致描写格外传神：冰天雪地之中，结伴而行，回归到大自然里，将烦恼、疲惫甚至一切都抛之脑后，寻找一种忘我的享受。滑雪运动固然很精彩，但其中也隐藏了不少危险和不确定因素。这需要有冒险精神。而小说中尼克和乔治都称赞滑雪运动妙不可言，可见他们对于这项惊险刺激的运动的热衷，体现出他们的硬汉精神和男性情谊 (male bonding)。两人在滑雪之时并没有太多言语，而是将精力都投入到雪中。即使没有表达自己的滑雪感受，可他们还是能够做到心有灵犀一点通。不过，乔治与尼克看起来很亲密，但他们之间还是刻意地保留着一定的距离，比如：乔治将尼克喊为“迈克”。这似乎意味着尼克和乔治没有向彼此表明真实身份，有所隐瞒，没有坦诚相待。虽然我们不知道这是有意的，还是无意的，但是他们之间的那种愉悦、默契和共鸣是可以清楚地感觉到的。

The funicular car bucked once more and then stopped. It could not go farther, the snow drifted solidly across the track. The gale scouring the exposed surface of the mountain had swept the snow surface into a wind-board crust. Nick, waxing his skis in the baggage car, pushed his boots into the toe irons and shut the clamp tight. He jumped from the car sideways onto the hard wind-board, made a jump turn① and crouching and trailing his sticks slipped in a rush down the slope.

On the white below George dipped and rose and dipped out of sight. The rush and the sudden swoop as he dropped down a steep undulation in the mountain side plucked Nick's mind out and left him only the wonderful flying, dropping sensation in his body. He rose to a slight up-run and then the snow seemed to drop out from under him as he went down, down, faster and faster in a rush down the last, long steep slope. Crouching so he was almost sitting back on his skis, trying to keep the center of gravity low, the snow driving like a sand-storm, he knew the pace was too much. But he held it. He would not let go and spill. Then a patch of soft snow, left in a hollow by the wind, spilled him and he went over and over in a clashing of skis, feeling like a shot rabbit, then stuck, his legs crossed, his skis sticking straight up and his nose and ears jammed full of snow.

George stood a little farther down the slope, knocking the snow from his wind jacket with big slaps.

"You took a beauty, Mike," he called to Nick. "That's lousy

---

① jump turn："跳跃转弯"是一种滑雪技术（首先撑一下滑雪杖，再快速地跳跃以掉转滑雪者的方向）。通常用在起伏比较大或者狭窄的地方，比如峡谷等地。

缆索车又颠簸了一下，便停了下来。再也不能往前开了，厚厚的大雪覆盖在轨道上。狂风扫过大山，而山上一无遮拦，上面的雪都给吹成了冰。尼克在行李车厢里一边给他的滑雪板上蜡，一边把靴子塞进鞋尖铁夹里，扣紧夹子。他从车厢的一边向前跳到硬实的雪壳上，来个跳跃转弯，然后蹲下身子，再拖着滑雪杖俯冲滑下了山坡。

在下方的白雪之上，乔治时落时起，时而不见了踪影。当尼克滑向山边一个起伏较大的山坡时，那股冲势再加上猛然下滑，让他忘却了一切，只觉得身体上有一种奇妙的飞翔、下落的感觉。他直起身来稍稍向上翻转，然后又不断往下滑，往下滑，越滑越快，冲下最后一个陡峭的长坡，积雪仿佛是从他身后纷纷落下的。他一边蹲下身子，几乎坐到了滑雪板上，一边尽量把重心放低，只见飞雪来得犹如沙暴，他知道自己速度太快了。但他还是稳住了。他是不会失控摔倒的。接着一团被风刮进坑里的松软的雪让他摔了一跤，随着滑雪板一阵磕磕碰碰，他接连翻了几个筋斗就不动了，就像只中了弹的兔子，两腿交叉，滑雪板朝天立着，鼻子耳朵里都是雪。

乔治站在坡下稍远的地方，正用力拍去防风夹克上的雪。

“你刚才滑得太漂亮了，迈克，”他对尼克喊道。“那令人讨厌的松软的雪。我也是这么绊倒的。”

soft snow. It bagged[②] me the same way."

"What's it like over the khud?" Nick kicked his skis around as he lay on his back and stood up.

"You've got to keep to your left. It's a good fast drop with a Christy[①] at the bottom on account of a fence."

"Wait a sec and we'll take it together."

"No, you come on and go first. I like to see you take the khuds."

Nick Adams came up past George, big back and blond head still faintly snowy, then his skis started slipping at the edge and he swooped down, hissing in the crystalline powder snow and seeming to float up and drop down as he went up and down the billowing khuds. He held to his left and at the end, as he rushed toward the fence, keeping his knees locked tight together and turning his body like tightening a screw brought his skis sharply around to the right in a smother of snow and slowed into a loss of speed parallel to the hillside and the wire fence.

He looked up the hill. George was coming down in telemark[②] position, kneeling; one leg forward and bent, the other trailing; his sticks hanging like some insect's thin legs, kicking up puffs of snow as they touched the surface and finally the whole kneeling, trailing figure coming around in a beautiful right curve, crouching, the legs shot forward and back, the body leaning out against the swing, the sticks accenting the curve like points of light, all in a

② bagged：在这里译为“使……绊倒”，其本意为“猎获捕获；捕杀（猎物）”。
① Christy：一种滑雪技术。通常滑行速度很快时，需要依靠改变身体前倾重量才能使滑雪板平行转弯刹住，用以掉转下坡方向。
② telemark：“屈膝旋转法”或“弓步式转弯”是滑雪中的一种转弯方法（外滑雪板在前，再逐渐向内转，然后顺势绕过去）。

“不知道在峡谷那边滑雪会是怎样？”尼克仰面躺着，将滑雪板乱踢一气，然后站起身。

“你得一直靠左滑。由于谷底有道围栏，飞速冲下去时可以来个漂亮的克里斯汀转弯。”

“待会儿吧，我们再一起到那儿去滑。”

“不，你得赶快先滑。我想看着你滑下峡谷。”

尼克·亚当斯滑到乔治的前面去了，宽大的背和金黄色的头发上还有点雪花，然后他开始靠滑雪板的一边侧滑，再俯冲下去，晶莹的雪糁儿都被磨得嘶嘶作响。当他在起伏不定的峡谷里时上时下的那会儿，那看起来就像是浮了上来又沉了下去。他始终靠左滑，末了，当他冲向栅栏时，就保持双膝紧紧并拢，像拧紧螺旋般旋转着身子，这使得滑雪板也向右急转，扬起阵阵白雪，然后再慢慢减速直至跟山坡和铁丝栅栏平行滑驶。

他抬头看着山上。乔治正屈膝以弓步转弯姿势滑下山来；一条腿在前面弯着，另一条腿在后面拖着；两支滑雪杖犹如昆虫的细腿一般荡着，触及地面时，激起阵阵白雪，最后，他一腿弯曲，一腿拖随，整个身子就以一个漂亮的右弧线绕了过来，蹲下身子，双腿一前一后，飞快移动，身子向前倾，以避免任何摆动，两支滑雪杖将弧线衬托得像许多光点，一切都在茫茫白雪之中。

wild cloud of snow.

"I was afraid to Christy," George said, "the snow was too deep. You made a beauty."

"I can't telemark with my leg," Nick said.

Nick held down the top strand of the wire fence with his ski and George slid over. Nick followed him down to the road. They thrust bent-kneed along the road into a pine forest. The road became polished ice, stained orange and a tobacco yellow from the teams hauling logs. The skiers kept to the stretch of snow along the side. The road dipped sharply to a stream and then ran straight uphill. Through the woods they could see a long, low-eaved, weather-beaten building. Through the trees it was a faded yellow. Closer the window frames were painted green. The paint was peeling. Nick knocked his clamps loose with one of his ski sticks and kicked off the skis.

"We might as well carry them up here," he said.

He climbed the steep road with the skis on his shoulder, kicking his heel nails into the icy footing. He heard George breathing and kicking in his heels just behind him. They stacked the skis against the side of the inn and slapped the snow off each other's trousers, stamped their boots clean, and went in.

Inside it was quite dark. A big porcelain stove shone in the corner of the room. There was a low ceiling. Smooth benches back of dark, wine-stained tables were along each side of the rooms. Two Swiss sat over their pipes and two decies of cloudy new wine next to the stove. The boys took off their jackets and sat against the wall on the other side of the stove. A voice in the next room

“我怕做克里斯汀转弯，”乔治说，“雪好深。你滑得很漂亮。”

“我的腿也做不了弓步转弯，”尼克说。

尼克用滑雪板把铁围栏最上面的铁丝压弯了些，乔治滑了过去。尼克跟着他一直到了大路上。他们一路屈膝滑行，冲进一片松树林。路面上都是磨得光溜溜的冰，都让运木料的马队给弄得一片橙红，一片烟草黄。两人一直沿着两边的雪地滑行。路面陡然下降，通往小河，然后又笔直地往上坡伸展。透过林子，他们看到一长排饱经日晒雨淋、屋檐低矮的房子。隔着树林看，房子外面的黄颜色已经开始褪色了。走近点一看，窗框漆成了绿色。不过油漆也在剥落。尼克用支滑雪杖把滑雪板的夹子敲松，再踢掉滑雪板。

“我们还是从这里开始带着滑雪板上去吧，”他说。

他扛着滑雪板，用鞋跟的铁钉扎进冰封的立足点，就这样爬上了陡峭的山路。他听见紧跟在后面的乔治一边喘着气，一边跺着鞋跟上的雪。他们把滑雪板堆放在客栈墙边，相互拍掉彼此裤子上的雪，再把靴子弄干净了才走进去。

客栈里面非常昏暗。一只大瓷炉在屋角闪着火光。低矮的天花板。屋子四周都有酒渍斑斑的暗黑色桌子，桌子后面都是光滑的长椅。两个瑞士人坐在炉边，抽着烟斗，喝着两杯混浊的新酒。尼克和乔治脱去夹克衫，在炉子另一边靠墙坐了下来。

stopped singing and a girl in a blue apron came in through the door to see what they wanted to drink.

"A bottle of Sion[①]," Nick said. "Is that all right, Gidge?"

"Sure" said George. "You know more about wine than I do. I like any of it."

The girl went out.

"There's nothing really can touch skiing, is there?" Nick said. "The way it feels when you first drop off on a long run."

"Huh," said George. "It's too swell to talk about."

The girl brought the wine in and they had trouble with the cork. Nick finally opened it. The girl went out and they heard her singing in German in the next room.

"Those specks of cork in it don't matter," said Nick.

"I wonder if she's got any cake."

"Let's find out."

The girl came in and Nick noticed that her apron covered swellingly her pregnancy. I wonder why I didn't see that when she first came in, he thought.

"What were you singing?" he asked her.

"Opera, German opera." She did not care to discuss the subject. "We have some apple strudel if you want it."

"She isn't so cordial, is she?" said George.

"Oh, well. She doesn't know us and she thought we were going to kid her about her singing, maybe. She's from up where they speak German probably and she's touchy about being here,

① Sion：西昂，位于瑞士日内瓦湖东南，接近瑞士、意大利、法国三国的交界处，属于法语区，盛产名酒，尤其是葡萄酒。

隔壁房里的歌声停了，一个围着蓝围裙的女孩走出门来看看他们想喝点什么。

“一瓶西昂酒，”尼克说，“行不行，吉奇？”

“好的，”乔治说，“你在酒这方面比我懂得多。我什么酒都爱喝。”

那女孩出去了。

“没什么能真正比得上滑雪，对吧？”尼克说，“当你滑了很长一段路第一次停下来的时候就有这种感觉。”

“嘿，”乔治说，“这种满足感是难以言表的。”

那女孩拿了酒进来，他们打不开瓶塞。最后还是尼克打开的。那女孩出去了，他们听见她在隔壁房间里唱德语歌。

“里面的那些瓶塞渣子不要紧的，”尼克说。

“不知道她这儿有没有糕点。”

“我们问问就知道了。”

那姑娘进屋来了，尼克这才注意到她那围裙遮着高高隆起的肚子。她先前进来时我怎么没发现呢，他心里想着。

“你刚才唱的是什么？”他问她。

“歌剧，德国歌剧。”她不愿谈论这个话题，“如果你们要吃点什么的话，我们这儿有苹果馅卷饼。”

“她不是那么热情友好，对吗？”乔治说。

“哦，行啦！她又不认识我们，也许还以为我们拿她唱歌的事开玩笑呢。她可能是从北方讲德语的地区来的，待在这里让她很恼火了，再加上还没结婚就怀了孕，她就更敏感了。”

and then she's got that baby coming without being married and she's touchy."

"How do you know she isn't married?"

"No ring. Hell, no girls get married around here till they're knocked up."

The door came open and a gang of woodcutters from up the road came in, stamping their boots and steaming in the room. The waitress brought in three litres of new wine for the gang and they sat at the two tables, smoking and quiet, with their hats off, leaning back against the wall or forward on the table. Outside the horses on the wood sledges made an occasional sharp jangle of bells as they tossed their heads.

George and Nick were happy. They were fond of each other. They knew they had the run back home ahead of them.

"When have you got to go back to school?" Nick asked.

"Tonight," George answered. "I've got to get the ten-forty from Montreux. "

"I wish you could stick over and we could do the Dent du Lys① tomorrow."

"I got to get educated," George said. "Gee, Mike, don't you wish we could just bum together? Take our skis and go on the train to where there was good running and then go on and put up at pubs and go right across the Oberland② and up the Valais③ and all through the Engadine④ and just take repair kit and extra sweaters

① Dent du Lys：又称"Dent de Lys"，瑞士境内伯尔尼兹阿尔卑斯山的山峰之一，高2014米。
② Oberland：奥伯兰，瑞士地名，是瑞士最知名的滑雪区之一。
③ Valais：瓦莱，瑞士州名，山峰颇多且山谷风景秀丽，为疗养胜地。
④ Engadine：恩加，位于瑞士格劳宾登州 (Graubunden) 因河 (Inn River) 上游。其上方就是圣莫里茨 (Sankt Moritz 著名滑雪山城)。

"你怎么知道她还没结婚?"

"她没戴戒指。该死,这一带的女孩都是肚子大了才结婚的。"

门开了,一帮从大路另一头来的伐木工人进来了,他们跺跺靴子上的雪,身上直冒水汽。女招待给这帮人拿来了三升新酒,他们坐两桌,抽着烟,不说话,帽子也取了下来,有的靠着墙,有的趴在桌上。屋外,拉木制雪橇的马一摆头,使得铃铛偶尔也跟着清脆地叮当作响。

乔治和尼克都开心着呢。两人彼此比较谈得来。他们知道前方还有漫漫回程路在等着他们。

"你什么时候得回学校?"尼克问。

"今晚,"乔治答。"我得赶上10点40分从蒙特勒开出的那趟车。"

"我真希望你能留下来,明天我们就可以去赖斯峰滑雪了。"

"我得上学啊,"乔治说,"哎呀,迈克,你难道不希望我们就这样一起游荡吗?带着滑雪板,乘上火车,哪儿有好的滑雪场地我们就去哪儿,滑好就上路,找个客栈投宿,再直接穿过奥伯兰,到瓦莱去,跑遍恩加丁,随身只带修理工具和换洗的毛衣和睡衣,将学校啊什么的,全都抛之脑后。"

and pyjamas in our rucksacks and not give a damn about school or anything."

"Yes, and go through the *Schwarzwald* that way. Gee, the swell places."

"That's where you went fishing last summer, isn't it?"

"Yes."

They ate the strudel and drank the rest of the wine.

George leaned back against the wall and shut his eyes.

"Wine always makes me feel this way," he said.

"Feel bad?" Nick asked.

"No, I feel good, but funny."

"I know," Nick said.

"Sure," said George.

"Should we have another bottle?" Nick asked.

"Not for me," George said.

They sat there, Nick leaning his elbows on the table, George slumped back against the wall.

"Is Helen going to have a baby?" George said, coming down to the table from the wall.

"Yes."

"When?"

"Late next summer."

"Are you glad?"

"Yes. Now."

"Will you go back to the States?"

"I guess so."

"Do you want to?"

"嗯，就那样走遍黑森林。哎呀，多么好的地方啊。"

"那就是你这个夏天钓鱼的地方，是吗？"

"是的。"

他们吃着苹果馅卷饼，把剩下的酒也都喝光了。

乔治靠在墙上，闭着眼睛。

"喝酒总让我有这种感觉，"他说。

"感觉很糟糕吗？"尼克问。

"不。感觉还可以，只是有点不舒服。"

"我明白，"尼克说。

"当然，"乔治说。

"我们再喝一瓶？"尼克问。

"我不喝了，"乔治说。

他们坐在那儿，尼克双肘撑在桌上，乔治颓然地靠在墙上。

"海伦快生了吗？"乔治说，离开墙那儿，来到桌边。

"是啊。"

"什么时候？"

"明年夏末。"

"你高兴吗？"

"高兴。此刻就很高兴。"

"你会回美国去吗？"

"我想会的。"

"你想回去吗？"

"No."

"Does Helen?"

"No."

George sat silent. He looked at the empty bottle and the empty glasses.

"It's hell, isn't it?" he said.

"No. Not exactly," Nick said.

"Why not?"

"I don't know," Nick said.

"Will you ever go skiing together in the States?" George said.

"I don't know," said Nick.

"The mountains aren't much," George said.

"No," said Nick. "They're too rocky. There's too much timber and they're too far away."

"Yes," said George, "that's the way it is in California."

"Yes," Nick said, "that's the way it is everywhere I've ever been."

"Yes," said George, "that's the way it is."

The Swiss got up and paid and went out.

"I wish we were Swiss," George said.

"They've all got goiter[①]," said Nick.

"I don't believe it," George said.

"Neither do I," said Nick.

They laughed.

"Maybe we'll never go skiing again, Nick," George said.

① goiter：即"甲状腺肿"，是由于缺碘而引起的。瑞士阿尔卑斯山地区的人们之所以容易得大脖子病（即地方性甲状腺肿），是因为他们住的地方海拔较高，土壤受雨水冲洗很严重，土壤里的碘成分就慢慢地流失掉了。

"不想。"

"海伦呢？"

"也不想。"

乔治默默地坐着。他看着空空的酒瓶和空空的酒杯。

"真麻烦，不是吗？"他说。

"不。并不完全是这样，"尼克说。

"为什么不完全是这样呢？"

"我不知道，"尼克说。

"你们在美国会一块儿去滑雪吗？"乔治说。

"我不清楚，"尼克说。

"山不是很多，"乔治说。

"不，"尼克说，"石头太多。树林也太多，而且路程遥远。"

"对啊，"乔治说，"加利福尼亚也是这样。"

"是啊，"尼克说，"我去过的地方都这样。"

"是啊，"乔治说，"都是这样。"

那两个瑞士人站起身来，结了账，出去了。

"真希望我们就是瑞士人，"乔治说。

"他们都得大脖子病，"尼克说。

"我不信，"乔治说。

"我也不信，"尼克说。

两人大笑起来。

"也许我们再也不会去滑雪了，尼克，"乔治说。

"We've got to," said Nick. "It isn't worth while if you can't."

"We'll go, all right," George said.

"We've got to," Nick agreed.

"I wish we could make a promise about it," George said.

Nick stood up. He buckled his wind jacket tight. He leaned over George and picked up the two ski poles from against the wall. He stuck one of the ski poles into the floor.

"There isn't any good in promising," he said.

They opened the door and went out. It was very cold. The snow had crusted hard. The road ran up the hill into the pine trees.

They took down their skis from where they leaned against the wall in the inn. Nick put on his gloves. George was already started up the road, his skis on his shoulder. Now they would have the run home together.

“我们一定得去，”尼克说，“不能滑就没意义了。”

“对，我们就要去滑，”乔治说。

“我们一定得滑，”尼克附和说。

“但愿我们就这么说定了，”乔治说。

尼克站起身，扣紧防风夹克。他朝乔治那边弯下身子，拿起靠墙放着的两支滑雪杖。他把一支滑雪杖插在地上。

“说定了没什么好处，”他说。

他们把门打开，出去了。外面很冷。雪都结得硬邦邦的。大路一直从山上通到松树林里。

他们把刚才放置在客栈墙边的滑雪板拿起来。尼克戴上了手套。乔治已经扛着滑雪板上路了。现在他们将要一起踏上回家的路途。

The Mother of a Queen[1]
一个同性恋者的母亲

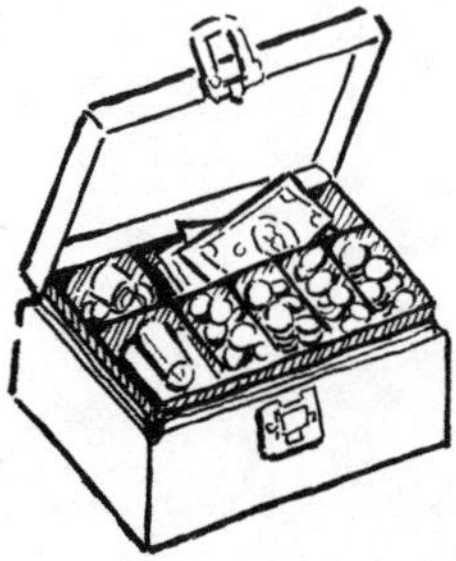

① queen：美国俚语，指的是“女性化的男同性恋者”。

《一个同性恋者的母亲》(*The Mother of a Queen,* 1933) 是海明威在 20 世纪 30 年代写下的一篇同性恋题材小说。小说中并没有任何来自作者对同性恋态度的表述迹象。小说从第一人称“我”的有限视角来叙述整个故事情节的发展过程。虽然帕科是主人公,但他并没有直接出现并陈述自己的观点，而是由小说中的“我”即他的情人在传达着相关信息。然而这样的叙述眼光往往较为主观且带有个人偏见和感情色彩，只限于“我”的所见所闻所感。正是因为如此，小说中出现了“我”几次主动提出处理帕科母亲墓地续用的事宜，却总是得到空头的回应; 随着帕科一次又一次地对通知漠不关心，“我”为此气得说了好几次粗话和脏话；最后帕科对“我”和小混混之间的差别对待再加上对“我”的戏弄把“我”完全激怒了，放弃了钱柜的管理并与帕科断绝任何联系。然而正是通过这一次次的通知和“我”的主观表达，帕科的生活方式、人生价值观和为人都一一展现在读者面前。

When his father died he was only a kid and his manager buried him perpetually. That is, so he would have the plot permanently. But when his mother died his manager thought they might not always be so hot on each other. They were sweethearts; sure he's a queen, didn't you know that, of course he is. So he just buried her for five years.

Well, when he came back to Mexico from Spain he got the first notice. It said it was the first notice that the five years were up and would he make arrangements for the continuing of his mother's grave. It was only twenty dollars for perpetual. I had the cash box then and I said let me attend to it, Paco. But he said no, he would look after it. He'd look after it right away. It was his mother and he wanted to do it himself.

Then in a week he got the second notice. I read it to him and I said I thought he had looked after it.

No, he said, he hadn't.

"Let me do it," I said. "It's right here in the cash box."

No, he said. Nobody could tell him what to do. He'd do it himself when he got around to it. "What's the sense in spending money sooner than necessary?"

"All right," I said, "but see you look after it." At this time he had a contract for six fights at four thousand pesos[1] a fight besides his benefit fight. He made over fifteen thousand dollars there in the capital alone. He was just tight, that's all.

The third notice came in another week and I read it to him. It said that if he did not make the payment by the following Saturday

① peso：拉丁美洲一些国家和菲律宾的货币单位。

当他父亲过世时，他还是个毛头小子，是他的经纪人将他父亲永久地安葬下来的。换句话说，那么，他父亲就可以一直享用这块墓地。然而当他母亲去世时，经纪人认为，他们之间不可能老是那么的热情。他们是亲密的爱人；而他肯定是个同性恋。难道你不知道，他当然是。因此经纪人只将他母亲暂且安葬五年。

喔，当他从西班牙回到墨西哥时，他就收到第一份通知。通知说，这是第一份通知——五年期到了，他该办理一下关于他母亲继续享用墓地的相关事宜。只要花20美元就可以永久享用了。那时钱柜是由我来掌管的，于是我就说让我来办理这件事，帕科。但是他拒绝了我，说他自己会处理。他会尽快办妥。那是他母亲，他得亲自去办。

然后一个星期后，他又收到了第二份通知。我念给他听的，我说我还以为他已经处理好了呢。

没有，他说，他还没有处理。

“让我去办吧，”我说，“钱就放在钱柜里。”

不行，他说。没人说得动他去做任何事情。等他抽出空来时，就会亲自去办的。“还没到那个时候就这么急着把钱送出去有啥意思啊？”

“好吧，”我说，“不过务必要处理这件事。”这时他除了参加义赛外，还签了份合同，参加六场斗牛比赛，每场的报酬是4 000比索。光是在首都，他就挣了一万五千多美元。总之，他很忙。

又一星期过去了，第三份通知到了，我又念给他听。通知上说，如果在下星期六之前他还没有来付钱的话，就要把他母亲的

his mother's grave would be opened and her remains dumped on the common boneheap. He said he would go attend to it that afternoon when he went to town.

"Why not have me do it?" I asked him.

"Keep out of my business," he said. "It's my business and I'm going to do it."

"All right, if that's the way you feel about it," I said. "Do your own business."

He got the money out of the cash box, although then he always carried a hundred or more pesos with him all the time, and he said he would look after it. He went out with the money and so of course I thought he had attended to it.

A week later the notice came that they had no response to the final warning and so his mother's body had been dumped on the boneheap; on the public boneheap.

"Jesus Christ," I said to him, "you said you'd pay that and you took money out of the cash box to do it and now what's happened to your mother? My God, think of it! The public boneheap and your own mother. Why didn't you let me look after it? I would have sent it when the first notice came."

"It's none of your business. It's *my* mother."

"It's none of *my* business, yes, but it was *your* business. What kind of blood is it in a man that will let that be done to his mother? You don't deserve to have a mother."

"It is my mother," he said. "Now she is so much dearer to me. Now I don't have to think of her buried in one place and be sad. Now she is all about me in the air, like the birds and the flowers.

坟墓挖开，将尸骨扔在万人冢上。他说下午到城里去，他会处理这个事情的。

“为什么不让我来处理呢？”我问他。

“别插手我的事，”他说。“我自己的事情，我自己会办。”

“好吧，既然你是这么认为的，那就你自己办吧，”我说。

虽然那时他身上老带着100比索或者是更多的钱，但他还是从钱柜拿钱，他说他会亲自去办的。他拿了钱出去，因此我理所当然地以为他已经把这事办好了。

一星期之后，通知又来了，由于他们发出的最后警告没有得到任何回应，所以他母亲的尸骨已经被扔到万人冢上去了。

“我的天啊，”我跟他说。“你答应过会去付钱，你还从钱柜里拿了钱去处理这事情，可如今你母亲又怎么样了呢？天哪，想想看！想想那万人冢，还有你自己的母亲。你为什么不让我去处理呢？第一份通知到的时候，我就可以去付清的。”

“与你无关。这是我的母亲。”

“对，这确实与我无关，可这是你该做的啊。任由别人对自己的母亲做那样的事，还是人吗？你真不配有母亲。”

“这是我母亲，”他说，“现在她跟我更亲近了。现在我不必去想该把她葬在什么地方，更不必悲伤。现在她就像鸟儿和花儿一样在我的周围。现在她时刻跟我在一起。”

Now she will always be with me."

"Jesus Christ," I said, "what kind of blood have you anyway? I don't want you to even speak to me."

"She is all around me," he said. "Now I will never be sad."

At that time he was spending all kinds of money around women trying to make himself seem a man and fool people, but it didn't have any effect on people that knew anything about him. He owed me over six hundred pesos and he wouldn't pay me. "Why do you want it now?" he'd say. "Don't you trust me? Aren't we friends?"

"It isn't friends or trusting you. It's that I paid the accounts out of my own money while you were away and now I need the money back and you have it to pay me."

"I haven't got it."

"You have it," I said. "It's in the cash box now and you can pay me."

"I need that money for something," he said. "You don't know all the needs I have for money."

"I stayed here all the time you were in Spain and you authorized me to pay these things as they came up, all these things of the house, and you didn't send any money while you were gone and I paid over six hundred pesos in my own money and now I need it and you can pay me."

"I'll pay you soon," he said. "Right now I need the money badly."

"For what?"

"For my own business."

“天啊，”我说，“你还是不是人啊？我甚至不想你跟我讲话。”

“她就在我的身旁，”他说，“现在我再也不会伤心了。”

那时，他在女人身上花了不少钱，努力将自己弄得像模像样地好去哄骗别人，不过对他底细略知一二的人都不会上他的当。他欠我六百多比索，还没给我。“你为什么现在要钱呢？”他说，“难道你不相信我？我们不是朋友了吗？”

“这与是不是朋友，信任不信任无关。问题在于你不在的时候，我拿自己的钱替你付了账，现在我要讨还这笔钱，你有钱就得还给我。”

“我没钱。”

“你有钱，”我说，“就放在钱柜里，你可以还给我的。”

“我需要这笔钱办事，”他说，“你并不知道我需要钱去干很多事情。”

“你在西班牙时，我一直待在这里，你委托我凡是碰到有什么账要付的时候，屋里的一切开支均由我支付，你在外时没寄一分钱回来，我拿自己的钱付了六百多比索，现在我缺钱用，你还给我吧。”

“我会尽快还给你，”他说，“目前我急需钱用。”

“你需要钱干什么呢？”

“个人私事。”

"Why don't you pay me some on account?"

"I can't," he said. "I need that money too badly. But I will pay you."

He had only fought twice in Spain, they couldn't stand him there, they saw through him quick enough, and he had seven new fighting suits made and this is the kind of thing he was: he had them packed so badly that four of them were ruined by sea water on the trip back and he couldn't even wear them.

"My God," I said to him, "you go to Spain. You stay there the whole season and only fight two times. You spend all the money you took with you on suits and then have them spoiled by salt water so you can't wear them. That is the kind of season you have and then you talk to me about running your own business. Why don't you pay me the money you owe me so I can leave?"

"I want you here," he said, "and I will pay you. But now I need the money."

"You need it too badly to pay for your own mother's grave to keep your mother buried. Don't you?" I said.

"I am happy about what has happened to my mother," he said. "You cannot understand."

"Thank Christ I can't," I said. "You pay me what you owe me or I will take it out of the cash box."

"I will keep the cash box myself," he said.

"No, you won't," I said.

That very afternoon he came to me with a punk, some fellow from his own town who was broke, and said, "Here is a *paisano*

"你为什么不先预付一些给我呢？"

"不行，"他说，"我太缺钱了。可我会还给你的。"

在西班牙，他只斗过两场，他们那儿可受不了他，很快就看穿了他，他都做了七套新的斗牛装，他就是那样的人，把这些服装包裹得如此的随意以至其中的四套在回国途中被海水浸坏了，穿都不能穿了。

"我的天啊，"我跟他说，"你去了西班牙。整个斗牛季节[1]，你都在那儿，却只斗了两场。你把带去的钱都花在做衣服上，结果又让海水给糟蹋了，弄得穿都穿不了。那就是你过的斗牛季节，如今你倒跟我说要自己处理自己的事情。你为什么不把欠我的钱还清好让我走？"

"我这儿离不开你，"他说，"我会还你的。但是我现在缺钱用。"

"你急需钱来付墓地租金好安葬你母亲，对吧？"我说。

"对于我母亲墓地那件事，我倒是挺高兴的，"他说，"你无法理解的。"

"谢天谢地，幸亏我不能理解，"我说，"你把欠我的钱还给我，不然我就自己从钱柜里拿钱。"

"钱柜我自己保管，"他说。

"不，你不行，"我说。

就在那天下午，他带了个小混混来找我，这小混混是他老

① the whole season：指的是整个斗牛季节。西班牙的斗牛季节一般从每年的 3 月到 10 月，因为这段时间为西班牙的春季、夏季和秋季，天气比较暖和，而 7、8 月份更是欣赏斗牛表演的黄金时期。

who needs money to go home because his mother is very sick." This fellow was just a punk, you understand, a nobody he'd never seen before, but from his home town, and he wanted to be the big, generous matador with a fellow townsman.

"Give him fifty pesos from the cash box," he told me.

"You just told me you had no money to pay me," I said. "And now you want to give fifty pesos to this punk."

"He is a fellow townsman," he said, "and he is in distress."

"You bitch," I said. I gave him the key of the cash box. "Get it yourself. I'm going to town."

"Don't be angry," he said. "I'm going to pay you."

I got the car out to go to town. It was his car but he knew I drove it better than he did. Everything he did I could do better. He knew it. He couldn't even read and write. I was going to see somebody and see what I could do about making him pay me. He came out and said, "I'm coming with you and I'm going to pay you. We are good friends. There is no need to quarrel."

We drove into the city and I was driving. Just before we came into the town he pulled out twenty pesos.

"Here's the money," he said.

"You motherless bitch," I said to him and told him what he could do with the money. "You give fifty pesos to that punk and then offer me twenty when you owe me six hundred. I wouldn't take a nickel from you. You know what you can do with it."

I got out of the car without a peso in my pocket and I didn't know where I was going to sleep that night. Later I went out with a friend and got my things from his place. I never spoke to him again

乡，穷得叮当响。他说："这位老乡由于母亲病重需要点钱回家。"这同乡只不过是个小流氓，要知道他以前从没见过这个人，仅仅是从他的家乡来的罢了。而他竟要在同乡面前充当慷慨大方的斗牛士。

"从钱柜里拿50比索给他，"他跟我说。

"你刚告诉我没钱还我，"我说，"现在你却要给这小流氓50比索。"

"他是同乡，"他说，"他有难了。"

"你个混蛋，"我骂着。我将钱柜的钥匙给了他。"你自己去拿。我要上城里去。"

"别生气，"他说，"我会还钱给你的。"

我把车子开出来，准备到城里去。这是他的车子，不过他知道我车开得比他好。凡是他能做的事情我都可以做得比他好。这他也是知道的。他甚至连读书写字都不会。我打算去找个人，看看有什么办法好让他还我钱。他走出来说："我要跟你一起去，我打算还钱给你。我们是好朋友。没必要吵架。"

我们开车进了城，我开的车。就在我们进城之前，他掏出了20比索。

"钱在这儿，"他说。

"你这没教养的东西，"我朝他骂道，还告诉他拿着钱能干些什么事情。"你给那小流氓50比索，却还我20，你欠我的可是六百多比索。我决不会拿你一分钱。你也知道拿着这钱会怎么着。"

我下了车，兜里一分钱也没有，不知道晚上到哪儿去落脚。后来，我和一个朋友交往了，也把我的东西从他那儿拿走了。直到今年，我再也没跟他说过话。一天傍晚，我在马德里碰见他正

until this year. I met him walking with three friends in the evening on the way to the Callao cinema in the Gran Via in Madrid. He put his hand out to me.

"Hello Roger, old friend," he said to me. "How are you? People say you are talking against me. That you say all sorts of unjust things about me."

"All I say is you never had a mother," I said to him. That's the worst thing you can say to insult a man in Spanish.

"That's true," he said. "My poor mother died when I was so young it seems as though I never had a mother. It's very sad."

There's a queen for you. You can't touch them. Nothing, nothing can touch them. They spend money on themselves or for vanity, but they never pay. Try to get one to pay. I told him what I thought of him right there on the Gran Via, in front of three friends, but he speaks to me now when I meet him as though we were friends. What kind of blood is it that makes a man like that?

跟三个朋友一起去格兰维亚的卡略电影院。他向我招手。

“嗨，罗杰，我的老朋友，”他对我说，“你过得怎么样啊？大家说你在讲我坏话。你讲了很多冤枉我的坏话。”

“我所说的就是你根本没有母亲，”我跟他说。这句话在西班牙语里是最侮辱人的。

“没错，”他说，“我可怜的母亲过世时，我还不懂事。这看起来就像是我从来就没有母亲。太悲伤了。”

你所面对的是个同性恋啊。你怎么也感动不了他们。也没有东西可以感动他们。他们为自己花钱，或者是为了虚荣心，可是他们从不自己出钱。想方设法要别人来付。我在格兰维亚大道那当着他三个朋友的面，跟他说了我对他的看法；可这会儿我碰到他，他跟我说话时竟像两个朋友似的。他这样还算是人吗？

The Snows of Kilimanjaro[1]
乞力马扎罗山的雪

① Kilimanjaro：赤道雪峰乞力马扎罗山，在非洲斯瓦希里语中意为“光明之山”，位于坦桑尼亚东北部，是坦桑尼亚和肯尼亚的分水岭。

《乞力马扎罗山的雪》(*The Snows of Kilimanjaro,* 1936) 讲述的是美国作家哈里在非洲度过的他生命中最后半天的情形。哈里与其富有的妻子从巴黎来到肯尼亚狩猎，不料在狩猎时被荆棘划伤，也许是由于疏忽，也许是由于卡车抛锚而得不到及时救治，他的伤口转变成了坏疽，救治无望。这个故事从两个层面展开叙述。一个层面是按照时间顺序叙述的故事：通过人物对话叙述了一个正值盛年、名大于实的作家临死前的种种怪异、冷漠与不甘。另一个层面通过意识流的写法，展现了主人公哈里回忆中各个不同的画面，让读者窥探到了哈里人生经历的各个侧面及其内心世界的复杂感受。在这个故事里，海明威通过内心独白、自由联想、时空跳跃等意识流技巧，展现了哈里的旧日世界里曾经有过的片刻的美好、理想的破灭以及随后行尸走肉般的生活。终年积雪的乞力马扎罗山山巅是非洲人心中的圣殿，是哈里弥留之际的意识所抵达的地方，是他最后的精神诉求，或许也是海明威自己寻求灵魂升华与心理救赎的圣殿。小说主人公哈里的经历中有着海明威的真实生活的部分缩影。《乞力马扎罗山的雪》于1952 年被拍成电影。

Kilimanjaro is a snow-covered mountain 19, 710 *feet high, and is said to be the highest mountain in Africa. Its western summit is called the Masai*[①] *"Ngàje Ngài," the House of God. Close to the western summit there is the dried and frozen carcass of a leopard. No one has explained what the leopard was seeking at that altitude.*

"The marvellous thing is that it's painless," he said. "That's how you know when it starts."

"Is it really?"

"Absolutely. I'm awfully sorry about the odor though. That must bother you."

"Don't! Please don't."

"Look at them," he said. "Now is it sight or is it scent[②] that brings them like that?"

The cot the man lay on was in the wide shade of a mimosa tree and as he looked out past the shade onto the glare of the plain there were three of the big birds squatted obscenely, while in the sky a dozen more sailed, making quick-moving shadows as they passed.

"They've been there since the day the truck broke down," he said. "Today's the first time any have lit on the ground. I watched the way they sailed very carefully at first in case I ever wanted to use them in a story. That's funny now."

"I wish you wouldn't," she said.

"I'm only talking," he said. "It's much easier if I talk. But I

① Masai：马塞人，是肯尼亚和坦桑尼亚的一个游牧狩猎民族。
② "sight"和"scent"在英语里押头韵。

乞力马扎罗山，白雪皑皑，海拔19 710英尺，据称是非洲最高的山。西高峰在马塞语中称作“恩加奇—恩加伊”，即上帝之殿。接近西高峰处有一具风干冻僵了的猎豹尸骸。猎豹到这样的高度到底要寻求什么，尚无人做出过解释。

“让人感到奇妙的是，它一点都不疼，”他说，“你知道，开始的时候它就是这样。”

“真的吗？”

“千真万确。不过对这气味我却抱歉万分。那一定让你心烦。”

“别这样说！请别这样说。”

“看看那些鸟儿，”他说道，“是视觉还是嗅觉使它们像那样子？”

男人躺在帆布床上，床在一棵合欢树的阔荫下。他朝阴凉外望去，旷野上阳光炫目，三只巨鸟蹲伏在那里，模样让人恶心。空中，还有十多只在滑翔。巨鸟过处，鸟影迅即随形闪动。

“卡车抛锚那天起它们就在那儿了，”他说，“今天它们可是第一次落到地面上来。起初我曾非常仔细地观察它们飞翔呢！以为在故事中我也许会用得着。现在想起来却很好笑了。”

“我倒是希望你不要写，”她说。

“我只是说说而已，”他说，“如果我说说话，就感觉轻松多了。但我不想让你心烦。”

don't want to bother you."

"You know it doesn't bother me," she said. "It's that I've gotten so very nervous not being able to do anything. I think we might make it as easy as we can until the plane comes."

"Or until the plane doesn't come."[①]

"Please tell me what I can do. There must be something I can do."

"You can take the leg off and that might stop it, though I doubt it. Or you can shoot me. You're a good shot now. I taught you to shoot, didn't I?"

"Please don't talk that way. Couldn't I read to you?"

"Read what?"

"Anything in the book that we haven't read."

"I can't listen to it," he said. "Talking is the easiest. We quarrel and that makes the time pass."

"I don't quarrel. I never want to quarrel. Let's not quarrel any more. No matter how nervous we get. Maybe they will be back with another truck today. Maybe the plane will come."

"I don't want to move," the man said. "There is no sense in moving now except to make it easier for you."

"That's cowardly."

"Can't you let a man die as comfortably as he can without calling him names?[②] What's the use of clanging me?"

"You're not going to die."

① "Or until the plane doesn't come." means "Or the plane won't come even if I die.", 意为"即使我死了，飞机也不会来"。

② 对于一个自诩为具有阳刚气质的男人来说，被人称作是"coward"就相当于是在骂他 (call him names)。

“你知道的，这不会让我心烦。我如此焦虑紧张，是由于我对此束手无策。飞机来之前，我想我们还是尽可能地放松放松。”

“或者等到飞机来不了。”

“求你告诉我，我能做点什么。一定有什么是我能做的。”

“你可把这条腿拿掉，那也许会让它止住。尽管对此我持怀疑态度。或者你可以打死我。如今你可是神枪手啦。我教你学会开枪的，对吧？”

“求你别像那样说话。我难道不能给你读点什么吗？”

“读什么？”

“读书本里我们没读过的。”

“我听不进去的，”他说，“说话是最轻松的了。我们吵吵嘴吧，那样能打发时间。”

“我不吵嘴。我从来都不想吵嘴。我们不要再吵嘴了。即便我们再紧张无措也不要。也许他们今天会随另一辆卡车回来呢。也许飞机会来呢。”

“我不想挪动了，”男人说，“现在，挪动毫无意义了，除非这样能让你好过点。”

“那样放弃是懦夫的行为。”

“你能不能让一个男人舒服点死去，而不诅咒他呢？辱骂我有什么用？”

“你不会死的。”

"Don't be silly. I'm dying now. Ask those bastards." He looked over to where the huge, filthy birds sat, their naked heads sunk in the hunched feathers. A fourth planed down, to run quick-legged and then waddle slowly toward the others.

"They are around every camp. You never notice them. You can't die if you don't give up."

"Where did you read that? You're such a bloody fool."

"You might think about some one else."

"For Christ's sake," he said, "that's been my trade."

He lay then and was quiet for a while and looked across the heat shimmer of the plain to the edge of the bush. There were a few Tommies that showed minute and white against the yellow and, far off, he saw a herd of zebra, white against the green of the bush. This was a pleasant camp under big trees against a hill, with good water, and close by, a nearly dry water hole where sand grouse flighted in the mornings.

"Wouldn't you like me to read?" she asked. She was sitting on a canvas chair beside his cot. "There's a breeze coming up."

"No thanks."

"Maybe the truck will come."

"I don't give a damn about the truck."

"I do."

"You give a damn about so many things that I don't."

"Not so many, Harry."

"What about a drink?"

“别犯傻了。现在我已经命悬一线了。问问那些杂种。”他向那些巨大的、模样让人作呕的鸟盘踞的地方望过去，它们裸露的头部掖在隆起的羽毛里。第四只鸟飞落下来，快步跑着，然后慢慢地摇向另外几只。

“有营地的地方就有它们。你一直没注意它们而已。你若不放弃，就不会死。”

“你在哪里读到的？你是这样一个大蠢蛋。”

“你不妨想想别人。”

“看在上帝的分上，”他说，“那可是我的本行。”

他随即躺着，安静了一会。他的目光透过旷野的灼灼热浪，落到灌木丛边缘。有几只野羊，在黄色的映衬下显得娇小又白皙。再远些地方，他看到一群斑马，映衬着绿色的灌木丛，显得白花花的。这个营地令人心旷神怡。营地在几棵大树底下，背靠着小山岭，水源充足。邻近的地方，在一起几近干涸的水洼处，清晨有沙鸡飞行。

“你难道不想我给你读点什么吗？”她问道。她坐在他帆布床边的一把帆布椅子上。“有一阵微风刮过来呢。”

“不，谢了。”

“也许卡车会来。”

“我压根不在乎卡车。”

“我在乎。”

“你在乎的很多事情，我压根儿都不在乎。”

“不是很多，哈里。”

“来点酒怎样？”

"It's supposed to be bad for you. It said in Black's[①] to avoid all alcohol. You shouldn't drink."

"Molo!" he shouted.

"Yes Bwana."

"Bring whiskey-soda."

"Yes Bwana."

"You shouldn't," she said. "That's what I mean by giving up. It says it's bad for you. I know it's bad for you."

"No," he said. "It's good for me."

So now it was all over, he thought. So now he would never have a chance to finish it. So this was the way it ended, in a bickering over a drink. Since the gangrene started in his right leg he had no pain and with the pain the horror had gone and all he felt now was a great tiredness and anger that this was the end of it. For this, that now was coming, he had very little curiosity. For years it had obsessed him; but now it meant nothing in itself. It was strange how easy being tired enough made it.

Now he would never write the things that he had saved to write until he knew enough to write them well. Well, he would not have to fail at trying to write them either. Maybe you could never write them, and that was why you put them off and delayed the starting. Well he would never know, now.

"I wish we'd never come," the woman said. She was looking at him holding the glass and biting her lip. "You never would have gotten anything like this in Paris. You always said you loved

① Black：指詹姆士·布拉克 (James Black1823—1893) 禁酒主义者，曾于 1869 年创建禁酒党，并出书宣扬其禁酒主张。

“它对你该是有害无益。在布拉克的书里说，要杜绝所有酒精。你不该沾酒。”

“莫洛！”他喊道。

“是，先生。”

“拿威士忌苏打来。”

“是，先生。”

“你不应该这样，”她说，“我说的放弃就是指这。书里说对你有害处，我晓得这对你有害处。”

“不，”他说，“这对我有好处。”

就这样，现在什么都结束了，他想。就这样，现在他永远不会有机会来完成它了。就这样，为一口酒产生口角，这就是它了结的方式了。自从右腿开始生坏疽以来，他不再感到疼痛了，恐惧也随疼痛消失得无影无踪；这会儿，他感到的是极度的疲惫和愤懑，因为这样竟成为大结局。对这点，对即将到来的这点，他一点也不觉诧异。多年来，这感觉一直笼罩着他；但现在，它本身已毫不重要了。奇怪的是，倦怠之极，竟可如此轻而易举地引发它。

现在，他将再也不会写作他曾经积累下来的那些题材了。他本想积累下来，等他知道如何很好地把它们写出来时再写的。也罢，他也不会经历尝试写作它们时可能遭遇的失败了。也许是因为你永远都无法将它们写出来，所以你就一再拖延，迟迟未动笔。唉，这当儿，他将永远无法知道了。

“我多希望我们没来过这儿，”女人说。她看着他，手握玻璃杯，咬着唇。“在巴黎，你绝不会惹这样的事情上身。你过去总

Paris. We could have stayed in Paris or gone anywhere. I'd have gone anywhere. I said I'd go anywhere you wanted. If you wanted to shoot we could have gone shooting in Hungary and been comfortable."

"Your bloody money," he said.

"That's not fair," she said. "It was always yours as much as mine. I left everything and I went wherever you wanted to go and I've done what you wanted to do. But I wish we'd never come here."

"You said you loved it."

"I did when you were all right. But now I hate it. I don't see why that had to happen to your leg. What have we done to have that happen to us?"

"I suppose what I did was to forget to put iodine on it when I first scratched it. Then I didn't pay any attention to it because I never infect. Then, later, when it got bad, it was probably using that weak carbolic solution when the other antiseptics ran out that paralyzed the minute blood vessels and started the gangrene." He looked at her, "What else?"

"I don't mean that."

"If we would have hired a good mechanic instead of a half-baked Kikuyu[1] driver, he would have checked the oil and never burned out that bearing in the truck."

"I don't mean that."

"If you hadn't left your own people, your goddamned Old

① Kikuyu：基库尤人又称阿基库尤人，是非洲班图人中的一支。基库尤人是肯尼亚第一大部族。

说你热爱巴黎。我们本可待在巴黎或者去别的什么地方。我但愿我们是去了别的地方。我说过，只要是你愿意去的地方，我都愿意去。如果你只是想打猎，我们本来也可以去匈牙利打猎，舒舒心心地过日子。”

“用你的大把的钞票吧，”他说。

“那样说不公正啊，”她说，“有我多少钞票，就有你多少钞票。我放弃了一切，只要你想去的地方我都跟着。只要你想做的事儿我都做了。可我多么希望我们根本就没来过这里。”

“你说过你爱它。”

“你好端端的时候，我确实如此。但这会儿我恨它。我不明白那为什么会降临到你的腿上。我们到底做过些什么，竟让它降临到我们身上？”

“我揣想，我所做过的事情，就是我第一次挠它的时候，忘记在上面抹碘酒了。接下来的是，我对它置之不理，因为我从来没有感染过。接着，后来，当它恶化的时候，其他的抗菌剂都用完了，可能是用了药性很弱的碳酸溶液，损坏了毛细血管，于是开始生坏疽。”他望着她，“还能有什么别的呢？”

“我不是这个意思。”

“如果我们雇一个好技师，而不是一个半吊子基库尤司机，他就会检查油量，而不会烧坏了卡车的轴承。”

“我不是这个意思。”

“如果你没有离开你的那群人，没离开你的在旧西布雷、萨拉托加、棕榈滩的那群人，而转而跟我勾搭上的话——”

Westbury, Saratoga, Palm Beach[②] people to take me on—"

"Why, I loved you. That's not fair. I love you now. I'll always love you. Don't you love me?"

"No," said the man. "I don't think so. I never have."

"Harry, what are you saying? You're out of your head."

"No. I haven't any head to go out of."

"Don't drink that," she said. "Darling, please don't drink that. We have to do everything we can."

"You do it," he said. "I'm tired."

Now in his mind he saw a railway station at Karagatch and he was standing with his pack and that was the headlight of the Simplon-Orient[①] *cutting the dark now and he was leaving Thrace*[②] *then after the retreat. That was one of the things he had saved to write, with, in the morning at breakfast, looking out the window and seeing snow on the mountains in Bulgaria and Nansen's*[③] *Secretary asking the old man if it were snow and the old man looking at it and saying, No, that's not snow. It's too early for snow. And the Secretary repeating to the other girls, No, you see. It's not snow and them all saying, It's not snow we were mistaken. But it was the snow all right and he sent them on into it when he evolved exchange of populations. And it was snow they tramped along in until they died that winter.*

---

② Old WestburySaratogaPalm Beach：这三个地点都在美国，都是富人居住区。

① The Simplon-Orient：1919年辛普伦隧道贯通，使得原来往返于巴黎至伊斯坦布尔的豪华列车东方快车几乎贯穿欧洲。

② Thrace：色雷斯是东欧的历史学和地理学上的概念，经历了巴尔干战争、第一次世界大战以及希腊—土耳其战争后，色雷斯被希腊、土耳其和保加利亚所瓜分。

③ Nansen：这里指挪威外交官弗里特约夫·南森(Fridtjof Nansen, 1861—1930)国际难民事务的先驱，于1922年获得诺贝尔和平奖。

“嗨，我那时可是爱你来着。这样说不公平。我现在也爱着你。我会一直爱你的。你难道不爱我吗？

“是的，”男人说。“我认为不爱。我从来都没爱过你。”

“哈里，你在说些什么呢！你脑子进水啦？”

“没呢！我没有脑子，所以无从进水。”

“别喝了，”她说，“宝贝，求你了，别喝酒了。我们必须竭尽全力去做咱们能办到的事。”

“你去办吧，”他说，“我累了。”

现在，在他脑海里，他看到，在卡拉加奇的一个火车站，他携行李而立。这会儿，穿透黑幕的，是辛普伦东方快车的前车灯。撤退后的他，此刻正离开色雷斯。那是他积累下来想写的一段情景。还有，清晨，早餐后，向窗外看去，可以看到保加利亚群山的白雪。南森的秘书问老人这是否是雪；老人看着它说，不，那不是雪。还太早了，哪会有雪。接着她对其他的女孩子们重复：不，你知道的。这不是雪，她们都在说。这不是雪，我们看错了。但那场却真的是雪。那时他提倡交换人质，他把她们送到雪地里去。那年冬天，她们踩着的恰恰是雪，直到她们死去。

It was snow too that fell all Christmas week that year up in the Gauertal, that year they lived in the woodcutter's house with the big square porcelain stove that filled half the room, and they slept on mattresses filled with beech leaves, the time the deserter came with his feet bloody in the snow. He said the police were right behind him and they gave him woolen socks and held the gendarmes talking until the tracks had drifted over.

In Schrunz[①], *on Christmas day, the snow was so bright it hurt your eyes when you looked out from the Weinstube and saw every one coming home from church. That was where they walked up the sleigh-smoothed urine-yellowed road along the river with the steep pine hills, skis heavy on the shoulder, and where they ran that great run down the glacier above the Madlenerhaus, the snow as smooth to see as cake frosting and as light as powder and he remembered the noiseless rush the speed made as you dropped down like a bird.*

They were snow-bound a week in the Madlenerhaus that time in the blizzard playing cards in the smoke by the lantern light and the stakes were higher all the time as Herr Lent lost more. Finally he lost it all. Everything, the Skischule money and all the season's profit and then his capital. He could see him with his long nose, picking up the cards and then opening, "Sans Voir." There was always gambling then. When there was no snow you gambled and when there was too much you gambled. He thought of all the time in his life he had spent gambling.

But he had never written a line of that, nor of that cold, bright

① Schrunz：希伦兹村庄，位于奥地利福拉尔贝格州的布卢登茨区。20 世纪 20 年代，希伦兹是海明威非常喜欢的滑雪胜地。

那年圣诞节，在高厄塔耳山，一整个星期下的也是雪。那年他们住在伐木工人的房子里，巨大的方形瓷炉子占据了一半空间。他们睡在塞有山毛榉叶子的垫子上。那次，逃兵来了。雪中，他双脚血迹斑斑。他说宪兵就尾随其后；他们给了他羊毛袜子，缠着宪兵说话，直到逃兵的足迹被雪湮没。

在希伦兹，圣诞节那天，白雪是如此的耀眼，耀眼得刺疼你的眼睛。你从小酒吧向外望去，看到人们一个个地从教堂回家。那里，他们曾肩扛沉沉的滑雪板，沿着河流，走在被雪橇磨得滑溜溜的斑黄的道路上。河流夹岸有长满松树的陡峭的山丘。也是在那里，在玛德莱屋的上方，他们沿着冰川滑了一次大滑雪。雪花纷纷扬扬，看起来如同在蛋糕上撒糖霜一样，又轻柔得像粉末。他仍记得，当你像鸟儿一样飞落到地上的时候，速度飞快，滑冲时毫无声息。

那次，在暴风雪中，他们一星期的时间都拘囿于玛德莱屋，就着灯光，在弥漫的烟雾中打牌。随着伦特先生输得越来越多，赌注也越来越大。最后他囊空如洗，输光了所有的一切，包括滑雪学校的钱，那一季的全部收益以及他的老本。他看到他伸着长长的鼻子，捡起他的牌，然后摊开说，“不看。”那时总是赌博。不下雪的时候，你赌；雪下得太大，你还是赌。他想起一生中他花在赌博中的那些时光。

但他从未对此写过只言片语。也未写到过寒冷的、雪光耀

Christmas day with the mountains showing across the plain that Barker had flown across the lines to bomb the Austrian officers' leave train, machine-gunning them as they scattered and ran. He remembered Barker afterwards coming into the mess and starting to tell about it. And how quiet it got and then somebody saying, ''You bloody murderous bastard.''

Those were the same Austrians they killed then that he skied with later. No not the same. Hans, that he skied with all that year, had been in the Kaiser-Jagers and when they went hunting hares together up the little valley above the saw-mill they had talked of the fighting on Pasubio and of the attack on Perticara and Asalone and he had never written a word of that. Nor of Monte Corona, nor the Sette Communi, nor of Arsiero.

*How many winters had he lived in the Vorarlberg and the Arlberg*①*? It was four and then he remembered the man who had the fox to sell when they had walked into Bludenz, that time to buy presents, and the cherry-pit taste of good kirsch, the fast-slipping rush of running powder-snow on crust, singing "Hi! Ho! Said Rolly!*②*" as you ran down the last stretch to the steep drop, taking it straight, then running the orchard in three turns and out across the ditch and onto the icy road behind the inn. Knocking your bindings loose, kicking the skis free and leaning them up against the wooden wall of the inn, the lamplight coming from the window, where inside, in the smoky, new-wine smelling warmth, they were playing the accordion.*

① *Arlberg*：阿尔贝格是奥地利的滑雪胜地。
② "*Hi! Ho! Said Rolly*！" 是一首字母歌中的句子。

眼的圣诞节，旷野尽头，群山屹立，巴克飞跃边境，轰炸奥地利军官们的休假火车。当他们逃散时，他用机关枪扫射他们。他记得巴克随后走进这一片狼藉中，开始绘声绘色地描述。空气一下子肃静下来，接着有人说："你这个可耻的嗜血成性的杂种。"

他们那时杀死的那些奥地利人，就是不久前与之一起滑过雪的奥地利人。不，不是一模一样。那年他整年与之一起滑雪的汉斯，一直待在"皇家—猎人"客栈里。他们在锯木厂上游的小山谷一起猎兔的时候，曾谈起帕苏比奥的战役以及对波蒂卡和阿萨罗纳的进攻。对此他在写作中只字未提。也未提及蒙特科尔诺，未提及西特科姆蒙，未提及阿尔西陀。

有几个冬天他是在福拉尔贝格和阿尔贝格度过的？有四个。接着他想起来，当他们那次去买礼物时，步行到布卢登茨，那里有个卖狐狸的男人；还有上好的樱桃酒所特有的那种樱桃核味儿；你们一边唱着"嗨！嗬！罗利说！"，一面越过最后一程冲向险峻的陡坡。其时，纷纷扬起的粉似的雪花飞速飘落到路面上。然后，径直朝前滑；接着拐了三个弯穿过果园，从果园出来后越过一道沟壑，冲向了酒吧后面冰冻的路面。敲松绑腿带，踢开滑雪板，把滑雪板斜靠在酒吧的木板墙上，窗户投射出灯光；窗户里面，在烟雾缭绕、新酒飘香的暖意里，他们在拉手风琴。

“Where did we stay in Paris?” he asked the woman who was sitting by him in a canvas chair, now, in Africa.

“At the Crillon. You know that.”

“Why do I know that?”

“That’s where we always stayed.”

“No. Not always.”

“There and at the Pavillion Henri-Quatre in St. Germain. You said you loved it there.”

“Love is a dunghill,” said Harry. “And I’m the cock that gets on it to crow.”

“If you have to go away,” she said, “is it absolutely necessary to kill off everything you leave behind? I mean do you have to take away everything? Do you have to kill your horse, and your wife and burn your saddle and your armour?”

“Yes,” he said. “Your damned money was my armour. My Swift and my Armour[①].”

“Don’t.”

“All right. I’ll stop that. I don’t want to hurt you.”

“It’s a little bit late now.”

“All right then. I’ll go on hurting you. It’s more amusing. The only thing I ever really liked to do with you I can’t do now.”

“No, that’s not true. You liked to do many things and everything you wanted to do I did.”

“Oh, for Christ sake stop bragging, will you?”

① Swift and Armour：姓氏名“斯威夫特”和“阿穆尔”。男主人公联想到的可能是美国两大姓斯威夫特和阿穆尔的富有家族，在这里有调侃意味。这两个姓氏名“Swift”和“Armour”与英语单词“swift”（骏马）“armour”（盔甲）同音。

“在巴黎我们待在什么地方？”此刻，在非洲，他问坐在身边帆布椅上的这个女人。

“在克里昂酒店。这你是知道的。”

“我怎么会知道？”

“那是我们总待的地方。”

“不，并不总是。”

“通常是待在那里，还有圣日耳曼区的亨利四世酒店。你说过你喜欢那个地方。”

“爱是一坨屎，”哈里说。“我就是那只爬到屎上面喔喔叫的公鸡。”

“如果你不得不离开，”她说道，“你真的有必要将留诸你身后的一切都蹂躏殆尽吗？我是说，你一定要把一切都带走吗？你一定要宰了你的马，杀死你的妻子，烧毁你的马鞍和盔甲吗？”

“是的，”他说。“你的大把的钞票就是我的盔甲。我的斯威夫特和我的阿穆尔。”

“别这样。”

“好吧。我打住。我无意去伤害你的。”

“这会儿却有点太迟了。”

“那好吧。我继续伤害你。这更有乐子。我曾经唯一真正喜欢和你干的那件事，这会儿我却干不了啦。”

“不，那不是真话。你喜欢做很多事情；每件你想做的事情，我都做了。”

“噢！看在上帝的分上别夸口了，行不？”

He looked at her and saw her crying.

"Listen," he said. "Do you think that it is fun to do this? I don't know why I'm doing it. It's trying to kill to keep yourself alive, I imagine. I was all right when we started talking. I didn't mean to start this, and now I'm crazy as a coot and being as cruel to you as I can be. Don't pay any attention, darling, to what I say. I love you, really. You know I love you. I've never loved any one else the way I love you."

He slipped into the familiar lie he made his bread and butter by.

"You're sweet to me."

"You bitch," he said. "You rich bitch①. That's poetry. I'm full of poetry now. Rot and poetry. Rotten poetry."

"Stop it. Harry, why do you have to turn into a devil now?"

"I don't like to leave anything," the man said. "I don't like to leave things behind."

* * *

It was evening now and he had been asleep. The sun was gone behind the hill and there was a shadow all across the plain and the small animals were feeding close to camp; quick dropping heads and switching tails, he watched them keeping well out away from the bush now. The birds no longer waited on the ground. They were all perched heavily in a tree. There were many more of them. His personal boy was sitting by the bed.

"Memsahib's gone to shoot," the boy said. "Does Bwana want?"

---

① rich bitch 在英语里押尾韵，所以男主人公说此刻他说话充满了诗意。

他看着她，看到她在哭。

“听我说，”他说，“你认为这么做我就有乐趣了？我不知道我为什么这么做。我想，这可能是想通过蹂躏来支撑着活下去。我们刚谈话那会儿我还是好端端的。我也不想变成这样。但现在我却像是个二百五，能对你多冷酷就有多冷酷。对于我说的话，亲爱的，别往心里去。我爱你，真的。你知道我爱你。我从来没有像爱你这样爱过别的任何女人。”

他又用上了他用来挣面包黄油的那种娴熟的谎言。

“你对我很贴心。”

“你这个婊子，”他说，“你这个有钱的婊子。那是诗歌。这会儿我诗兴大发。溃烂和诗歌。溃烂的诗歌。”

“别说了，哈里，你现在非要变成恶魔不可吗？”

“我不想留下任何东西，”男人说，“我不想在身后留下任何东西。”

* * *

这时，夜幕降临，他已睡过了一觉。太阳落到山后了，一片阴影笼罩着旷野，小动物们在营地附近觅食。他观察到，这会儿它们远离灌木丛，脑袋飞快地起落，尾巴飞速地摆动。那几只鸟不再在地面守候了。它们沉甸甸地栖息在一棵树上。来了更多的鸟。他的跟班仆人在床边坐着。

“尊夫人打猎去了，”仆人说，“先生想要什么？”

"Nothing."

She had gone to kill a piece of meat and, knowing how he liked to watch the game, she had gone well away so she would not disturb this little pocket of the plain that he could see. She was always thoughtful, he thought. On anything she knew about, or had read, or that she had ever heard.

It was not her fault that when he went to her he was already over. How could a woman know that you meant nothing that you said; that you spoke only from habit and to be comfortable? After he no longer meant what he said, his lies were more successful with women than when he had told them the truth.

It was not so much that he lied as that there was no truth to tell. He had had his life and it was over and then he went on living it again with different people and more money, with the best of the same places, and some new ones.

You kept from thinking and it was all marvellous. You were equipped with good insides so that you did not go to pieces that way, the way most of them had, and you made an attitude that you cared nothing for the work you used to do, now that you could no longer do it. But, in yourself, you said that you would write about these people; about the very rich; that you were really not of them but a spy in their country; that you would leave it and write of it and for once it would be written by some one who knew what he was writing of. But he would never do it, because each day of not writing, of comfort, of being that which he despised, dulled his ability and softened his will to work so that, finally, he did no work at all. The people he knew now were all much more comfortable

“什么都不要。”

她是去切片儿肉。她了解他有多么喜欢观看打猎，因此她离开的距离会刚好在这一小片旷野里他的视线范围之内。她总是体贴周到，他想，就她所知道的而言，就她所读到过的而言，或曾听到过的而言，都是如此。

当他接近她的时候，他早已玩完了。这可不是她的过错。一个娘们怎么可能知道，你说的话，其实都不过是虚与委蛇而已？她怎知你说话，只是出于习惯，只是为了要图个逍遥？自从他开始言不由衷以来，与告诉女人们真话相比，他的谎言在跟她们打交道时更为成功。

他撒谎并不是由于毫无真话可说。他曾生活过，但生活结束了。然后他又接着生活一遍，但这次却是和不同的人在一起，有更多的钱，在同样的地域里的最好的地方，或在一些新的地方。

你不再思考。一切都可那么美妙。你有着牢不可破的内心，因此那种方式并未让你体无完肤。那种方式曾让他们大多数人体无完肤。你积攒起这样一种姿态：既然你不再能够写作，这种姿态使得你对你曾习以为常的工作玩世不恭。但在你的内心深处，你说你将把这些人诉诸笔端，将写那些豪门巨富；你说你并不真正是他们中的一员，而是他们的国度的一个间谍；你说你将离开这个国度，写作这个国度；终于有一个知道自己在写什么的人来写作这个国度了。但是他却绝不会这样做，因为，日复一日的旷笔，日复一日的闲适，日复一日地做他所鄙夷的一切，疏懒了他的能力，软化了他的工作的意志；这样到后来，他根本就不工作了。当他不工作了以后，他现在认识的这些人较以往更为惬意舒适了。在他生命中的美好时日里，他曾在非洲度过了最

when he did not work. Africa was where he had been happiest in the good time of his life, so he had come out here to start again. They had made this safari with the minimum of comfort. There was no hardship; but there was no luxury and he had thought that he could get back into training that way. That in some way he could work the fat off his soul the way a fighter went into the mountains to work and train in order to burn it out of his body.

She had liked it. She said she loved it. She loved anything that was exciting, that involved a change of scene, where there were new people and where things were pleasant. And he had felt the illusion of returning strength of will to work. Now if this was how it ended, and he knew it was, he must not turn like some snake biting itself because its back was broken. It wasn't this woman's fault. If it had not been she it would have been another. If he lived by a lie he should try to die by it. He heard a shot beyond the hill.

She shot very well this good, this rich bitch, this kindly caretaker and destroyer of his talent. Nonsense. He had destroyed his talent himself. Why should he blame this woman because she kept him well? He had destroyed his talent by not using it, by betrayals of himself and what he believed in, by drinking so much that he blunted the edge of his perceptions, by laziness, by sloth, and by snobbery, by pride and by prejudice, by hook and by crook. What was this? A catalogue of old books?[①] What was his talent anyway? It was a talent all right but instead of using it, he had traded on it. It was never what he had done, but always what

① A catalogue of old books：指哈里试图为他自己的天赋被毁所找的一系列原因，就像是旧书所列举的目录那样繁多且鲜有意义。

幸福的时光。所以他远离尘嚣来到这里重新开始。他们的这次狩猎是尽可能地从简。没有举步维艰，但也没有穷奢极欲。他曾想，那样他也许能够恢复到锻炼状态。他曾想，在某种程度上他可以给灵魂去脂，就如一个战士走进崇山峻岭去工作，去锻炼，好燃尽身体的脂肪那样。

她曾喜欢这样子。她说过她爱极了这样子。她酷爱任何刺激的东西，任何风景的变换，以及有新面孔的地方，有愉快事情的地方。他体验到一种幻觉，似乎又恢复了工作的意志力。如今如果一切就这样结束，他也清楚一切都这样结束了，但他却没必要变得像某种蛇一样，因为脊梁已断便啃噬自己。这不是这个娘们的过错。如果不是这个娘们，也会有另一个。如果他靠谎言而活，他也应该携谎言而死。他听到山丘那边传来一声枪响。

她射得很准，这个不赖的、这个富有的婊子，这个好心的看护人以及他的天赋的摧毁者。瞎扯。他摧毁了自己的天赋。他凭什么推责于这个女人，难道就因为她把他保养得很好？他摧毁了他的天赋，因为他没有使用它，因为他背叛了他自己以及他的信仰，因为他纵酒过度，磨蚀了洞察力的锋芒，因为他的懒散、倦怠、势利，因为傲慢及偏见，因为不择手段。这是什么？旧书的目录吗？说到底，他的天赋又是什么呢？就算它是天赋吧，但是他不是在开发天赋，而是以之做交易。并不在于他曾经做过些

he could do. And he had chosen to make his living with something else instead of a pen or a pencil. It was strange, too, wasn't it, that when he fell in love with another woman, that woman should always have more money than the last one? But when he no longer was in love, when he was only lying, as to this woman, now, who had the most money of all, who had all the money there was, who had had a husband and children, who had taken lovers and been dissatisfied with them, and who loved him dearly as a writer, as a man, as a companion and as a proud possession; it was strange that when he did not love her at all and was lying, that he should be able to give her more for her money than when he had really loved.

We must all be cut out for what we do, he thought. However you make your living is where your talent lies. He had sold vitality, in one form or another, all his life and when your affections are not too involved you give much better value for the money. He had found that out but he would never write that, now, either. No, he would not write that, although it was well worth writing.

Now she came in sight, walking across the open toward the camp. She was wearing jodhpurs and carrying her rifle. The two boys had a Tommie slung and they were coming along behind her. She was still a good-looking woman, he thought, and she had a pleasant body. She had a great talent and appreciation for the bed, she was not pretty, but he liked her face, she read enormously, liked to ride and shoot and, certainly, she drank too much. Her husband had died when she was still a comparatively young woman and for a while she had devoted herself to her two just-grown children, who did not need her and were embarrassed at having her about, to

什么，而在于一直以来，他只能做什么。况且他选择了靠别计谋生，而不是靠钢笔或铅笔。并且，每当他变换新欢，这个新欢总应比上一个娘们更有钱，难道这不奇怪吗？但是当他不再爱，当他只是撒谎的时候，就像对这个女人一样的时候（这个女人是其中最有钱的，要多有钱就多有钱。她曾有夫有子，有不少相好但却不如意；她深爱着他，把他当作作家，当作男人，当作伴侣及令人自豪的财产）。奇怪的是，当他压根不爱她，并且谎话连篇的时候，他为了她的钱所给予她的，却比给予他真正爱过的女人的要多得多。

我们做什么，也许是天生的，他想。你如何谋生，便是你天赋之所在。他这辈子都在出卖生命的活力，不是这样便是那样。当你不再那么投入你的真情真性的时候，你让钱更有所值。他早已觉察到那一点，但现在，他再也不会将之诉诸笔端了。不，他不会写那事儿的，虽然它很值得一写。

这会儿，她走进视线了，正穿过空地向营地走来。她穿着马裤，拿着来复枪。两个杂役抬着一头野羊，他们跟在她身后。她仍旧是个蛮好看的娘们，他想，并且她有着让人赏心悦目的身体。对床笫之事她有着极高的天赋和鉴赏力。她不是那么楚楚动人，但他喜欢她的脸蛋。她阅读广泛，喜欢骑马和射击。当然，她也酗酒。当她相对来说还是个少妇的时候，她的丈夫过世了。有那么一阵子她全心扑到她的两个乳臭刚干的孩子身上，但是他们却不需要她，看到她在周围转悠便心烦意乱。她也全

her stable of horses, to books, and to bottles. She liked to read in the evening before dinner and she drank Scotch and soda while she read. By dinner she was fairly drunk and after a bottle of wine at dinner she was usually drunk enough to sleep.

That was before the lovers. After she had the lovers she did not drink so much because she did not have to be drunk to sleep. But the lovers bored her. She had been married to a man who had never bored her and these people bored her very much.

Then one of her two children was killed in a plane crash and after that was over she did not want the lovers, and drink being no anesthetic she had to make another life. Suddenly, she had been acutely frightened of being alone. But she wanted some one that she respected with her.

It had begun very simply. She liked what he wrote and she had always envied the life he led. She thought he did exactly what he wanted to. The steps by which she had acquired him and the way in which she had finally fallen in love with him were all part of a regular progression in which she had built herself a new life and he had traded away what remained of his old life.

He had traded it for security, for comfort too, there was no denying that, and for what else? He did not know. She would have bought him anything he wanted. He knew that. She was a damned nice woman too. He would as soon be in bed with her as any one; rather with her, because she was richer, because she was very pleasant and appreciative and because she never made scenes.

心扑到她的马厩里的马匹上、书本上、酒瓶上。她喜欢在晚餐前看书，边看书边喝苏格兰威士忌苏打。到晚餐时，她已经略有醉意；晚餐时再一瓶酒后，通常她就醉得可以入睡了。

那是在有那些相好之前。有了相好之后，她就不再喝那么多酒了，因为她再没必要借醉入睡了。但这些相好让她腻烦。她曾嫁给的那个男人从未让她烦过，可这些家伙让她索然至极。

接下来，两个孩子中的一个在飞机失事中丧命。丧事过后，她不再需要相好，酒也不再是麻醉剂。她不得不开始另一段生活。突然之间，她是那么真切地害怕独处。但她需要找一个她可敬重的人。

开始时简简单单。她喜欢他写的东西，她也一直羡慕他所过的生活。她以为他是在随心所欲地过活。她追求他时的步步逼近，她最终与他坠入情网的方式，都是一个再普通不过的进程中的伎俩。在这个进程中，她为自己构筑起了一种新生活；而他呢，则是以旧生活的残余作为交换的代价。

他出卖旧生活，是为了安全，也是为了安逸。这是毋庸置疑的。否则还能是为了什么呢？他不知道。无论他想要什么，她都会给他买来。这点，他再清楚不过了。她也是个非常好的女人。他和她上床的速度与和别的任何女人上床的速度一样快；他倒更宁愿跟她上床，因为她更有钱，因为她赏心悦目、品位不错，

And now this life that she had built again was coming to a term[1] because he had not used iodine two weeks ago when a thorn had scratched his knee as they moved forward trying to photograph a herd of waterbuck standing, their heads up, peering while their nostrils searched the air, their ears spread wide to hear the first noise that would send them rushing into the bush. They had bolted, too, before he got the picture.

Here she came now.

He turned his head on the cot to look toward her. "Hello," he said.

"I shot a Tommy ram," she told him. "He'll make you good broth and I'll have them mash some potatoes with the Klim. How do you feel?"

"Much better."

"Isn't that lovely? You know I thought perhaps you would. You were sleeping when I left."

"I had a good sleep. Did you walk far?"

"No. Just around behind the hill. I made quite a good shot on the Tommy."

"You shoot marvellously, you know."

"I love it. I've loved Africa. Really. If you're all right it's the most fun that I've ever had. You don't know the fun it's been to shoot with you. I've loved the country."

"I love it too."

"Darling, you don't know how marvellous it is to see you

① come to a term：即将结束。这里指海伦把自己的幸福建立在与哈里的关系上。哈里如果死亡，她的这一段幸福也将结束。

也因为她从未大吵大闹。可现在，她为自己再次构筑的生活正走向尽头。因为两星期前，蒺藜刮破了他的膝盖，而他，没有擦碘酒。当时他们正前行，试图拍下一群水羚。它们站着，头部上扬，鼻孔嗅着空气，眼睛警觉地张望。它们的耳朵张得开开的，一有风吹草动，它们就会冲进灌木丛。他尚未拍得照片，它们便飞驰开去。

这会儿她到这里了。

他在帆布床上扭过头来朝她看。"哈罗，"他说。

"我打中了一头野公羊，"她告诉他，"可以用它给你熬顿鲜美的肉汤了。我会要他们在克宁奶粉里捣些土豆泥的。你感觉怎样？"

"好多了。"

"这可太好了。你也知道，我本来就认为你会好转的。我走的时候，你还睡着呢。"

"我睡得可沉呢。你走得很远吗？"

"不远。就在那山丘后面转悠。我打野羊的那枪打得很漂亮。"

"你是个神枪手，你知道的。"

"我爱它。我一直爱着非洲。真的。如果你现在好端端的，这将是我一生中最快乐的时光。你不知道，能和你一起狩猎是多么快乐。我一直爱这片土地。"

"我也爱它。"

"宝贝儿，看到你好转，让人多么开心啊。刚才，你感觉那样

feeling better. I couldn't stand it when you felt that way. You won't talk to me like that again, will you? Promise me?"

"No," he said. "I don't remember what I said."

"You don't have to destroy me. Do you? I'm only a middle-aged woman who loves you and wants to do what you want to do. I've been destroyed two or three times already. You wouldn't want to destroy me again, would you?"

"I'd like to destroy you a few times in bed," he said.

"Yes. That's the good destruction. That's the way we're made to be destroyed. The plane will be here tomorrow."

"How do you know?"

"I'm sure. It's bound to come. The boys have the wood all ready and the grass to make the smudge. I went down and looked at it again today. There's plenty of room to land and we have the smudges ready at both ends."

"What makes you think it will come tomorrow?"

"I'm sure it will. It's overdue now. Then, in town, they will fix up your leg and then we will have some good destruction. Not that dreadful talking kind."

"Should we have a drink? The sun is down."

"Do you think you should?"

"I'm having one."

"We'll have one together. Molo, *letti dui* whiskey-soda!" she called.

"You'd better put on your mosquito boots," he told her.

"I'll wait till I bathe . . ."

While it grew dark they drank and just before it was dark and

糟糕，真叫我受不了。你不会再像那样和我说话了，对不？答应我？”

“不，”他说，“我说过什么我会记不住的。”

“你没必要毁灭我的。你说呢？我只不过是个对你一往情深、想如你所愿的中年妇人。我已经被毁灭两三次了。你不会再毁灭我的，对不？”

“我倒乐意在床上毁灭你好几次呢。”他说。

“哦！那可是美妙的毁灭。我们是为这种毁灭而生的。明天，飞机就会来这儿了。”

“你怎么知道？”

“我对此坚信不疑。它一定会来的。杂役们把木柴准备好了。点浓烟的草也准备好了。我今天又过去看了一下。有足够的空地可供飞机降落。我们准备在两头都点浓烟。”

“你凭什么认为它明天会来呢？”

“我坚信它会来。它早该来了。然后，在镇上，他们就能治好你的腿。然后，我们就能来点儿美妙的毁灭了。而不是像那种可怕的谈话。”

“我们来点酒怎么样？太阳都下去了。”

“你觉得你该喝酒吗？”

“我要喝。”

“我们一起喝。莫洛，两杯威士忌苏打。”

“你最好穿上你的防蚊靴子，”他叮嘱她。

“等洗澡后再说吧……”

他们饮着酒，天越来越黑。天完全黑下来之前那会儿，天光

there was no longer enough light to shoot, a hyena crossed the open on his way around the hill.

"That bastard crosses there every night," the man said. "Every night for two weeks."

"He's the one makes the noise at night. I don't mind it. They're a filthy animal though."

Drinking together, with no pain now except the discomfort of lying in the one position, the boys lighting a fire, its shadow jumping on the tents, he could feel the return of acquiescence in this life of pleasant surrender. She was very good to him. He had been cruel and unjust in the afternoon. She was a fine woman, marvellous really. And just then it occurred to him that he was going to die.

It came with a rush; not as a rush of water nor of wind; but of a sudden, evil-smelling emptiness and the odd thing was that the hyena slipped lightly along the edge of it.

"What is it, Harry?" she asked him.

"Nothing," he said. "You had better move over to the other side. To windward."

"Did Molo change the dressing?"

"Yes. I'm just using the boric now."

"How do you feel?"

"A little wobbly."

"I'm going in to bathe," she said. "I'll be right out. I'll eat with you and then we'll put the cot in."

So, he said to himself, we did well to stop the quarrelling. He had never quarrelled much with this woman, while with the women

已经暗得无法开枪瞄准，一只鬣狗穿过旷地，在山丘那头转悠。

“那狗日的每天夜里都经过那里，”男人说，“每天晚上，都两星期了。”

“夜里怪叫的就是它。我才不介意呢。不过这种动物可够叫人作呕的。”

他们一起饮着酒。这会儿毫无痛感，只有一点不舒适，那是老用同一种姿势躺着引起的。杂役们生起一堆火，火光的影子在帐篷上摇曳。他能够感觉到，在对这种生活心甘情愿的妥协中，听天由命之感又回来了。她对他相当好。下午他对她有点冷酷，对她有点不公。她是个优秀的女人，算得上是个妙人儿。就在那一刻，他忽然意识到，他就要死了。

这意识伴随着一股冲击而来。这冲击既不是一股水流，也不是一阵风；而是一丝突如其来、无影无踪的龌龊气味。古怪的是，鬣狗却循之悄然溜来了。

“那是什么，哈里？”她问他。

“没什么，”他说，“你最好挪到另一边，到背风的一边。”

“莫洛帮你换药了吗？”

“换了。这会儿我用着硼酸膏呢。”

“你感觉如何？”

“说不清。”

“我进去洗澡了，”她说，“我一会儿就出来。我和你吃完饭后，就把帆布床搬进来。”

不错，他自言自语道，我们就这样体面地熄灭了争吵。和这个娘们，他很少吵得起劲；和别的他所爱的娘们，他却吵得很凶。

that he loved he had quarrelled so much they had finally, always, with the corrosion of the quarrelling, killed what they had together. He had loved too much, demanded too much, and he wore it all out.

He thought about alone in Constantinople that time, having quarrelled in Paris before he had gone out. He had whored the whole time and then, when that was over, and he had failed to kill his loneliness, but only made it worse, he had written her, the first one, the one who left him, a letter telling her how he had never been able to kill it... How[①] *when he thought he saw her outside the Regence one time it made him go all faint and sick inside, and that he would follow a woman who looked like her in some way, along the Boulevard, afraid to see it was not she, afraid to lose the feeling it gave him. How every one he had slept with had only made him miss her more. How what she had done could never matter since he knew he could not cure himself of loving her. He wrote this letter at the Club, cold sober, and mailed it to New York asking her to write him at the office in Paris. That seemed safe. And that night missing her so much it made him feel hollow sick inside, he wandered up past Maxim's, picked a girl up and took her out to supper. He had gone to a place to dance with her afterward, she danced badly, and left her for a hot Armenian slut, that swung her belly against him so it almost scalded. He took her away from a British gunner subaltern after a row. The gunner asked him outside and they fought in the street on the cobbles in the dark. He'd hit him twice,*

① 以下的几个"How"所引导的状语从句都作"telling her"的直接宾语。

到后来，随着吵架的磨蚀，他们也总是会毁灭他们曾共有的东西。他曾经爱得太深，要求得太多，也是他亲手将之葬送。

他想起那次在君士坦丁堡，他形影孑立。来这之前他刚在巴黎吵了架。他竟日宿娼。当酒阑人散，他却不仅无法遣散他的孤独，反而使孤独更甚。他于是给她写信，这是第一个，第一个离开他的女人。他给她写信，告诉她，他是多么的难以忘怀……有一次，在摄政院门外，他以为他看到的是她，他是如何地几近晕眩，难以自持；他尾随着这个女人，这个女人有点像她。他沿着林荫街尾随着她，一面唯恐这并不是她，一面又唯恐失去此情此景在他心中唤起的感觉。每个他与之上床的女人是如何使他更想她。无论她做过什么事情，那都是多么的无关紧要啊，因为他知道，他对她的爱无药可医。他在夜总会写下这封信，心静神定。接着他将信寄到纽约，请求她把信寄到他在巴黎的事务所去。这样似乎万无一失。那夜，他是如此的想念她，以至于六神无主，难以自持。他在街头踯躅徘徊，经过马克西姆时，捎上一个女郎，带她出去吃晚饭。随后，他与她到某处跳舞，她跳得糟透了。他于是离开她，拥一个骚劲十足的亚美尼亚妓女入怀。她用肚皮蹭他，几乎蹭得发烫。一场争斗过后他从一个英国炮兵副官身边将她带走了。那炮兵在外面向他挑衅。在漆黑的铺着鹅卵石的路面上，他们打起架来。他两次打中了他，打得很重，打在一侧的下颚上；而他并未倒下，于是他知道将有一场恶斗了。炮兵打中了他的身体，然后又击中他的眼角。他又一次挥起了左拳，击中了。炮兵扑向他，抓住他的大衣，扯断了他的大衣袖子。他两次击在他的脑后，把他推开的时候，挥起右

*hard, on the side of the jaw and when he didn't go down he knew he was in for a figh. The gunner hit him in the body, then beside his eye. He swung with his left again and landed and the gunner fell on him and grabbed his coat and tore the sleeve off and he clubbed him twice behind the ear and then smashed him with his right as he pushed him away. When the gunner went down his head hit first and he ran with the girl because they heard the M. P.'s*① *coming. They got into a taxi and drove out to Rimmily Hissa along the Bosphorus, and around, and back in the cool night and went to bed and she felt as over-ripe as she looked but smooth, rose-petal, syrupy, smooth-bellied, big-breasted and needed no pillow under her buttocks, and he left her before she was awake looking blousy enough in the first daylight and turned up at the Pera Palace with a black eye, carrying his coat because one sleeve was missing.*

That same night he left for Anatolia and he remembered, later on that trip, riding all day through fields of the poppies that they raised for opium and how strange it made you feel, finally, and all the distances seemed wrong, to where they had made the attack with the newly arrived Constantine officers, that did not know a god-damned thing, and the artillery had fired into the troops and the British observer had cried like a child.

That was the day he'd first seen dead men wearing white ballet skirts and upturned shoes with pompons on them. The Turks had come steadily and lumpily and he had seen the skirted men running and the officers shooting into them and running then themselves and he and the British observer had run too until his

① M.P：Military Police 的缩写，意指“宪警”。

拳，将他彻底击溃。炮兵倒下了，头先着地。他和那女的逃之夭夭，因为他们听到宪警走近了。他们钻进的士，沿着博士普鲁士海峡，开向雷米利·希萨，又在冷夜里兜回来上床。她摸起来就像看起来那样，熟透了，但却柔滑得很，像玫瑰花瓣，像糖浆。她腹部光滑，双乳硕大，也根本无须在她屁股下面垫枕头。他离开时她尚未醒来，在第一线天光中，显得蓬头垢面。他现身在彼拉宫门口，一只眼睛淤青，大衣却拿在手上，因为大衣有只袖子没了。

就在那夜，他起身前往安纳托利亚。他想起来，后来在那次旅程中，竟日穿行于罂粟田里——他们种罂粟是为了鸦片——这种感觉让你觉得多么诡异。后来，似乎哪个方向都不对劲。最后终于来到了他们和新近抵达的君士坦丁堡军官们曾发动进攻的地方。那些军官都是大草包，炮弹竟然打到部队里去了。英国观察员像个孩子似的放声大哭起来。

那天是他第一次看到穿着白色芭蕾舞裙、鞋尖上翘、鞋上缀有绒球的死人。土耳其人排山倒海似的推进，他看到这些穿裙子的男人飞跑起来；军官们朝他们开枪，接着他们自己也逃跑了。英国观察员也逃跑起来，跑到他肺都痛了，口里满是铜腥味；他们在一堆岩石后面停了下来。土耳其人像先前那样仍在排山倒海似的推进。后来，他看到的都不堪回想；再后来，他看

*lungs ached and his mouth was full of the taste of pennies and they stopped behind some rocks and there were the Turks coming as lumpily as ever. Later he had seen the things that he could never think of and later still he had seen much worse. So when he got back to Paris that time he could not talk about it or stand to have it mentioned. And there in the cafe as he passed was that American poet with a pile of saucers in front of him and a stupid look on his potato face talking about the Dada*① *movement with a Roumanian who said his name was Tristan Tzara*②, *who always wore a monocle and had a headache, and, back at the apartment with his wife that now he loved again, the quarrel all over, the madness all over, glad to be home, the office sent his mail up to the flat. So then the letter in answer to the one he'd written came in on a platter one morning and when he saw the handwriting he went cold all over and tried to slip the letter underneath another. But his wife said, "Who is that letter from, dear?" and that was the end of the beginning of that.*

He remembered the good times with them all, and the quarrels. They always picked the finest places to have the quarrels. And why had they always quarrelled when he was feeling best? He had never written any of that because, at first, he never wanted to hurt any one and then it seemed as though there was enough to write without it. But he had always thought that he would write it finally. There was so much to write. He had seen the world change;

① Dada：达达主义一词在一战期间出现。达达主义者声称，达达运动不是艺术运动而是反艺术运动。

② Tristan Tzara：特里斯坦·采拉（1896—1953），罗马尼亚人，1919年移居法国，先锋派诗人，达达运动的领袖人物。

到的更加不堪。因此当他那次回到巴黎，他只能对此三缄其口，甚至别人提到时他都无法忍受。经过小饭店时，那儿有一位美国诗人，前面摆着一堆碟子，土豆似的脸上一副蠢相。他正与一个罗马尼亚人高谈达达运动。后者说他的名字叫特里斯坦·采拉，戴着单片眼镜，有头痛病。随后，与他又爱上的这一位妻子回到寓所，此刻争吵烟消云散，气恼也烟消云散。到家真好。事务所将他的邮件送到公寓来。有天早上，写给他曾写过的那封信的回信被托在一只盘子里送了进来。他一看到笔迹马上全身都冷却了，接着就试图将信塞在另一封信下面。但他的妻子问："那封信是谁寄来的，亲爱的？"于是，这一段的开始也随之结束。

他想起和她们所有人度过的快乐时光，以及争吵。她们总是挑最妙的场合和他吵架。为什么每次他心情最愉快的时候，她们就吵架？对此他从未写过只言片语，因为最初，他是出于不想伤害任何人；随后，是因为即便不写这些也似乎有足够的东西写。但他却是一直想着总有一天要将之写出来。要写的太多了。他曾眼见这世界天翻地覆；不仅仅是看到这些事件本身；尽管他

not just the events; although he had seen many of them and had watched the people, but he had seen the subtler change and he could remember how the people were at different times. He had been in it and he had watched it and it was his duty to write of it; but now he never would.

"How do you feel?" she said. She had come out from the tent now after her bath.

"All right."

"Could you eat now?" He saw Molo behind her with the folding table and the other boy with the dishes.

"I want to write," he said.

"You ought to take some broth to keep your strength up."

"I'm going to die tonight," he said. "I don't need my strength up."

"Don't be melodramatic, Harry, please," she said.

"Why don't you use your nose? I'm rotted half way up my thigh now. What the hell should I fool with broth for? Molo bring whiskey-soda."

"Please take the broth," she said gently.

"All right."

The broth was too hot. He had to hold it in the cup until it cooled enough to take it and then he just got it down without gagging.

"You're a fine woman," he said. "Don't pay any attention to me."

She looked at him with her well-known, well-loved face from

曾见证了许多事件，并且观察了其中的人；但他却注意到了更微妙的变化，他仍旧记得在不同的时候人们是如何表现的。他曾身临其境，曾观察入微，因此他有义务将之写出来。但现在他却永远不会了。

“你感觉怎样？”她说。她浴后走出了帐篷。

“还行。”

“你这会儿能吃点吗？”他看到莫洛在她身后拿着折叠桌，另一个杂役端着菜盘子。

“我要写东西，”他说。

“你该喝点肉汤，把精力养足。”

“今天夜里我就要死了，”他说，“我不需要养足什么精力。”

“别耸人听闻了，哈里，求你了，”她说。

“你干吗不用用你的鼻子？我已经烂了半茬了，这会儿都烂到大腿了。我他妈还拿肉汤开玩笑干吗？莫洛，拿威士忌苏打来。”

“请你喝点肉汤吧，”她温和地说。

“好吧。”

汤太烫了。他只好握着盛汤的杯子，等凉一会儿再喝。随后，他一股脑地把汤喝光了。

“你是个好女人，”他说，“你不用太在意我的。”

她抬起脸望着他。她那张脸在《潮流》及《城里城外》杂志上

Spur and *Town & Country*[①], only a little the worse for drink, only a little the worse for bed, but *Town & Country* never showed those good breasts and those useful thighs and those lightly small-of-back-caressing hands, and as he looked and saw her well-known pleasant smile, he felt death come again. This time there was no rush. It was a puff, as of a wind that makes a candle flicker and the flame go tall.

"They can bring my net out later and hang it from the tree and build the fire up. I'm not going in the tent tonight. It's not worth moving. It's a clear night. There won't be any rain."

So this was how you died, in whispers that you did not hear. Well, there would be no more quarrelling. He could promise that. The one experience that he had never had he was not going to spoil now. He probably would. You spoiled everything. But perhaps he wouldn't.

"You can't take dictation, can you?"

"I never learned," she told him.

"That's all right."

There wasn't time, of course, although it seemed as though it telescoped so that you might put it all into one paragraph if you could get it right.

There was a log house, chinked white with mortar, on a hill above the lake. There was a bell on a pole by the door to call the people in to meals. Behind the house were fields and behind the fields was the timber. A line of lombardy poplars ran from the

① *Spur* 和 *Town & Country* 为时尚杂志名。

人尽皆知、人见人爱；现在不过因为饮酒过度稍有逊色，由于床笫过度稍有逊色。但《城里城外》却从未登过这两只销魂的乳房，这两条美妙的大腿，以及这曾轻轻抚摩后腰的纤手。此刻，他看着，看到她那人尽皆知的动人微笑，他感到，死亡又来光顾了。这次，并不是突如其来。它一阵阵地吹来，如同一阵风，吹过蜡烛，烛光摇曳，火焰腾得更高了。

“待会儿叫他们把我的帐子拿出来，挂在树上，生一堆火。今天夜里我就不进帐篷里去了。不值得再移动了。夜空晴朗。不会下雨的。”

那么你就将这样死去了，死在你听不到的悄然低语中。也罢，不会再有任何吵嘴了。这点他能保证。对这次他从未有过的经历，他不想让它泡汤。他也许会。你让一切都泡汤了。但也许他不会。

“你不会速记，对不？”

“我从未学过，”她告诉他。

“不要紧。”

没时间了，当然，尽管缩短之后，如果你能表述清楚的话，你仿佛都能在一段话里浓缩一切。

湖畔，山上，木屋墙上抹的泥灰浆泛白。门边柱上有一个铃，那是用来招呼人们进餐的。屋后是田野，田野后是树林。一排箭杆杨从木屋一直伸展到码头。其他的箭杆杨从地岬那里迤逦开去。在树林的边上，有条路直通山里，他曾沿那条路拾黑莓。后来，那座木屋被烧毁了。搁在生火的地方上面的鹿角架

house to the dock. Other poplars ran along the point. A road went up to the hills along the edge of the timber and along that road he picked blackberries. Then that log house was burned down and all the guns that had been on deer foot racks above the open fire place were burned and afterwards their barrels, with the lead melted in the magazines, and the stocks burned away, lay out on the heap of ashes that were used to make lye for the big iron soap kettles, and you asked Grandfather if you could have them to play with, and he said, no. You see they were his guns still and he never bought any others. Nor did he hunt any more. The house was rebuilt in the same place out of lumber now and painted white and from its porch you saw the poplars and the lake beyond; but there were never any more guns. The barrels of the guns that had hung on the deer feet on the wall of the log house lay out there on the heap of ashes and no one ever touched them.

In the Black Forest, after the war, we rented a trout stream and there were two ways to walk to it. One was down the valley from Triberg and around the valley road in the shade of the trees that bordered the white road, and then up a side road that went up through the hills past many small farms, with the big Schwarzwald houses, until that road crossed the stream. That was where our fishing began.

The other way was to climb steeply up to the edge of the woods and then go across the top of the hills through the pine woods, and then out to the edge of a meadow and down across this meadow to the bridge. There were birches along the stream and it was not big, but narrow, clear and fast, with pools where it

上的枪全都着了火；接下来，弹盒里的铅都被火烧熔了，枪托也报销了，只有枪筒直愣愣地堆在一堆灰上。这些灰是用来给那口大铁锅烧制肥皂时烧碱液的。你问爷爷你是否能玩那些枪筒，可他说，不行。你明白了，它们仍旧是他的枪，而且他也从未再买过别的枪。他也不再打猎了。后来，又用木材在同一个地方建起了房子，涂成了白色。从门廊那儿可以看到箭杆杨及远处的湖泊。但却不再有新枪了。曾挂在木屋鹿角架上的枪筒，仍直愣愣地堆在灰上，从未有人动过它们一下。

战后，在黑森林，我们租了一条有鳟鱼的溪流。有两条路可通向它。其中的一条路从特里贝格顺山谷而下。绕过山谷的小路，空寂的小路两旁树影荫翳；然后爬上一条羊肠小道。这条羊肠小道翻山越岭，沿途有许多小农场，农场里有些具有黑森林地区特色的高大房屋。这条路最终通向那条溪流。我们就在那里开始钓鱼。

另外一条路则首先要陡直地爬到树丛边缘，然后在山岭顶峰处穿出松林，接着来到一片草地的边缘。向下穿过草地，到达桥边。溪流沿岸是白桦树。它不是很宽阔，而是狭窄、清澈、湍

had cut under the roots of the birches. At the Hotel in Triberg the proprietor had a fine season. It was very pleasant and we were all great friends. The next year came the inflation and the money he had made the year before was not enough to buy supplies to open the hotel and he hanged himself.

You could dictate that, but you could not dictate the Place Contrescarpe[①] *where the flower sellers dyed their flowers in the street and the dye ran over the paving where the autobus started and the old men and the women, always drunk on wine and bad mare; and the children with their noses running in the cold; the smell of dirty sweat and poverty and drunkenness at the Cafe' des Amateurs and the whores at the Bal Musette they lived above. The concierge who entertained the trooper of the Garde Republicaine in her loge, his horse-hair-plumed helmet on a chair. The locataire across the hall whose husband was a bicycle racer and her joy that morning at the cremerie when she had opened L'Auto and seen where he placed third in Paris-Tours, his first big race. She had blushed and laughed and then gone upstairs crying with the yellow sporting paper in her hand. The husband of the woman who ran the Bal Musette drove a taxi and when he, Harry, had to take an early plane the husband knocked upon the door to wake him and they each drank a glass of white wine at the zinc of the bar before they started. He knew his neighbors in that quarter then because they all were poor.*

Around that Place there were two kinds; the drunkards and the sportifs. The drunkards killed their poverty that way;

① The Place Contrescarpe：护城墙广场，离卢森堡公园不远，位于巴黎左岸，拉丁区。

急，在白桦树根部冲积出了一些小水潭。特里贝格旅店的老板这个季节生意兴隆。这让人十分愉快，并且我们全都是好朋友。第二年，通货膨胀袭来，头一年他所赚的钱，却不够用来买旅店开业所需要的物品。他上吊了。

你可以口授如此这般，但你却无法口授护城墙广场那个地方。在那里，花贩子们当街染花；染料泼满路面，公共汽车从这里启动；年老的男人及女人们，喝葡萄酒及劣质白兰地，总喝得醉醺醺的；寒气凛冽中，孩子们鼻涕直流；“业余者小饭馆”里充斥着脏兮兮的汗臭味、穷苦味以及酒醉的味儿。还有“风笛舞厅”的妓女们。他们就住在这个舞厅上面。看门女人在她的小屋里款待共和国自卫队员，椅子上搁着他那顶插有马鬃的军帽。大厅另一端的女住户的丈夫是个自行车赛手。清晨，当她在牛奶房打开《机动车》报时，看到他在巴黎环城比赛中得了第三名，她是如此的喜不自禁。这是他的第一次重大比赛。她满脸绯红，放声大笑，手舞着那黄色的体育报纸，边上楼边大声嚷嚷。经营风笛舞厅的女人的老公是开出租车的。那天，哈里他要赶早班飞机。那老公敲门叫醒他，他们每人都在酒吧的锌桌上喝了一杯白葡萄酒，然后才动身。他熟知那个街区的左邻右舍，因为他们全都穷困潦倒。

在那个地方有两种人：酒徒和运动员。酒徒喝酒浇忘贫困，运动员锻炼排遣贫困。他们是巴黎公社成员的后裔。要他们懂得他们的政治处境并不难。他们清楚，是谁杀死了他们的父辈、

*the sportifs took it out in exercise. They were the descendants of the Communards and it was no struggle for them to know their politics. They knew who had shot their fathers, their relatives, their brothers, and their friends when the Versailles troops came in and took the town after the Commune and executed any one they could catch with calloused hands, or who wore a cap, or carried any other sign he was a working man. And in that poverty, and in that quarter across the street from a Boucherie Chevaline and a wine cooperative he had written the start of all he was to do. There never was another part of Paris that he loved like that, the sprawling trees, the old white plastered houses painted brown below, the long green of the autobus in that round square, the purple flower dye upon the paving, the sudden drop down the hill of the rue Cardinal Lemoine to the River, and the other way the narrow crowded world of the rue Mouffetard. The street that ran up toward the Pantheon and the other that he always took with the bicycle, the only asphalted street in all that quarter, smooth under the tires, with the high narrow house and the cheap tall hotel where Paul Verlaine*① *had died. There were only two rooms in the apartments where they lived and he had a room on the top floor of that hotel that cost him sixty francs a month where he did his writing, and from it he could see the roofs and chimney pots and all the hills of Paris.*

From the apartment you could only see the wood and coal man's place. He sold wine too, bad wine. The golden horse's

① Paul Verlaine：保尔·魏尔伦 (1844—1895)，法国象征派诗人，曾是巴黎公社中央委员会的宣传部长。

亲戚、兄弟和朋友。当凡尔赛的军队开进来，继公社之后占领了这座城镇，他们见人就杀：只要抓到的那人手上有老茧，或戴着便帽，或有任何痕迹表明他是个工人。就是在那种贫困中，就在那街对面有一家鲜马肉和酒合营店的街区里，他开始了他的写作生涯。巴黎任何别的地方从未使他像对这个地方如此钟爱。那里有枝叶蔓延的树木，涂着泛白的灰泥的老房子，房子下面涂成土黄色；在那个圆形广场上的公共汽车，长长的，涂成绿色；那路面上紫色的染花颜料；莱蒙昂红衣主教大街的山势陡降至那河流；另一侧则是莫菲塔德路上那狭窄而又拥挤的世界。一直通向潘神殿的那条街道以及另一条他老是骑自行车的街道；这是那个街区唯一的一条柏油马路，马路在车轮下平滑无阻；路边是一间间又高又狭窄的房屋，还有一家廉价的高耸的客栈，保尔·魏尔伦就是在这里咽气的。他们住的这套公寓只有两个房间。他在旅店的顶楼有一间屋子，每月要花上他60法郎的租金，他在那里写作。从那里他可以看到鳞次栉比的屋顶和烟囱，以及巴黎所有的山岭。

从公寓里你却只看得到那个卖木材和煤炭的人的住处。他也卖酒，劣质酒。马肉铺外挂着个金色的马头，开着的橱窗里悬挂着黄黄红红的马肉。这家涂成绿色的合营店是他们买酒的地方：酒好，且廉价。其余的则是左邻右舍的灰墙及窗户。夜里，

head outside the Boucherie Chevaline where the carcasses hung yellow gold and red in the open window, and the green painted co-operative where they bought their wine; good wine and cheap. The rest was plaster walls and the windows of the neighbors. The neighbors who, at night, when some one lay drunk in the street, moaning and groaning in that typical French ivresse that you were propaganded to believe did not exist, would open their windows and then the murmur of talk.

"*Where is the policeman? When you don't want him the bugger is always there. He's sleeping with some concierge. Get the Agent.*" *Till some one threw a bucket of water from a window and the moaning stopped.* "*What's that? Water. Ah, that's intelligent.*" *And the windows shutting. Marie, his femme de menage, protesting against the eight-hour day saying,* "*If a husband works until six he gets only a little drunk on the way home and does not waste too much. If he works only until five he is drunk every night and one has no money. It is the wife of the working man who suffers from this shortening of hours.*"

"Wouldn't you like some more broth?" the woman asked him now.

"No, thank you very much. It is awfully good."

"Try just a little."

"I would like a whiskey-soda."

"It's not good for you."

"No. It's bad for me. Cole Porter [1] wrote the words and the

① Cole Porter：柯尔·波特 (1891—1964)，美国印第安纳州的作曲家和歌词作家。

有人在街上醉倒，发出哼哼声和咕噜声。这是一种典型的法国式的酩酊大醉，有人曾说服你，要你相信这种醉并不存在。此时，左邻右舍打开窗子，接着是一阵喃喃的低语。

“那警察哪去了？你不需要这家伙的时候他却老在那儿。他正和某个看门的女人睡觉呢。把奸细找来！”直到有人从窗户泼下一桶水，哼哼声才会停止。“那是啥？水！啊，那样做可真聪明。”于是窗户一一关上了。他的女佣玛丽抗议八小时工作时说道：“如果一个丈夫工作到六点钟，他在回家的路上只会喝得小醉，浪费的钱不多。但如果他只工作到五点钟，他是每夜必醉，那样人们就分文全无啦。上班时间缩短，受苦的可是这些上班的男人的婆娘们咯。”

“你不想再来点肉汤吗？”女人这会儿问他道。

“不，不用劳你大驾了。这样很好。”

“就喝一点点嘛。”

“我想喝威士忌苏打。”

“这对你不好。”

“是的。这对我有害。柯尔·波特写的词曲。知道你为我都要急疯了。”

music. This knowledge that you're going mad for me."

"You know I like you to drink."

"Oh yes. Only it's bad for me."

When she goes, he thought, I'll have all I want. Not all I want but all there is. Ayee he was tired. Too tired. He was going to sleep a little while. He lay still and death was not there. It must have gone around another street. It went in pairs, on bicycles, and moved absolutely silently on the pavements.

No, he had never written about Paris. Not the Paris that he cared about. But what about the rest that he had never written?

What about the ranch and the silvered gray of the sage brush, the quick, clear water in the irrigation ditches, and the heavy green of the alfalfa. The trail went up into the hills and the cattle in the summer were shy as deer. The bawling and the steady noise and slow moving mass raising a dust as you brought them down in the fall. And behind the mountains, the clear sharpness of the peak in the evening light and, riding down along the trail in the moonlight, bright across the valley. Now he remembered coming down through the timber in the dark holding the horse's tail when you could not see and all the stories that he meant to write.

About the half-wit chore boy who was left at the ranch that time and told not to let any one get any hay, and that old bastard from the Forks who had beaten the boy when he had worked for him stopping to get some feed. The boy refusing and the old man saying he would beat him again. The boy got the rifle from the kitchen and shot him when he tried to come into the barn and when

“你清楚，我原本是不介意你喝酒的。”

“噢，对。不过这对我有害。”

她走开后，他想，我就会要什么有什么了。不是要什么有什么，而是有什么要什么。他累了。累极了。他要小睡一会儿。他静静地躺着，死神不在那儿。它一定是到另一条街道上溜达去了。它成双结对，骑着自行车，在人行道上寂静无声地行驶。

没有，他从来没有写过巴黎。未写过他在意的那个巴黎。可是，他从未写过的其他事物又如何呢？

那大牧场以及北美艾灌丛的那银灰色，灌溉渠里的湍急而又清澈的流水，那苜蓿的深绿色等等又如何呢？小路迤逦沿山而上，夏天的牛群胆小如鹿。秋天，当你把它们赶下山去的时候，吆喝声伴随着持续的嘈杂声，牛群缓缓移动，扬起一片尘灰。群峦后面，最高的山峰清晰地凸显在暮霭里；在月色中骑马沿小路而下，穿越山谷时一片皎洁。这会儿，他想起来，当时在黝黑中穿过树林的时候，你什么也看不见，紧紧揪着马尾巴。以及他曾想写的凡此种种又如何呢？

还有关于那个打杂的笨男孩的事。那次，留下他一个人在大牧场，告诉他不可让任何人弄走一根牧草。从福克斯来的那个老杂种停在那儿偏偏想弄点饲料。这男孩为他打工时，他曾揍过这男孩。此刻，男孩拒绝了，老家伙说他要再揍他。男孩从厨房拿到了步枪。当他企图走进牲口棚的时候，他朝他开枪了。当他们回到大牧场时，他已经死了一星期了，僵挺在畜栏里，一

they came back to the ranch he'd been dead a week, frozen in the corral, and the dogs had eaten part of him. But what was left you packed on a sled wrapped in a blanket and roped on and you got the boy to help you haul it, and the two of you took it out over the road on skis, and sixty miles down to town to turn the boy over. He having no idea that he would be arrested. Thinking he had done his duty and that you were his friend and he would be rewarded. He'd helped to haul the old man in so everybody could know how bad the old man had been and how he'd tried to steal some feed that didn't belong to him, and when the sheriff put the handcuffs on the boy he couldn't believe it. Then he'd started to cry. That was one story he had saved to write. He knew at least twenty good stories from out there and he had never written one. Why?

"You tell them why," he said.

"Why what, dear?"

"Why nothing."

She didn't drink so much, now, since she had him. But if he lived he would never write about her, he knew that now. Nor about any of them. The rich were dull and they drank too much, or they played too much backgammon. They were dull and they were repetitious. He remembered poor Julian and his romantic awe of them and how he had started a story once that began, "The very rich are different from you and me."[1] And how some one had said to Julian, Yes, they have more money. But that was not humorous to Julian. He thought they were a special glamourous race and

① 这句话是 F. S. 菲茨杰拉德 1926 年的小说《阔少爷》第三段的第二句话。

群狗啃吃了他的尸体。可接下来，你却将剩下的躯干裹上毯子，装上雪橇，系上绳子。你要男孩帮你拖着，你们两个将他弄出来，穿着滑雪板，赶了60里路到镇上，把男孩交出去。他万万没料到他会被逮捕。还以为他是忠于职守呢，并且你又是他的朋友，他理应得到奖励呢。他还帮着把这个老家伙拖来，这样人人就能知道这个老家伙曾有多坏，知道他是怎样企图去偷不属于他的饲料。当治安官给男孩戴上手铐时，他不敢相信这是真的。接着他放声大哭起来。这个故事，他曾留着想写的。在那个地方他知道至少有20个好故事。他却一个也未曾写过。为什么呢？

"你告诉他们为什么，"他说。

"什么为什么，亲爱的？"

"没什么为什么。"

如今，自从她有了他，她不再喝那么多了。但是，倘若他活着，他绝不会写她。这会儿他明白那点了。也不会写他们中的任何人。富人无聊，于是要么大量饮酒，要么老玩十五子游戏。他们无聊且无趣。他想起可怜的朱利安以及他对他们所持的不切实际的敬畏之心；想起他是如何构思一篇这样开头的故事："豪门巨富，与你我有天壤之别。"想起有人曾对朱利安怎样说的，是啊，他们有更多的钱。但那对朱利安来说却不是幽默。他认为他们是魅力无限的一类人；当他发现他们并非如此时，他就毁了，毁的程度之深就像任何其他毁过他的事情一样。

when he found they weren't it wrecked him just as much as any other thing that wrecked him.

He had been contemptuous of those who wrecked. You did not have to like it because you understood it. He could beat anything, he thought, because no thing could hurt him if he did not care.

All right. Now he would not care for death. One thing he had always dreaded was the pain. He could stand pain as well as any man, until it went on too long, and wore him out, but here he had something that had hurt frightfully and just when he had felt it breaking him, the pain had stopped.

He remembered long ago when Williamson, the bombing officer, had been hit by a stick bomb some one in a German patrol had thrown as he was coming in through the wire that night and, screaming, had begged every one to kill him. He was a fat man, very brave, and a good officer, although addicted to fantastic shows. But that night he was caught in the wire, with a flare lighting him up and his bowels spilled out into the wire, so when they brought him in, alive, they had to cut him loose. Shoot me, Harry. For Christ sake shoot me. They had had an argument one time about our Lord never sending you anything you could not bear and some one's theory had been that meant that at a certain time the pain passed you out automatically. But he had always remembered Williamson, that night. Nothing passed out Williamson until he gave him all his morphine tablets that he had always saved to use himself and then they did not work right away.

他曾睥睨那些毁了的人。你根本没必要去喜欢这一套，因为你了解这是怎么回事。他能击败一切，他想，因为如果他是心无所系，则无懈可击。

正好。现在他的心也非死亡所系。他曾一直担心的是疼痛。他能如任何常人那样忍受疼痛，除非疼痛持续太久，让他精疲力竭。这儿曾有什么东西痛得撕心裂肺，可当他刚一觉得它要弄垮他的时候，痛感却戛然而止了。

他想起很久以前的威廉森，那个投弹军官。那晚，他试图穿过铁丝网回来，却被一枚手榴弹炸中了。炸弹是一名德国巡逻兵扔的。他嚎声凄厉，求人把他干掉。他是个胖子，非常勇敢，是个好军官，尽管有点耽于耸人听闻的作秀。但那夜，他陷于铁丝网中，一道照明灯照到他身上，可他的肠子淌了出来，淌到铁丝网中。当他们把他弄回来时，他还活着，他们不得不把肠子割断。打死我，哈里。看在上帝的面上，打死我。他们曾有过一次辩论，辩论的焦点是说我们的主从来不会给你降临你无法承受的东西。某人的理论是说过段时间痛苦就会自动消失。可他一直记得那夜的威廉森。威廉森身上什么都没自动消失，直到后来他给了他所有的吗啡片。这是他自备用的。可即便是这些吗啡片也未立即生效。

Still this now, that he had, was very easy; and if it was no worse as it went on there was nothing to worry about. Except that he would rather be in better company.

He thought a little about the company that he would like to have. No, he thought, when everything you do, you do too long, and do too late, you can't expect to find the people still there. The people all are gone. The party's over and you are with your hostess now.

I'm getting as bored with dying as with everything else, he thought.

"It's a bore," he said out loud.

"What is, my dear?"

"Anything you do too bloody long."

He looked at her face between him and the fire. She was leaning back in the chair and the firelight shone on her pleasantly lined face and he could see that she was sleepy. He heard the hyena make a noise just outside the range of the fire.

"I've been writing," he said. "But I got tired."

"Do you think you will be able to sleep?"

"Pretty sure. Why don't you turn in?"

"I like to sit here with you."

"Do you feel anything strange?" he asked her.

"No. Just a little sleepy."

"I do," he said.

He had just felt death come by again.

"You know the only thing I've never lost is curiosity," he said to her.

相对而言，现在他所经历的，只是小菜一碟。如果情形持续下去，不再恶化，则什么也不用担心。只有一点除外，即他宁愿同行的另有更好的同伴。

他略微想了想他愿意拥有的同伴。没了，他想，但凡你做的事情，只要你做得太久，且做得太晚，你不能指望人家还在那儿。人家都已经离开了。酒阑席终，这会儿和你在一起的，只有女主人。

如所有别的东西一样，这种垂死的感觉让我讨厌，他想。

“真讨厌。”他脱口而出。

“什么讨厌，我亲爱的？”

“任何你干了太久的东西。”

越过火堆，他看着她的脸。她靠在椅子上，火光映照到她线条动人的脸上。他瞧出来，她瞌睡了。他听到，就在火光范围之外，鬣狗的吠声响起。

“我一直在写，”他说，“可我累了。”

“你觉得你能不能睡着觉？”

“肯定能。你干吗不去睡呢？”

“我喜欢和你在这儿坐着。”

“你是否觉察到有点怪？”他问她。

“没呀。只是有点瞌睡罢了。”

“我可是觉察到了。”

刚才他觉得死神又来串门儿了。

“你晓得的，好奇是我唯一没有失去的东西，”他对她说。

"You've never lost anything. You're the most complete man I've ever known."

"Christ," he said. "How little a woman knows. What is that? Your intuition?"

Because, just then, death had come and rested its head on the foot of the cot and he could smell its breath.

"Never believe any of that about a scythe and a skull[①]," he told her. "It can be two bicycle policemen as easily, or be a bird. Or it can have a wide snout like a hyena."

It had moved up on him now, but it had no shape any more. It simply occupied space.

"Tell it to go away."[②]

It did not go away but moved a little closer.

"You've got a hell of a breath," he told it. "You stinking bastard."

It moved up closer to him still and now he could not speak to it, and when it saw he could not speak it came a little closer, and now he tried to send it away without speaking, but it moved in on him so its weight was all upon his chest, and while it crouched there and he could not move or speak, he heard the woman say, "Bwana is asleep now. Take the cot up very gently and carry it into the tent."

He could not speak to tell her to make it go away and it crouched now, heavier, so he could not breathe. And then, while they lifted the cot, suddenly it was all right and the weight went from his chest.

---

① a scythe and a skull：西方死神的形象，多半以骷髅为主，传说中大多手持收割头颅的镰刀。

② "Tell it to go away." 这句话表明处于半昏迷状态的哈里已经分不清楚现实与幻觉。

“你从来没失去过任何东西。据我所知，你是最无可挑剔的男人。”

“天啊，”他说，“一个女人所知的可太有限了。那是什么？你的直觉吗？”

因为，就在刚才，死神来了，将它的头憩息在帆布床床脚那儿，他能嗅到它的鼻息。

“永远别相信那关于镰刀和骷髅的话，”他告诉她，“它可能是简简单单的两个骑自行车的警察，抑或是只鸟儿。甚至可能和鬣狗一样，有张阔大的猪一样的嘴巴。”

现在，它爬了上来，爬到他身上了，可它现在却化于无形了。它只是盘踞在空间中。

“叫它走开。”

它非但没走开，反而挪得更近些了。

“你的鼻息太难闻了，”他对它说，“你这个臭杂种。”

它仍在一步步地逼近他。这会儿他无法对它发话了。当它看到他无法说话，它逼得更近些了。于是他现在企图不开口就将它驱开，但它挤进来压到他身上，直到它全部的重量都压到他胸口上。它蹲在那儿，他动弹不得，无法开口。他听到女人说“先生现在睡着了。轻轻地抬起帆布床，抬进帐篷里。”

他无法开口告诉她，让她将它弄开。现在它蹲在那儿，越来越重，以致他呼吸维艰。接下来，当他们把帆布床抬起，刹那间一切都好了，重压从他胸口消失了。

*　*　*

It was morning and had been morning for some time and he heard the plane. It showed very tiny and then made a wide circle and the boys ran out and lit the fires, using kerosene, and piled on grass so there were two big smudges at each end of the level place and the morning breeze blew them toward the camp and the plane circled twice more, low this time, and then glided down and levelled off and landed smoothly and, coming walking toward him, was old Compton in slacks, a tweed jacket and a brown felt hat.

"What's the matter, old cock?" Compton said.

"Bad leg," he told him. "Will you have some breakfast?"

"Thanks. I'll just have some tea. It's the Puss Moth you know. I won't be able to take the Memsahib. There's only room for one. Your lorry is on the way."

Helen had taken Compton aside and was speaking to him. Compton came back more cheery than ever.

"We'll get you right in," he said. "I'll be back for the Mem①. Now I'm afraid I'll have to stop at Arusha to refuel. We'd better get going."

"What about the tea?"

"I don't really care about it, you know."

The boys had picked up the cot and carried it around the green tents and down along the rock and out onto the plain and along past the smudges that were burning brightly now, the grass all consumed, and the wind fanning the fire, to the little plane. It was difficult getting him in, but once in he lay back in the leather seat,

① Mem. 为 Memsahib 的缩写形式。

*　*　*

天亮了。天亮了有会儿了。他听到飞机的声音。飞机显得很小，接着转了个大圈儿。杂役们跑出去，生起了火，浇上煤油，堆在草上，在平地的两端生起两股浓烟。清晨的微风将烟吹向营地。飞机又绕了两圈，这次接近地面了；接着滑翔下来，平飞，平稳着陆。向他迎面走来的是老康普顿。他穿着宽松的裤子及花呢夹克，戴一顶棕色的毡帽。

"出什么事了，老兄？"康普顿说道。

"腿坏了，"他告诉他，"你是否来点早餐？"

"谢了。我喝点茶就行了。你知道，这是一架'天社蛾'，我无法捎上尊夫人啦。只够带一个人的空间。你的卡车正在路上。"

海伦把康普顿拉向一边，对他叽咕着什么。康普顿走回来时，脸色比先前灿烂多了。

"我们马上把你弄进来，"他说，"我会回来接夫人的。不过我恐怕要在阿鲁沙停一下加点油。我们最好马上动身。"

"那还喝不喝茶？"

"我喝不喝其实无所谓的，你知道。"

杂役们已经抬起了帆布床，抬着它，绕过绿色的帐篷，沿着那块岩石而下，来到平地上；穿过平地，途经那一堆堆浓烟。浓烟此时变成了熊熊大火，草都燃起来了，有风助着火势；最后来到了小飞机旁。把他弄进来还真费劲。可一旦进来了，他就躺到了皮革座位上，腿伸得直直的，伸向座位的另一侧康普顿坐的地方。康普顿发动了马达，上了飞机。他向海伦和杂役们挥挥

and the leg was stuck straight out to one side of the seat where Compton sat. Compton started the motor and got in. He waved to Helen and to the boys and, as the clatter moved into the old familiar roar, they swung around with Compie [1] watching for warthog holes and roared, bumping, along the stretch between the fires and with the last bump rose and he saw them all standing below, waving, and the camp beside the hill, flattening now, and the plain spreading, clumps of trees, and the bush flattening, while the game trails ran now smoothly to the dry waterholes, and there was a new water that he had never known of. The zebra, small rounded backs now, and the wildebeeste, big-headed dots seeming to climb as they moved in long fingers across the plain, now scattering as the shadow came toward them, they were tiny now, and the movement had no gallop, and the plain as far as you could see, gray-yellow now and ahead old Compie's tweed back and the brown felt hat. Then they were over the first hills and the wildebeeste were trailing up them, and then they were over mountains with sudden depths of green-rising forest and the solid bamboo slopes, and then the heavy forest again, sculptured into peaks and hollows until they crossed, and hills sloped down and then another plain, hot now, and purple brown, bumpy with heat and Compie looking back to see how he was riding. Then there were other mountains dark ahead.

And then instead of going on to Arusha they turned left, he evidently figured that they had the gas, and looking down he saw a pink sifting cloud, moving over the ground, and in the air, like the first snow in a blizzard, that comes from nowhere, and he knew the

① Campie 是 Campton 的昵称。

手。这时“咔嗒咔嗒”声变成了惯常熟悉的轰鸣声，他们掉头时，康普顿留神着一个个疣猪洞。飞机轰鸣着，颠簸着，行驶在两堆火之间的平地上；随着最后的一次颠簸拉向空中。他看到，他们全站在下面，挥着手。山丘旁的营地，变得越来越扁平；平原伸展开来，树林成团成簇，那片灌木丛也越来越扁了。猎踪一览无余地延伸至一道道干涸的水洼。有一道他从不知道的水流。现在，斑马的背部又小又圆；牛羚呢，变成了一个个有着巨头的圆点，当它们在平原上列成指状纵队移动时，圆点像是在地面上爬行。现在，当飞机的影子逼近它们时，它们四散开去，看起来像小不点儿，看不出任何疾驶的动静。你极目望去，这会儿平原一览无余，呈灰黄色。向前，看到老康皮的穿花呢夹克的背影和棕色的毡帽。接着，他们飞行到了第一群山丘，一头头牛羚正尾随他们而上。随后，他们飞行到了崇山峻岭之上，陡峭的深谷里乍然涌现出一片葱郁的森林，山间是一道道生长着茂密的翠竹的山坡；接着又见一片浓密的森林，在他们飞越经过时目睹其被削成了一处处尖峰和空谷。山丘坡势平缓，接着又见一片平原，这片平原炽热一片，呈棕红色。热气掀得飞机一颠一颠的。康皮回过头来，看看他在飞行中的状态如何。再往前，又是黑压压的连绵的崇山峻岭。

可接下来，他们不是往阿鲁沙方向飞，而是折向左。他清楚地估算了一下，他们有着充足的燃料呢。向下俯瞰，他看到一片翻滚着的沙沙作响的云团，正掠过地面。这团云在空中看来，就像一场暴风雪伊始时的雪团，凭空而降。他明白蝗虫正从南部飞涌而来。接着，他们爬高了，看起来是向东部飞去。接下来眼

locusts were coming, up from the South. Then they began to climb and they were going to the East it seemed, and then it darkened and they were in a storm, the rain so thick it seemed like flying through a waterfall, and then they were out and Compie turned his head and grinned and pointed and there, ahead, all he could see, as wide as all the world, great, high, and unbelievably white in the sun, was the square top of Kilimanjaro. And then he knew that there was where he was going.

Just then the hyena stopped whimpering in the night and started to make a strange, human, almost crying sound. The woman heard it and, stirred uneasily. She did not wake. In her dream she was at the house on Long Island and it was the night before her daughter's debut. Somehow her father was there and he had been very rude. Then the noise the hyena made was so loud she woke and for a moment she did not know where she was and she was very afraid. Then she took the flashlight and shone it on the other cot that they had carried in after Harry had gone to sleep. She could see his bulk under the mosquito bar but somehow he had gotten his leg out and it hung down alongside the cot. The dressings had all come down and she could not look at it.

"Molo," she called, "Molo! Molo！"

Then she said, "Harry, Harry!" Then her voice rising, "Harry! Please. Oh Harry!"

There was no answer and she could not hear him breathing.

Outside the tent the hyena made the same strange noise that had awakened her. But she did not hear him for the beating of her heart.

前一黑，他们遭遇上暴雨了，雨流如注，就像穿行于瀑布之中。总算飞出来了。康皮扭过头来，咧嘴而笑，用手指指。就在那儿，在前方，扑入他整个眼帘的，像整个宇宙那样宽广无垠，宏伟无边，高耸无岸，在阳光下，是那样的令人难以置信的雪白夺目。那是乞力马扎罗山的方形的山巅。于是他明白，他正驶向的地方，就是那里。

就在那时，鬣狗在夜里停止了呜咽，开始发出一种诡异的、类似人的、几乎是号哭的声音。那女人听到这声音，不安地翻了翻身。她并未醒来。在她梦中，她正在长岛的房子里。此时是她的女儿初进社交界的前夜。她的父亲不知为何出现在那里，并且他的态度一直很恶劣。后来，鬣狗发出的声响是如此之大，她醒了。一时间她不知身在何处，不禁十分担忧起来。然后，她拿起手电筒，照到另一张帆布床上。哈里睡着后，他们将床弄了进来。她看到蚊帐下他的身躯，但他的腿却不知为何伸出来了，在帆布床沿耷拉着。敷料全掉落了下来。她不忍再看。

“莫洛，”她喊道，“莫洛！莫洛！”

然后她说：“哈里，哈里！”随后她声音抬高了：“哈里！求你了。哦哈里！”

没有回应。她也听不到他的呼吸。

帐篷之外，鬣狗又发出了那诡异的叫声。刚才正是这叫声惊醒了她。可她，却听不到他的声音了，因为此刻的她，心跳如雷。

The Killers
杀手

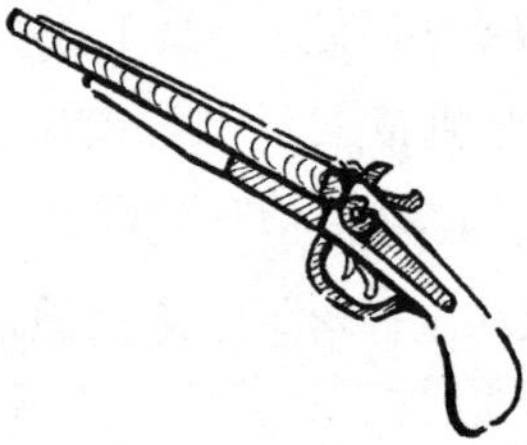

《杀手》(*The Killers,* 1927) 是现代美国短篇小说的经典之作：两名杀手挟持了一家快餐厅的工作人员，并布置好杀人现场，准备枪杀一名拳击手；然而，这名拳击手始终未曾出现；杀手离开之后，服务员尼克向被杀目标人通风报信，却得知早已知晓此事的他并未采取任何应对措施；尼克对此颇为震惊，决定离开小镇。

这篇描写暗杀事件的小说情节简单，大半篇幅都是人物对话，对事情的来龙去脉也没做只言片语的交代，其实，这正是海明威的春秋笔法，是他著名的“冰山理论”的具体化。在短篇小说《死在午后》中，海明威联系自己的创作，提出了著名的经验总结：“冰山在海里移动很是庄严、雄伟，这是因为它只有八分之一露在水面。”海明威把文学创作比喻成漂浮在大洋上的冰山，看得见的只是露在水面上的八分之一，而隐藏在水下的则是八分之七。这“八分之七”虽然没有写出来，却能为读者所感受到。海明威在自己的小说中成功地创建了一种现代英语文学的叙事文体。正是这种创新精神，使他突破了传统的小说美学，形成了自己独特的小说创作手法——海明威风格。

The door of Henry's lunch—room opened and two men came in. They sat down at the counter. "What's yours?" George asked them.

"I don't know," one of the men said. "What do you want to eat, Al?"

"I don't know," said Al. "I don't know what I want to eat."

Outside it was getting dark. The street-light came on outside the window. The two men at the counter read the menu. From the other end of the counter Nick Adams watched them. He had been talking to George when they came in.

"I'll have a roast pork tenderloin with apple sauce and mashed potatoes," the first man said.

"It isn't ready yet."

"What the hell[①] do you put it on the card for?"

"That's the dinner," George explained. "You can get that at six o'clock."

George looked at the clock on the wall behind the counter.

"It's five o'clock."

"The clock says twenty minutes past five," the second man said.

"It's twenty minutes fast."

"Oh, to hell with the clock," the first man said. "What have you got to eat?"

"I can give you any kind of sandwiches," George said. "You can have ham and eggs, bacon and eggs, liver and bacon, or a steak."

"Give me chicken croquettes with green peas and cream sauce

① What the hell：用于加强语气或咒骂，"究竟、到底"的意思。

亨利快餐厅的门开了，进来两个人。他们在柜台边坐下。“你们要什么？”乔治问他们。

“我不知道，”其中一个人说，“你想吃什么，艾尔？”

“我不知道，”艾尔说，“我不知道我想吃什么。”

外面，天色渐黑。窗外的路灯亮了起来。坐在柜台边上的那两个人在看菜单。尼克·亚当斯从柜台的另一头看着他们。他们进来时，他正在跟乔治聊天。

“我要一份加苹果酱和马铃薯泥的烤猪里脊，”第一个人说。

“这个还没有准备好。”

“那你把它写在菜单上干什么？”

“那是晚饭，”乔治解释说，“6点你们就可以吃了。”

乔治看了看柜台后面墙上的那只钟。

“5点了。”

“钟面上是5点20，”第二个人说。

“它快了20分钟。”

“啊，让这钟见鬼去吧！”第一个人说，“那你们有什么吃的？”

“我可以供应你们任何一种三明治，”乔治说，“你们可以要火腿加蛋，熏肉加蛋，肝加熏肉，或者牛排。”

“给我来份炸鸡肉饼，配上青豆，奶油沙司和马铃薯泥。”

and mashed potatoes."

"That's the dinner."

"Everything we want's the dinner, eh? That's the way you work it."

"I can give you ham and eggs, bacon and eggs, liver—"

"I'll take ham and eggs," the man called Al said. He wore a derby hat[①] and a black overcoat buttoned across the chest. His face was small and white and he had tight lips. He wore a silk muffler and gloves.

"Give me bacon and eggs," said the other man. He was about the same size as Al. Their faces were different, but they were dressed like twins. Both wore overcoats too tight for them. They sat leaning forward, their elbows on the counter.

"Got anything to drink?" Al asked.

"Silver beer, bevo[②], ginger-ale," George said.

"I mean you got anything to *drink*[③]?"

"Just those I said."

"This is a hot town," said the other. "What do they call it?"

"Summit."

"Ever hear of it?" Al asked his friend.

"No," said the friend.

"What do you do here nights?" Al asked.

"They eat the dinner," his friend said. "They all come here and eat the big dinner."

---

① derby hat：常礼帽一种圆顶、带有窄的弯曲帽檐的硬毡帽。
② bevo：是一种不含酒精的麦芽酒精饮料。
③ 作品中的艾尔强调"drink"一词，其实是问服务员乔治有什么"烈酒"可以喝，但乔治并没有理解到这层含义。

“那是晚饭。”

“我们要的都是晚饭，嗯？你们就是这么招呼客人的啊。”

“我可以供应你们火腿加蛋，熏肉加蛋，肝——”

“我要份火腿加蛋，”名叫艾尔的人说。他头戴一顶常礼帽，身穿一件纽扣横扣在胸前的黑大衣。他的脸又小又白，嘴唇闭得紧紧的。他围着一条真丝围巾，戴着手套。

“给我来份熏肉加蛋，”另一个人说。他的体形跟艾尔差不多。他们的长相不一样，但是却穿得跟双胞胎似的。他们两个都穿着过于紧身的大衣，前倾着身体坐在那儿，把胳膊肘放在柜台上。

“有什么喝的？”艾尔问。

“淡啤酒，麦芽酒，干姜水，”乔治说。

“我是说你们有什么喝的？”

“就是我说的那些啊。”

“这还真是个热闹[1]的小镇，”另一个人说，“人们叫它什么？”

“萨米特。”

“听过吗？”艾尔问他的朋友。

“没有，”那个朋友说。

“你们这儿的人晚上都干些什么？”艾尔问。

“人们来吃晚饭，”他的朋友说，“人们都来这儿大吃一顿。”

① hot：在美国俚语中可指“有生气的、活跃的、繁忙的”的意思。此外它还有“危险的”意思。因此文中麦克斯说小镇充满活力，其实是在暗示小镇是个犯罪活动频繁发生的危险地方。

"That's right," George said.

"So you think that's right?" Al asked George.

"Sure."

"You're a pretty bright boy, aren't you?"

"Sure," said George.

"Well, you're not," said the other little man. "Is he, Al?"

"He's dumb," said Al. He turned to Nick. "What's your name?"

"Adams."

"Another bright boy," Al said. "Ain't he a bright boy, Max?"

"The town's full of bright boys," Max said.

George put the two platters, one of ham and eggs, the other of bacon and eggs, on the counter. He set down two side-dishes[①] of fried potatoes and closed the wicket into the kitchen.

"Which is yours?" he asked Al.

"Don't you remember?"

"Ham and eggs."

"Just a bright boy," Max said. He leaned forward and took the ham and eggs. Both men ate with their gloves on. George watched them eat.

"What are *you* looking it?" Max looked at George.

"Nothing."

"The hell you were. You were looking at me."

"Maybe the boy meant it for a joke, Max," Al said.

George laughed.

"*You* don't have to laugh," Max said to him. "*You* don't have

① side-dish："配菜"与主菜一起上的一道菜。另外它还可以指"盛配菜用的小碟"。

“对，”乔治说。

“这么说你觉得对了？”艾尔问乔治。

“当然。”

“你是个相当聪明的小伙子，不是吗？”

“当然是，”乔治说。

“喔，你不是，”另一个小个子说，“他是吗，艾尔？”

“他是个笨蛋，”艾尔说。他转身面对尼克：“你叫什么名字？”

“亚当斯。”

“又一个聪明的小伙子，”艾尔说，“他不是个聪明的小伙子吗，麦克斯？”

“这个小镇聪明的小伙子很多，”麦克斯说。

乔治在柜台上放下两盘菜，一盘是火腿加蛋，另一盘是熏肉加蛋。接着他又放下了两碟炸土豆作配菜，然后关上了通向厨房的那扇便门。

“哪一盘是你的？”他问艾尔。

“你不记得了？”

“火腿加蛋。”

“真是个聪明的小伙子，”麦克斯说。他向前欠了欠身子，拿了火腿加蛋。两人都戴着手套吃。乔治看着他们吃。

“你在看什么？”麦克斯望着乔治说。

“没什么。”

“你就在看。你刚才在看我。”

“或许这小子是闹着玩的，麦克斯，”艾尔说。

乔治大笑。

“你用不着笑，”麦克斯对他说，“你根本就用不着笑，知道吗？”

to laugh at all, see?"

"All right," said George.

"So he thinks it's all right." Max turned to Al. "He thinks it's all right. That's a good one."

"Oh, he's a thinker," Al said. They went on eating.

"What's the bright boy's name down the counter?" Al asked Max.

"Hey, bright boy," Max said to Nick. "You go around on the other side of the counter with your boy friend."

"What's the idea?" Nick asked.

"There isn't any idea."

"You better go around, bright boy," Al said. Nick went around behind the counter.

"What's the idea?" George asked.

"None of your damned business," Al said. "Who's out in the kitchen?"

"The nigger①."

"What do you mean the nigger?"

"The nigger that cooks."

"Tell him to come in."

"What's the idea?"

"Tell him to come in."

"Where do you think you are?"

"We know damn well where we are," the man called Max said. "Do we look silly?"

"You talk silly," Al said to him. "What the hell do you argue

① nigger："黑鬼"，无礼用语，是一个对黑人带有侮辱性的称呼。

“没关系，”乔治说。

“这么说他认为没关系，”麦克斯对艾尔说，“他认为没关系。这话说得真好。”

“哦，他是个思想家，”艾尔说。他们继续吃。

“柜台那头那个聪明的小伙子叫什么？”艾尔问麦克斯。

“嗨，聪明的小伙子，”麦克斯对尼克说，“你到柜台对面去陪陪你的男朋友。”

“你这是干什么？”尼克问。

“不干什么。”

“你还是过去吧，聪明的小伙子，”艾尔说。尼克走到了柜台的后面。

“你这是干什么？”乔治问。

“该死的别管闲事，”艾尔说，“谁在厨房里？”

“那个黑鬼。”

“那个黑鬼是什么意思？”

“做菜的那个黑鬼。”

“让他进来。”

“你这是干什么？”

“让他进来。”

“你们以为你们在哪儿？”

“我们在哪儿，我们清楚得很，”名叫麦克斯的人说，“我们看起来傻吗？”

“你在说傻话。”艾尔对他说。“你干吗要跟这小子吵？听着，”他对乔治说，“让那个黑鬼出来，到这儿来。”

with this kid for? Listen," he said to George, "tell the nigger to come out here."

"What are you going to do to him?"

"Nothing. Use your head, bright boy. What would we do to a nigger?"

George opened the slit that opened back into the kitchen. "Sam," he called. "Come in here a minute."

The door to the kitchen opened and the nigger came in. "What was it?" he asked. The two men at the counter took a look at him.

"All right, nigger. You stand right there," Al said.

Sam, the nigger, standing in his apron, looked at the two men sitting at the counter. "Yes, sir," he said. Al got down from his stool.

"I'm going back to the kitchen with the nigger and bright boy," he said. "Go on back to the kitchen, nigger. You go with him, bright boy." The little man walked after Nick and Sam, the cook, back into the kitchen. The door shut after them. The man called Max sat at the counter opposite George. He didn't look at George but looked in the mirror that ran along back of the counter. Henry's had been made over from a saloon into a lunch-counter.

"Well, bright boy," Max said, looking into the mirror, "why don't you say something?"

"What's it all about?"

"Hey, Al," Max called, "bright boy wants to know what it's all about."

"Why don't you tell him?" Al's voice came from the kitchen.

"What do you think it's all about?"

“你们要对他做什么？”

“不做什么。你动动脑子，聪明的小伙子。我们能对一个黑鬼做什么？”

乔治打开通向厨房的小门。“萨姆，”他叫道，“进来一会儿。”

通向厨房的那扇门一开，那个黑鬼走了进来。“什么事？”他问。柜台边的那两个人朝他看了看。

“好，黑鬼。你就站在那儿，”艾尔说。

黑鬼萨姆穿着围裙站在那里，看着坐在柜台边的那两个人。“是，先生，”他说。艾尔从凳子上下来。

“我和这个黑鬼，还有聪明的小伙子一起回厨房去，”他说，“回厨房去，黑鬼。你跟他一起，聪明的小伙子。”那个小个子跟在尼克和厨师萨姆的身后，回到厨房里。他们进去后便关上了门。名叫麦克斯的人则面对着乔治坐在柜台前。但是他没有看乔治，而是看着柜台后面的那面长镜。亨利快餐厅是由一家酒吧改装而成的。

“哎，聪明的小伙子，”麦克斯一边说，一边照着镜子，“你怎么不说话？”

“这一切是怎么回事？”

“嗨，艾尔，”麦克斯喊道，“聪明的小伙子想知道这一切是怎么回事。”

“你怎么不告诉他？”艾尔的声音从厨房里传来。

“你认为这一切是怎么回事？”

"I don't know."

"What do you think?"

Max looked into the mirror all the time he was talking.

"I wouldn't say."

"Hey, Al, bright boy says he wouldn't say what he thinks it's all about."

"I can hear you, all right," Al said from the kitchen. He had propped open the slit that dishes passed through into the kitchen with a catsup bottle. "Listen, bright boy," he said from the kitchen to George. "Stand a little further along the bar. You move a little to the left, Max." He was like a photographer arranging for a group picture.

"Talk to me, bright boy," Max said. "What do you think's going to happen?"

George did not say anything.

"I'll tell you," Max said. "We're going to kill a Swede. Do you know a big Swede named Ole Andreson?"

"Yes."

"He comes here to eat every night, don't he?"

"Sometimes he comes here."

"He comes here at six o'clock, don't he?"

"If he comes."

"We know all that, bright boy," Max said. "Talk about something else. Ever go to the movies?"

"Once in a while."

"You ought to go to the movies more. The movies are fine for a bright boy like you."

"我不知道。"

"你认为呢？"

麦克斯说话的时候一直在照镜子。

"我不想说。"

"嗨，艾尔，聪明的小伙子说他不想说他认为这一切是怎么回事。"

"我听到了，好，"艾尔在厨房里说。他用一个番茄酱瓶把那个往厨房送盘子的门撑开。"听着，聪明的小伙子，"他从厨房里对乔治说，"你沿着柜台边站远点。你往左边移点，麦克斯。"他像个在安排拍合影的摄影师一样。

"跟我说说啊，聪明的小伙子，"麦克斯说，"你认为将会发生什么事？"

乔治一言不发。

"我来告诉你，"麦克斯说，"我们准备杀一个瑞典人。你认识一个叫奥利·安德森的大个儿瑞典人吗？"

"认识。"

"他每天晚上都来这儿吃饭，不是吗？"

"他有时候来。"

"他6点来，不是吗？"

"如果他来的话。"

"这些我们全都知道，聪明的小伙子，"麦克斯说，"说点别的事儿吧。去看过电影吗？"

"偶尔去一次。"

"你应该多去看看电影。对于像你这样聪明的小伙子来说，看电影是很好的。"

"What are you going to kill Ole Andreson for? What did he ever do to you?"

"He never had a chance to do anything to us. He never even seen us."

"And he's only going to see us once," Al said from the kitchen.

"What are you going to kill him for, then?" George asked.

"We're killing him for a friend. Just to oblige a friend, bright boy."

"Shut up," said Al from the kitchen. "You talk too goddamn much."

"Well, I got to keep bright boy amused. Don't I, bright boy?"

"You talk too damn much," Al said. "The nigger and my bright boy are amused by themselves. I got them tied up like a couple of girl friends in the convent."

"I suppose you were in a convent?"

"You never know."

"You were in a kosher convent. That's where you were."

George looked up at the clock.

"If anybody comes in you tell them the cook is off, and if they keep after it, you tell them you'll go back and cook yourself. Do you get that, bright boy?"

"All right," George said. "What you going to do with us afterward?"

"That'll depend," Max said. "That's one of those things[①] you

① one of those things: 口语用法，意思是"命中注定的事、不可避免的事"或"必须接受(或承认)的事"。

“你们为什么要杀奥利·安德森？他对你们做过什么？”

“他从来都没机会对我们做什么。他从来都没有见过我们。”

“而且他只会见我们一次，”艾尔在厨房里说。

“那你们为什么要杀他呢？”乔治问。

“我们是替一个朋友杀他的。只是为了帮一个朋友的忙，聪明的小伙子。”

“闭嘴，”艾尔从厨房里说，“你说得他妈的太多了。”

“喔，我得逗聪明的小伙子乐一乐。不是吗，聪明的小伙子？”

“你说得他妈的太多了，”艾尔说，“这个黑鬼和我这个聪明的小伙子会自己逗自己乐。我把他们捆得像修道院里的一对女朋友那样。”

“我看你在女修道院里待过吧？”

“不好说啊。”

“你在一个犹太教的女修道院里待过。你是在那儿待过。”

乔治抬头看了看钟。

“如果有人进来，你就跟他们说厨师出去了，如果他们还是不走，你就跟他们说你可以到后面亲自做给他们吃。明白了吗，聪明的小伙子？”

“好吧，”乔治说，“那事后你们打算把我们怎么办？”

“那就要看情况了，”麦克斯说，“那是你们现在绝不会知道的命中注定的事。”

never know at the time."

George looked up at the clock. It was a quarter past six. The door from the street opened. A street-car motorman came in.

"Hello, George," he said. "Can I get supper?"

"Sam's gone out," George said. "He'll be back in about half an hour."

"I'd better go up the street," the motorman said. George looked at the clock. It was twenty minutes past six.

"That was nice, bright boy," Max said. "You're a regular little gentleman."

"He knew I'd blow his head off," Al said from the kitchen.

"No," said Max. "It ain't that. Bright boy is nice. He's a nice boy. I like him."

At six-fifty-five George said: "He's not coming."

Two other people had been in the lunch-room. Once George had gone out to the kitchen and made a ham-and-egg sandwich "to go" that a man wanted to take with him. Inside the kitchen he saw Al, his derby hat tipped back, sitting on a stool beside the wicket with the muzzle of a sawed-off shotgun resting on the ledge. Nick and the cook were back to back in the corner, a towel tied in each of their mouths. George had cooked the sandwich, wrapped it up in oiled paper, put it in a bag, brought it in, and the man had paid for it and gone out.

"Bright boy can do everything," Max said. "He can cook and everything. You'd make some girl a nice wife, bright boy."

"Yes?" George said, "Your friend, Ole Andreson, isn't going to come."

乔治抬头看了看时间。六点一刻。临街的那扇门开了。一个电车司机走了进来。

“嗨，乔治，”他说，“我可以吃晚饭了吗？”

“萨姆出去了，”乔治说，“他大概半个钟头后回来。”

“那我还是沿街走走看吧，”那个司机说。乔治看了看钟表。6点20。

“做得好，聪明的小伙子，”麦克斯说，“你真是个十足的小绅士。”

“他知道我会崩了他的脑袋的，”艾尔从厨房里说。

“不，”麦克斯说，“不是这样的。聪明的小伙子很好。他是个好小伙儿。我喜欢他。”

6点55分的时候，乔治说：“他不会来了。”

这期间，餐厅里还来过另外两个人。乔治曾到厨房里为一位想打包带走的客人做了一份火腿加蛋三明治外卖。在厨房里，他看到把常礼帽朝后戴着的艾尔正坐在小窗旁边的一张凳子上，并把一支锯短了的猎枪的枪口搁在壁架上。尼克和那个厨师背靠背地待在角落里，嘴里各塞着一块毛巾。乔治做好了三明治，用油纸包好，放进一个纸袋里，拿进餐厅，那人付了钱后便走了。

“聪明的小伙子什么都会做，”麦克斯说，“他会做菜，什么都会。你会教出一个好老婆来的，聪明的小伙子。”

“是吗？”乔治说，“你们的朋友奥利·安德森不会来了。”

"We'll give him ten minutes," Max said.

Max watched the mirror and the clock. The hands of the clock marked seven o'clock, and then five minutes past seven.

"Come on, Al," said Max. "We better go. He's not coming."

"Better give him five minutes," Al said from the kitchen.

In the five minutes a man came in, and George explained that the cook was sick.

"Why the hell don't you get another cook?" the man asked. "Aren't you running a lunch-counter?" He went out.

"Come on, Al," Max said.

"What about the two bright boys and the nigger?"

"They're all right."

"You think so?"

"Sure. We're through with it."

"I don't like it," said Al. "It's sloppy. You talk too much."

"Oh, what the hell," said Max.?"We got to keep amused, haven't we?"

"You talk too much, all the same," Al said. He came out from the kitchen. The cutoff barrels of the shotgun made a slight bulge under the waist of his too tight-fitting overcoat. He straightened his coat with his gloved hands.

"So long, bright boy," he said to George. "You got a lot of luck."

"That's the truth," Max said. "You ought to play the races, bright boy."

The two of them went out the door. George watched them, through the window, pass under the arc-light and cross the street.

“我们再等他10分钟，”麦克斯说。

麦克斯看看镜子，又看看时钟。时针指着7点，接着是7点5分。

“走吧，艾尔，”麦克斯说，“我们还是走吧。他不会来了。”

“还是再等5分钟吧，”艾尔从厨房里说。

5分钟过后，一个男人走了进来，乔治解释说厨师生病了。

“真是的，你们怎么不再找个厨师？”那人问，“你们不是开餐馆吗？”说完，他走了出去。

“走吧，艾尔，”麦克斯说。

“这两个聪明的小伙子和这个黑鬼怎么办？”

“他们不要紧。”

“你这样认为？”

“当然。咱们完事了。”

“我不喜欢这样，”艾尔说，“马马虎虎的。你话太多了。”

“哎，这没什么，”麦克斯说。“我们逗他们乐的，不是吗？”

“反正你话太多了，”艾尔说，他从厨房里出来。他的大衣太过紧身了，以至于那支锯掉了枪筒的猎枪在他的腰下微微鼓起。他用戴着手套的手把大衣拽平。

“再见，聪明的小伙子，”他对乔治说，“你运气太好了。”

“这是实话，”麦克斯说，“你应该去赌马，聪明的小伙子。”

他们俩走出门去。乔治透过窗户看着他们从弧光灯下走过，穿过街道。他们穿着紧大衣，戴着常礼帽，看起来像是杂耍表演

In their tight overcoats and derby hats they looked like a vaudeville team. George went back through the swinging-door into the kitchen and untied Nick and the cook.

"I don't want any more of that," said Sam, the cook. "I don't want any more of that."

Nick stood up. He had never had a towel in his mouth before.

"Say," he said. "What the hell?" He was trying to swagger it off.

"They were going to kill Ole Andreson," George said. "They were going to shoot him when he came in to eat."

"Ole Andreson?"

"Sure."

The cook felt the corners of his mouth with his thumbs.

"They all gone?" he asked.

"Yeah," said George. "They're gone now."

"I don't like it," said the cook. "I don't like any of it at all."

"Listen," George said to Nick. "You better go see Ole Andreson."

"All right."

"You better not have anything to do with it at all," Sam, the cook, said. "You better stay way out of it."

"Don't go if you don't want to," George said.

"Mixing up in this ain't going to get you anywhere," the cook said. "You stay out of it."

"I'll go see him," Nick said to George. "Where does he live?"

The cook turned away.

"Little boys always know what they want to do," he said.

组合。乔治转过身，推开双开式的弹簧门，走进厨房，为尼克和那个厨师松绑。

“我再也不想这样了，”厨师萨姆说，“我再也不想这样了。”

尼克站起来。他以前从没有让人往他嘴里塞过毛巾。

“哼，”他说，“真是的！”他想说句大话消消气。

“他们本来打算杀死奥利·安德森，”乔治说，“他们原本准备趁他进来吃饭的时候，把他枪杀了。”

“奥利·安德森？”

“是的。”

厨师用他的拇指摸摸嘴角。

“他们都走了？”他问。

“是啊，”乔治说，“他们这会儿都走了。”

“我不喜欢这事，”厨师说，“我一点儿也不喜欢。”

“听着，”乔治对尼克说，“你还是去看一下奥利·安德森吧。”

“好。”

“你们最好别跟这事扯上任何关系，”厨师萨姆说，“你们最好躲得远远的。”

“你不想去就别去，”乔治说。

“跟这种事掺和在一起，对你们没什么好处，”厨师说，“你们别插手了。”

“我去看看他，”尼克对乔治说，“他住在哪儿？”

厨师转身离开了。

“哪怕是小孩儿，也总知道自己该做什么，”他说。

"He lives up at Hirsch's rooming — house," George said to Nick.

"I'll go up there."

Outside the arc-light shone through the bare branches of a tree. Nick walked up the street beside the car-tracks and turned at the next arc-light down a side-street. Three houses up the street was Hirsch's rooming-house. Nick walked up the two steps and pushed the bell. A woman came to the door.

"Is Ole Andreson here?"

"Do you want to see him?"

"Yes, if he's in."

Nick followed the woman up a flight of stairs and back to the end of a corridor. She knocked on the door.

"Who is it?"

"It's somebody to see you, Mr. Andreson," the woman said.

"It's Nick Adams."

"Come in."

Nick opened the door and went into the room. Ole Andreson was lying on the bed with all his clothes on. He had been a heavyweight① prizefighter and he was too long for the bed. He lay with his head on two pillows. He did not look at Nick.

"What was it?" he asked.

"I was up at Henry's," Nick said, "and two fellows came in and tied up me and the cook, and they said they were going to kill you."

① heavyweight："最重量级拳击手"的意思是体重超过 175 磅（约合 79.5 公斤）的职业拳击手。

“他住在赫希的公寓里，”乔治对尼克说。

“我上他那儿去。”

外面，弧光灯穿过光秃秃的树枝照射下来。尼克挨着车轨沿街走去，在另一盏弧光灯下拐进了一条小街。街上的第三幢房子便是赫希的公寓。尼克踏上两级台阶，按了按门铃。一个女人应了门。

“奥利·安德森住在这儿吗？”

“你想见他吗？”

“是的，如果他在的话。”

尼克跟着那个女人走上一段楼梯，又折回到走廊的尽头。她敲了敲门。

“谁啊？”

“有人要见你，安德森先生，”那个妇女说。

“我是尼克·亚当斯。”

“进来。”

尼克推开门，走进房里。奥利·安德森和衣躺在床上。他曾是位最重量级职业拳击手，他的身体由于太长而无法在床上伸直。他枕着两个枕头。他并没有看尼克。

“什么事？”他问。

“我现在在亨利快餐厅里做事，”尼克说，“有两个人进来，把我和厨师捆了起来，他们说要杀死你。”

It sounded silly when he said it. Ole Andreson said nothing.

"They put us out in the kitchen," Nick went on. "They were going to shoot you when you came in to supper."

Ole Andreson looked at the wall and did not say anything.

"George thought I better come and tell you about it."

"There isn't anything I can do about it," Ole Andreson said.

"I'll tell you what they were like."

"I don't want to know what they were like," Ole Andreson said. He looked at the wall.

"Thanks for coming to tell me about it."

"That's all right."

Nick looked at the big man lying on the bed.

"Don't you want me to go and see the police?"

"No," Ole Andreson said. "That wouldn't do any good."

"Isn't there something I could do?"

"No. There ain't anything to do."

"Maybe it was just a bluff."

"No. It ain't just a bluff."

Ole Andreson rolled over toward the wall.

"The only thing is," he said, talking toward the wall, "I just can't make up my mind to go out. I been in here all day."

"Couldn't you get out of town?"

"No," Ole Andreson said. "I'm through with all that running around."

He looked at the wall.

"There ain't anything to do now."

"Couldn't you fix it up some way?"

他说这些话时，让人觉得可笑。奥利·安德森一言不发。

“他们把我们关在厨房里，”尼克接着说，“他们打算趁你进去吃饭的时候枪杀你。”

奥利·安德森望着墙壁，什么也没说。

“乔治认为还是让我来把这事告诉你。”

“对此，我没有什么好做的，”奥利·安德森说。

“我来给你说说他们长什么样。”

“我不想知道他们长什么样，”奥利·安德森说。他望着墙壁。

“谢谢你来告诉我这个。”

“这没什么。”

尼克看着躺在床上的那个大汉。

“你不需要我去报警吗？”

“不用，”奥利·安德森说，“去了也没什么用。”

“有什么我能帮忙的吗？”

“没有，没什么好帮的。”

“或许那只是虚张声势吧。”

“不。那不仅仅是虚张声势。”

奥利·安德森翻过身去，面朝墙壁。

“唯一的问题就是，”他对着墙壁说，“我只是无法下定决心出去。我躺在这儿一整天了。”

“你不能离开这个小镇吗？”

“不能，”奥利·安德森说，“那样东奔西跑的，我已经烦了。”

他望着墙壁。

“现在没什么好做的。”

“你不能想个办法，把这事解决了吗？”

"No. I got in wrong[1]. " He talked in the same flat voice. "There ain't anything to do. After a while I'll make up my mind to go out."

"I better go back and see George," Nick said.

"So long," said Ole Andreson. He did not look toward Nick. "Thanks for coming around."

Nick went out. As he shut the door he saw Ole Andreson with all his clothes on, lying on the bed looking at the wall.

"He's been in his room all day," the landlady said down-stairs. "I guess he don't feel well. I said to him: Mr. Andreson, you ought to go out and take a walk on a nice fall day like this, ' but he didn't feel like it."

"He doesn't want to go out."

"I'm sorry he don't feel well," the woman said. "He's an awfully nice man. He was in the ring[2], you know."

"I know it."

"You'd never know it except from the way his face is," the woman said. They stood talking just inside the street door. "He's just as gentle."

"Well, good-night, Mrs. Hirsch," Nick said.

"I'm not Mrs. Hirsch," the woman said. "She owns the place. I just look after it for her. I'm Mrs. Bell."

"Well, good-night, Mrs. Bell," Nick said.

"Good-night," the woman said.

Nick walked up the dark street to the corner under the arc-light, and then along the car-tracks to Henry's eating-house. George

① get in wrong：常用于美国口语，意思是"使某人讨厌"。另外它还可指"使某人陷入困境、使某人失去众望"的意思。
② ring：在文中的意思是"(呈方形并由绳子拦隔的)拳击台"。

“不能。我得罪了人。”他用同样无力的声音说。“没什么好做的。过一会儿，我会拿定主意出去。”

“我该回去见乔治了，”尼克说。

“再见，”奥利·安德森说。他并没有朝尼克看。“谢谢你来这一趟。”

尼克出去了。他关门时，看到奥利·安德森和衣躺在床上，眼睛望着墙壁。

“他一整天都待在屋里，”女房东在楼下说，“我想他是身体不舒服。我跟他说：‘安德森先生，像今天这么好的秋日，你应该出去散散步，’可是他不愿出去。”

“他不想出去。”

“他身体不舒服，真叫人难过，”那妇女说，“他是个非常好的人。他以前是打拳击的，你知道的。”

“我知道。”

“要不是看了他那张脸的样子，你是决不会知道的，”那个女人说。他们就站在临街的门廊里说话。“他真是很和善。”

“好吧，晚安，赫希太太，”尼克说。

“我不是赫希太太，”那个女人说，“这地方是她的。我只是替她看管房子。我是贝尔太太。”

“啊，晚安，贝尔太太，”尼克说。

“晚安，”那妇女说。

尼克沿着黑暗的街道走到弧光灯下的拐角处，然后沿着车轨走到亨利餐馆。乔治在里面，在柜台的后面。

was inside, back of the counter.

"Did you see Ole?"

"Yes," said Nick. "He's in his room and he won't go out."

The cook opened the door from the kitchen when he heard Nick's voice.

"I don't even listen to it," he said and shut the door.

"Did you tell him about it?" George asked.

"Sure. I told him but he knows what it's all about."

"What's he going to do?"

"Nothing."

"They'll kill him."

"I guess they will."

"He must have got mixed up in something in Chicago."

"I guess so," said Nick.

"It's a hell of a thing."

"It's an awful thing," Nick said.

They did not say anything. George reached down for a towel and wiped the counter.

"I wonder what he did?" Nick said.

"Double-crossed[①] somebody. That's what they kill them for."

"I'm going to get out of this town," Nick said.

"Yes," said George. "That's a good thing to do."

"I can't stand to think about him waiting in the room and knowing he's going to get it. It's too damned awful."

"Well," said George, "you better not think about it."

① double-cross：口语用法，意思是"欺骗、出卖"。

"你见到奥利了吗？"

"见到了，"尼克说，"他待在屋子里，不愿出去。"

那个厨师一听见尼克的声音，就推开了厨房的门。

"这事我听也不要听，"他说完便关上了门。

"你把情况都告诉他了吗？"乔治问。

"当然。我告诉他了，不过他什么都知道了。"

"他打算怎么做？"

"什么也不做。"

"他们要杀死他啊。"

"我看他们会。"

"他一定是在芝加哥惹上了什么事。"

"我猜是这样，"尼克说。

"这事真不像话。"

"是件很糟糕的事，"尼克说。

他们不再说什么了。乔治伸手到下面拿了一条毛巾来擦柜台。

"不知道他干了什么？"尼克说。

"出卖了什么人。因此他们要杀死他。"

"我要离开这个小镇，"尼克说。

"好啊，"乔治说，"离开是好事。"

"他明知道自己会送命，还那样在屋里干等，一想到这个我就受不了。这太他妈的可怕了。"

"好了，"乔治说，"你还是别想了。"

The Short Happy Life of Francis Macomber
弗朗西斯·麦康伯短促的幸福生活

《弗朗西斯·麦康伯短促的幸福生活》(*The Short Happy Life of Francis Macomber,* 1936) 讲述的是美国富豪麦康伯夫妇及其雇用的白人职业猎手威尔逊在肯尼亚两天两夜狩猎大型猎物的故事。这篇并不短的短篇小说有两条主线：以狩猎为显性线索，以麦康伯及其妻子的关系为隐性线索。

从一定程度上来说，麦康伯是男权社会对于社会性别角色进行僵化定位的牺牲品。麦康伯尽管极其有钱，他本身却是个“长不大的美国老顽童”。他性格懦弱，拙于言辞，委曲求全。他的生活看似洒脱不羁，但他却时常为自己没有具备十足的阳刚气而自责、自卑和自惭。他的妻子玛格丽特充分把握了他的这种追寻所谓“硬汉形象”的心态，并且加以充分地利用，时常将他缺乏阳刚气的表现用来作为自己红杏出墙的借口。海明威在这部小说的结尾让麦康伯生平第一次彻底摆脱了前怕狼后怕虎的忧惧，让他第一次勇敢地与死神交手而完全摆脱了患得患失的心态，让他第一次寻觅到男子汉的勇敢无畏与坚强自信。海明威将麦康伯拾得阳刚气质后的短暂的生活定义为麦康伯的“幸福生活”，在一定程度上也反映了海明威本人对男人阳刚气质的推崇。

这部小说于1947年被拍成电影，名为《麦康伯韵事》(*The Macomber Affair*)。

It was now lunch time and they were all sitting under the double green fly of the dining tent pretending that nothing had happened.

"Will you have lime juice or lemon squash?" Macomber asked.

"I'll have a gimlet[①]," Robert Wilson told him.

"I'll have a gimlet too. I need something," Macomber's wife said.

"I suppose it's the thing to do," Macomber agreed. "Tell him to make three gimlets."

The mess boy had started them already, lifting the bottles out of the canvas cooling bags that sweated wet in the wind that blew through the trees that shaded the tents.

"What had I ought to give them?"[②] Macomber asked.

"A quid would be plenty," Wilson told him. "You don't want to spoil them."

"Will the headman distribute it?"

"Absolutely."

Francis Macomber had, half an hour before, been carried to his tent from the edge of the camp in triumph on the arms and shoulders of the cook, the personal boys, the skinner and the porters. The gun-bearers had taken no part in the demonstration. When the native boys put him down at the door of his tent, he had shaken all their hands, received their congratulations, and then gone into the tent and sat on the bed until his wife came in. She did

① gimlet：一种鸡尾酒，味道辛辣。
② "What had I ought to give them?"麦康伯在这里征询威尔逊的意见时，既用"had to"又用"ought to"，这表明他是个性格懦弱、毫无主见且又迂腐的男人。

现在是午饭时间，他们都坐在就餐帐篷的双层绿色帆布门帘下，装作什么事情都没发生过似的。

“你们来点酸橙汁还是柠檬汽水？”麦康伯问道。

“我要杯兑酸橙汁的杜松子酒，”罗伯特·威尔逊告诉他。

“我也要杯兑酸橙汁的杜松子酒。我需要提提神，”麦康伯的妻子说。

“我想这东西正合适，”麦康伯附和着说，“告诉他调三杯兑酸橙汁的杜松子酒。”

那个杂役男孩早就在调酒了。他把酒瓶从帆布冷藏袋里掏出来。风吹过给帐篷遮阴的树木，瓶子在风中渗出水滴。

“我应该给他们多少呢？”麦康伯问。

“一英镑就够了，”威尔逊告诉他，“你不想惯坏他们吧？”

“头人会把它分了吗？”

“肯定会的。”

半个钟头前，凯旋的弗朗西斯·麦康伯被一群人（一个厨师、几个跟班杂役、一个剥皮匠，还有几个脚夫）从营地的边上肩手并用地抬回他的帐篷。几个扛枪的人压根没参加这场作秀。当土著杂役们在帐篷门口把他放下来时，他跟他们一一握手，接受他们的祝贺；然后，他走进帐篷，就此坐在床上，一直到他妻子走

not speak to him when she came in and he left the tent at once to wash his face and hands in the portable wash basin outside and go over to the dining tent to sit in a comfortable canvas chair in the breeze and the shade.

"You've got your lion," Robert Wilson said to him, "and a damned fine one too."

Mrs. Macomber looked at Wilson quickly. She was an extremely handsome and well-kept woman of the beauty and social position which had, five years before, commanded five thousand dollars as the price of endorsing, with photographs, a beauty product which she had never used. She had been married to Francis Macomber for eleven years.

"He is a good lion, isn't he?" Macomber said. His wife looked at him now. She looked at both these men as though she had never seen them before.

One, Wilson, the white hunter, she knew she had never truly seen before. He was about middle height with sandy hair, a stubby mustache, a very red face and extremely cold blue eyes with faint white wrinkles at the corners that grooved merrily when he smiled. He smiled at her now and she looked away from his face at the way his shoulders sloped in the loose tunic he wore with the four big cartridges held in loops where the left breast pocket should have been, at his big brown hands, his old slacks, his very dirty boots and back to his red face again. She noticed where the baked red of his face stopped in a white line that marked the circle left by his Stetson hat① that hung now from one of the pegs of the tent

① Stetson hat：斯特森帽子公司生产的一种阔边高顶毡帽。

进来。她走进来时，并没有跟他打招呼；而他呢，则立马离开帐篷，到外边便携式脸盆里洗了脸和手，接着就向就餐帐篷走去，坐到一张舒服的帆布椅子上。这里，微风习习，树影婆娑。

“你打到狮子啦，”罗伯特·威尔逊对他说，“并且还是头蛮厉害的狮子。”

麦康伯太太飞快地向威尔逊瞟了一眼。她是个相当俊逸、保养良好的女人。五年前她的美貌及社会地位就赢得了五千美元：那是在广告中用几张照片为一种美容产品做宣传的报酬，这产品她从未使用过。她和弗朗西斯·麦康伯结婚已有十一个年头。

“那是头不错的狮子，是不？”麦康伯说。他妻子这时又望着他。她望着这两个男人，仿佛她以前从未看到过他们似的。

其中一个是威尔逊，这个白人猎手，她知道她以前确实不认识他。他大约中等个子，头发黄中带红，嘴上一抹密密扎扎的胡子，面部肤色很红很红，相当冷峻的蓝眼睛，眼角有细细的、浅浅的鱼尾纹。他微笑的时候，这些皱纹就奕奕地变深了。他这会儿正向她微笑来着。她把目光从他脸上挪开，看到他双肩在宽宽的短上衣下松开。短上衣左边本应有胸袋，现在却有一个套子，套着四颗子弹。她的目光又逐一移到他晒成古铜色的大手上、他的旧便装裤上、他脏透了的靴子上，然后又重新移回到他红红的脸上。她观察到，他的斯特森牛仔帽在他被太阳晒红的脸上留下了一道白圈，这帽子此刻正悬在帐篷柱子的一个木钉子上呢。

pole.

"Well, here's to the lion," Robert Wilson said. He smiled at her again and, not smiling, she looked curiously at her husband.

Francis Macomber was very tall, very well built if you did not mind that length of bone, dark, his hair cropped like an oarsman, rather thin-lipped, and was considered handsome. He was dressed in the same sort of safari clothes that Wilson wore except that his were new, he was thirty-five years old, kept himself very fit, was good at court games, had a number of big game fishing records, and had just shown himself, very publicly, to be a coward.

"Here's to the lion," he said. "I can't ever thank you for what you did."

Margaret, his wife, looked away from him and back to Wilson.

"Let's not talk about the lion," she said.

Wilson looked over at her without smiling and now she smiled at him.

"It's been a very strange day," she said. "Hadn't you ought to put your hat on even under the canvas at noon? You told me that, you know."

"Might put it on," said Wilson.

"You know you have a very red face, Mr. Wilson," she told him and smiled again.

"Drink," said Wilson.

"I don't think so," she said. "Francis drinks a great deal, but his face is never red."

"It's red today," Macomber tried a joke.

“唔，为这头狮子干杯吧，”罗伯特说道。他又朝她笑了笑；而她呢，并没有笑，而是用古怪的眼神打量着她的丈夫。

弗朗西斯个子老高老高，如果你不嫌弃他的骨架太长的话，他的身材倒可以说是相当匀称。他的皮肤呈棕褐色，头发剪得像水手那么平，嘴唇薄薄的。在别人眼里他也算得上是英俊潇洒了。他穿的猎装和威尔逊穿的一样，不过他穿的是崭新的。他35岁，身体非常健康，擅长各类球场运动，有着无数捕获危险鱼类的纪录。刚才，在众目睽睽之下，他却表明他是个胆小鬼。

“为这头狮子干杯。”他说，“你做的一切我都不胜感激。”

玛格丽特——他的妻子——的目光从他身上移开，又落到威尔逊身上了。

“我们还是别谈那头狮子了，”她说。

威尔逊朝她看过来，脸上的笑容不见了；而她，则望着他笑呢。

“今天可非常奇怪啊，”她说，“你不是中午待在帆布帐篷里时都必须戴着你的帽子的吗？你曾对我说是那样的，你记得吧。”

“是可以戴帽子，”威尔逊说。

“要知道，你的脸可是非常红呢，威尔逊先生，”她告诉他并朝他笑了笑。

“是酒的作用吧，”威尔逊说。

“我看可不见得。弗朗西斯喝得那么多，但他的脸从来都不红。”

“今天可红了，”麦康伯故作揶揄地说道。

"No," said Margaret. "It's mine that's red today. But Mr. Wilson's is always red."

"Must be racial," said Wilson. "I say, you wouldn't like to drop my beauty as a topic, would you?"

"I've just started on it."

"Let's chuck it," said Wilson.

"Conversation is going to be so difficult," Margaret said.

"Don't be silly, Margot," her husband said.

"No difficulty," Wilson said. "Got a damn fine lion."

Margot looked at them both and they both saw that she was going to cry. Wilson had seen it coming for a long time and he dreaded it. Macomber was past dreading it.

"I wish it hadn't happened. Oh, I wish it hadn't happened," she said and started for her tent. She made no noise of crying but they could see that her shoulders were shaking under the rose-colored, sun-proofed shirt she wore.

"Women upset," said Wilson to the tall man. " Amounts to nothing. Strain on the nerves and one thing'n another."

"No," said Macomber. "I suppose that I rate that for the rest of my life now."

"Nonsense. Let's have a spot of the giant killer," said Wilson. "Forget the whole thing. Nothing to it anyway."

"We might try," said Macomber. "I won't forget what you did for me though."

"Nothing," said Wilson. "All nonsense."

So they sat there in the shade where the camp was pitched under some wide-topped acacia trees with a boulder-strewn

“才没呢！”玛格丽特说，“今天脸红的人是我。威尔逊先生的脸可一直都是红通通的。”

“大概是种族遗传吧，”威尔逊说，“我说，你拿我的美貌当话题还有完没完？”

“我才刚刚提了一下而已嘛！”

“那就让它到此为止吧！”威尔逊说。

“聊聊天都这么困难吗？”玛格丽特说。

“别闹了，玛戈，”她丈夫说道。

“毫无困难可言，”威尔逊说，“弄到了头厉害的狮子呢。”

玛戈望望他们这个，又望望那个。他俩都观察到她有点要哭了。威尔逊观察到她已经有好久都是欲哭无泪了，因此有点忐忑不安。麦康伯呢，却早已经不会为此忐忑不安了。

“我多么希望这一切从来都没发生过。哦，我多么希望这一切从来都没发生过，”她说道，起身向她的帐篷走去。他们听不到她的哭声，但可以看到她的双肩在她那件玫瑰红色的防晒衬衫下瑟瑟抖动。

“女人使使小性子，”威尔逊对高个男人说，“别太当回事。都是因为神经过敏，诸如此类的小事情而已。”

“不，”麦康伯说，“现在我料想我下半辈子都得面对这种情况啦。”

“胡说。咱们来点烈酒浇愁咋样？”威尔逊说。“忘了这档子事吧，没什么值得老提的。”

“我们会试试的，”麦康伯说，“但我不会忘记你为我所做的一切的。”

“没什么，”威尔逊说道，“不值一提”。

于是他们就坐在树荫下，喝着冰凉爽口的柠檬饮料。这营地安扎在几株枝繁叶茂的刺槐树底下，树后面是巨石林立的峭

cliff behind them, and a stretch of grass that ran to the bank of a boulder-filled stream in front with forest beyond it, and drank their just-cool lime drinks and avoided one another's eyes while the boys set the table for lunch. Wilson could tell that the boys all knew about it now and when he saw Macomber's personal boy looking curiously at his master while he was putting dishes on the table he snapped at him in Swahili①. The boy turned away with his face blank.

"What were you telling him?" Macomber asked.

"Nothing. Told him to look alive or I'd see he got about fifteen of the best."

"What's that? Lashes?"

"It's quite illegal," Wilson said. "You're supposed to fine them."

"Do you still have them whipped?"

"Oh, yes. They could raise a row if they chose to complain. But they don't. They prefer it to the fines."

"How strange！" said Macomber.

"Not strange, really," Wilson said. "Which would you rather do? Take a good birching or lose your pay?"

Then he felt embarrassed at asking it and before Macomber could answer he went on, "We all take a beating every day, you know, one way or another."

This was no better. "Good God," he thought. "I am a diplomat, aren't I?"

"Yes, we take a beating," said Macomber, still not looking at

① Swahili：斯瓦希里语，是非洲班图族人 (Bantu) 使用的一种语言。

壁；还有一溜草地，一直延伸到前面缀满卵石的小河岸，河对面是森林。当杂役们摆桌子准备午饭的时候，他俩都避免眼神接触。杂役们这会儿可全知道此事了，威尔逊对此心知肚明。当他看到麦康伯的跟班杂役一边把盘子放到桌上，一边怪里怪气地打量他的主人的时候，他用斯瓦希里语恶狠狠地斥责他。那杂役转身走了，表情漠然。

“你跟他说些什么来着呢？”麦康伯问道。

“没什么。是告诉他别一副死人相，否则我就要给他来十五下。”

“十五下什么，鞭子吗？”

“这么做是严重违法的，”威尔逊说，“你倒是可以扣他们工钱。”

“你们仍然可以叫人鞭打他们吗？”

“哦，是的。他们如果因此选择投诉的话，可就有好看的了。但是他们不会抱怨。他们情愿挨揍，不愿被扣钱。”

“多奇怪，”麦康伯说。

“不奇怪，真的，”威尔逊说，“你愿意挑哪一桩？被人用桦条狠狠抽一顿，还是拿不到工钱？”

此话一问出口，他立马觉得不妥。没等麦康伯回答，他又接着说道：“我们全都天天在挨揍，你知道的，方式不同罢了。”

这话于事无补。“老天，”他想，“我真是个圆通的人啊，难道不是吗？”

“是的，我们在挨揍，”麦康伯说着，仍然没有朝他看，“狮子那档子事，让我太难过了。这事没必要传开去，不是吗？我是说，

him. "I'm awfully sorry about that lion business. It doesn't have to go any further, does it? I mean no one will hear about it, will they?"

"You mean will I tell it at the Mathaiga Club[①]?" Wilson looked at him now coldly. He had not expected this. So he's a bloody four-letter man as well as a bloody coward, he thought. I rather liked him too until today. But how is one to know about an American?

"No," said Wilson. "I'm a professional hunter. We never talk about our clients. You can be quite easy on that. It's supposed to be bad form to ask us not to talk though."

He had decided now that to break would be much easier. He would eat, then, by himself and could read a book with his meals. They would eat by themselves. He would see them through the safari on a very formal basis—what was it the French called it? Distinguished consideration—and it would be a damn sight[②] easier than having to go through this emotional trash. He'd insult him and make a good clean break. Then he could read a book with his meals and he'd still be drinking their whisky. That was the phrase for it when a safari went bad. You ran into another white hunter and you asked, "How is everything going?" and he answered, "Oh, I'm still drinking their whisky," and you knew everything had gone to pot.

"I'm sorry," Macomber said and looked at him with his

① The Mathaiga Club 是英国殖民者在肯尼亚首都内罗毕的一家高级俱乐部。肯尼亚在1920—1963 年为英国殖民地。
② "a sight" 加上"比较级 (如 better/more/easier 等) + than" 时表达的意思是 "a lot; a great deal"，表示"很多"。

不会有人听到这件事了，好不？”

“你的意思是说我会到马撒加俱乐部去声张此事吗？”现在，威尔逊看着他，目光冷冷的。他没料到这一手。原来他不仅是个可怜的胆小鬼，还是个可耻的下流胚，他想道。到今天之前，我还一直相当喜欢他呢。但谁能摸得透一个美国佬呢？

“放心吧，”威尔逊说。“我是一名职业猎手。我们从不对我们的顾客说三道四。那件事你完全没必要老是如鲠在喉。不过，主动要求我们守口如瓶，好像不是很体面的做法。”

他现在觉得散伙将会好受得多。那么他就可以自个儿进餐，还可以边进餐边看本书。他们吃他们的，他将只会在狩猎的时候看到他们，公事公办——法国人管这叫什么来着？崇高的敬意——这样比不得不应付这种无聊的感情游戏要自在得多。他决定不给他留情面，分开得没有一点藕断丝连。那样他就可以边进餐边看本书，并且还可以继续喝他们的威士忌——这是当狩猎关系变得紧张时的一句口头禅。当你碰到另一个白人猎手时你问：“情况怎么样啊？”这时他回答：“哦，我还喝着他们的威士忌呢，”那么你就知道事情糟透了。

“对不起啊，”麦康伯说道，用他那张即便到了中年却仍是稚嫩的脸望着他。威尔逊注意到他的水手式的平头、漂亮的眼睛，摇曳不定的眼神、端正的鼻子、薄薄的嘴唇和好看的下巴。“对不起，我对此毫不知情。我不知道的事情太多了。”

American face that would stay adolescent until it became middle-aged, and Wilson noted his crew-cropped hair, fine eyes only faintly shifty, good nose, thin lips and handsome jaw. "I'm sorry I didn't realize that. There are lots of things I don't know."

So what could he do, Wilson thought. He was all ready to break it off quickly and neatly and here the beggar was apologizing after he had just insulted him. He made one more attempt. "Don't worry about me talking," he said. "I have a living to make. You know in Africa no woman ever misses her lion and no white man ever bolts."

"I bolted like a rabbit," Macomber said.

Now what in hell were you going to do about a man who talked like that, Wilson wondered.

Wilson looked at Macomber with his flat, blue, machine-gunner's eyes and the other smiled back at him. He had a pleasant smile if you did not notice how his eyes showed when he was hurt.

"Maybe I can fix it up on buffalo," he said. "We're after them next, aren't we?"

"In the morning if you like," Wilson told him. Perhaps he had been wrong. This was certainly the way to take it. You most certainly could not tell a damned thing about an American. He was all for Macomber again. If you could forget the morning. But, of course, you couldn't. The morning had been about as bad as they come.

"Here comes the Memsahib," he said. She was walking over from her tent looking refreshed and cheerful and quite lovely. She had a very perfect oval face, so perfect that you expected her to be

这样他还能怎么办呢，威尔逊想道。他本来准备好和他来个快刀斩乱麻，干净利落地散伙，但现在这个死乞白赖的家伙却在道歉，并且还是在自个儿被侮辱了之后向他道歉。他又试探了一下。“别担心我会说出去，”他说，“我不过是混口饭吃。你知道吧，在非洲，没有一个女人会打不中她的狮子，没有一个白种男人会临阵脱逃。”

“我却像只兔子一样溜掉了，”麦康伯说道。

真见鬼，对一个这样说话的男人，你还能有何技可施呢？威尔逊拿不定主意了。

威尔逊望着麦康伯。这是不动声色的蓝莹莹的机关枪手的眼神。后者对他报以微微一笑。如果没注意到他受伤时的眼神，他微笑起来可算是十分动人。

“也许我可以在野牛身上捞回本，”他说，“下次我们就要猎野牛了，是不是？”

“如果你喜欢的话，那就明早吧。”威尔逊告诉他。也许他搞错了。这才是泰然处之的方法。面对一个美国佬，你几乎不可能对他下任何决断。他又满心向着麦康伯了。如果你能够忘记这个早上的话。当然啦，你不能够。今天早上即便再糟糕，但的确到来过，就像他们的到来一样。

“尊夫人来了，”他说道。她正从她的帐篷那儿走过来，看起来精神抖擞、兴高采烈、楚楚动人。她的脸蛋呈完美的椭圆形，完美到你巴望她愚蠢一些。但是她并不愚蠢，威尔逊想，不，并

stupid. But she wasn't stupid, Wilson thought, no, not stupid.

"How is the beautiful red-faced Mr. Wilson? Are you feeling better, Francis, my pearl?"

"Oh, much," said Macomber.

"I've dropped the whole thing," she said, sitting down at the table. "What importance is there to whether Francis is any good at killing lions? That's not his trade. That's Mr. Wilson's trade. Mr. Wilson is really very impressive killing anything. You do kill anything, don't you?"

"Oh, anything," said Wilson. "Simply anything." They are, he thought, the hardest in the world; the hardest, the cruelest, the most predatory and the most attractive and their men have softened or gone to pieces nervously as they have hardened. Or is it that they pick men they can handle? They can't know that much at the age they marry, he thought. He was grateful that he had gone through his education on American women before now because this was a very attractive one.

"We're going after buff in the morning," he told her.

"I'm coming," she said.

"No, you're not."

"Oh, yes, I am. Mayn't I, Francis?"

"Why not stay in camp?"

"Not for anything," she said. "I wouldn't miss something like today for anything."

When she left, Wilson was thinking, when she went off to cry, she seemed a hell of a fine woman. She seemed to understand, to realize, to be hurt for him and for herself and to know how things

不愚蠢。

“漂亮的红脸威尔逊先生，你好啊！你感觉好点了吗，弗朗西斯，我的宝贝儿？”

“哦，好多啦，”麦康伯说道。

“整件事情我都完全看开了，”她一边说着，一边在饭桌旁坐下来。“关于弗朗西斯是否擅长猎狮子，那压根不重要！那又不是他的本行。那是威尔逊先生的本行。威尔逊先生杀任何东西都很在行。你确实什么东西都杀，对不？”

“嗯，无所不杀，”威尔逊说，“简单地讲，就是无所不杀。”她们真是世上最难以对付的，最难以对付、最冷酷无情、最暴掠成性、最撩惑人心，他想道。当她们变得难以对付以后，她们的男人就得软蛋下来，否则就会崩溃得稀里哗啦。要不就是她们只挑中自己能玩弄于股掌之中的男人。她们在结婚的那会儿年纪是不可能懂得这么多的，他想。想到在这之前他已经学完了如何同美国娘们打交道的门道，他就感到谢天谢地：因为眼前这个可是个尤物。

“我们明早去打野牛，”他告诉她。

“我要去，”她说。

“不，你不要去。”

“噢，不，我要去。我不可以去吗，弗朗西斯？”

“为什么不待在营地呢？”

“说什么也不成，”她说，“我怎么也不能错过像今天这样的事情啦。”

当她刚离开的时候，威尔逊想道，她刚走开去哭的时候，似乎是个相当说得过去的女人。她看上去好像懂情理、识好歹，为他和她自己感到痛心，并且知道将事物各归其位。她只不过离

really stood. She is away for twenty minutes and now she is back, simply enamelled in that American female cruelty. They are the damnedest women. Really the damnedest.

"We'll put on another show for you tomorrow," Francis Macomber said.

"You're not coming," Wilson said.

"You're very mistaken," she told him. "And I want so to see you perform again. You were lovely this morning. That is if blowing things' heads off is lovely."

"Here's the lunch," said Wilson. "You're very merry, aren't you?"

"Why not? I didn't come out here to be dull."

"Well, it hasn't been dull," Wilson said. He could see the boulders in the river and the high bank beyond with the trees and he remembered the morning.

"Oh, no," she said. "It's been charming. And tomorrow. You don't know how I look forward to tomorrow."

"That's eland he's offering you,"[①] Wilson said.

"They're the big cowy things that jump like hares, aren't they?"

"I suppose that describes them," Wilson said.

"It's very good meat," Macomber said.

"Did you shoot it, Francis?" she asked.

"Yes."

"They're not dangerous, are they?"

"Only if they fall on you," Wilson told her.

① 从"he's offering you"一句中的"he"可以看出此时威尔逊语气对麦康伯缺少尊重。

席了20分钟而已，现在她回来的时候，却涂上了那种美国女性冷酷的色彩。她们是最该受诅咒的女人。的确是最该受诅咒的。

“明天我们要为你表演另外一场秀，”弗朗西斯·麦康伯说。

“你不要来，”威尔逊说。

“你这是枉费心机，”她告诉他，“我可是好想好想再看到你们表演啊。今天早上你们太可爱了。如果把东西的脑袋敲开花也叫作可爱的话。”

“午饭来了，”威尔逊说。“你倒是很带劲啊，是不是？”

“为何不？我出门到这里来又不是自找没趣的。”

“唔，并不是没趣啊，”威尔逊说道。在这里他可以看到河里的一块块卵石以及树林背后高高的河岸。他想起了这个早晨。

“哦，当然啦，”她说，“一直都很迷人呢。还有明天。你不知道，我是多么期盼明天的到来啊！”

“他正给你上大角斑羚肉呢！”威尔逊说。

“它们是那种模样高大如牛、蹦起来像野兔的东西，是不是？”

“我想你描述得很到位，”威尔逊说道。

“肉非常不错，”麦康伯说。

“是你打到的吗，弗朗西斯？”她问道。

“是啊。”

“它们没有危险性，是吧？”

“除非它们扑到你身上来，”威尔逊告诉她。

"I'm so glad."

"Why not let up on the bitchery just a little, Margot," Macomber said, cutting the eland steak and putting some mashed potato, gravy and carrot on the down-turned fork that tined through the piece of meat.

"I suppose I could," she said, "since you put it so prettily."

"Tonight we'll have champagne for the lion," Wilson said. "It's a bit too hot at noon."

"Oh, the lion," Margot said. "I'd forgotten the lion!" ①

So, Robert Wilson thought to himself, she *is* giving him a ride, isn't she? Or do you suppose that's her idea of putting up a good show? How should a woman act when she discovers her husband is a bloody coward? She's damn cruel but they're all cruel. They govern, of course, and to govern one has to be cruel sometimes. Still, I've seen enough of their damn terrorism.

"Have some more eland," he said to her politely.

That afternoon, late, Wilson and Macomber went out in the motor car with the native driver and the two gun-bearers. Mrs. Macomber stayed in the camp. It was too hot to go out, she said, and she was going with them in the early morning. As they drove off Wilson saw her standing under the big tree, looking pretty rather than beautiful in her faintly rosy khaki, her dark hair drawn back off her forehead and gathered in a knot low on her neck, her face as fresh, he thought, as though she were in England. She waved to them as the car went off through the swale of high grass

① "I'd forgotten the lion！" 玛格丽特的这句话是提醒麦康伯不要忘记了他不久前在狮子面前的懦弱表现，提醒他没有资格在她面前逞威风教训她。

“这可让我长舒一口气了。”

“为何不把你那浪荡劲儿稍微收敛一点，玛戈？”麦康伯一边说着，一边切下一条斑羚肉排，用一把向下弯曲的叉子叉着肉，往上面放了些土豆泥、调味肉汁、胡萝卜。

“我想我能够做到这点，”她说，“因为你把话说得这么好听。”

“今晚我们要开香槟庆祝打到了狮子，”威尔逊说，“中午喝太热了点。”

“对了，还有狮子呢！”玛戈说，“我竟把狮子给忘了。”

原来如此，罗伯特·威尔逊暗自思忖，她是要送他一程呢，是不是？要不然，你以为她的想法就是要表演一场好戏？当一个女人发现她的丈夫是个可怜的胆小鬼的时候，她会做出些什么举动来呢？她冷酷得要死，她们都是冷酷无情的。不用说，她们掌控一切，有时为了掌控某人必须要冷酷无情。幸好，我把她们那套可怕的把戏已经看透了。

“多吃点羚羊肉吧！”他彬彬有礼地对她说。

当天下午临近天黑的时候，威尔逊和麦康伯坐汽车出去了一趟，带着土著司机和两个扛枪的人。麦康伯太太待在营地。她说这会儿出去太热啦，明天一大早她和他们出去好啦。当他们驱车而去的时候，威尔逊看到她站在那棵大树下，看起来与其说她是个美人儿，倒不如说更是个可人儿。她穿着浅玫瑰红的卡其衫，一头黑发从前额往后梳，低低地在后颈窝挽了个发髻。她的脸蛋光鲜得很，他想，仿佛她在英国似的。她向他们挥着手，这当儿，汽车正驶过长着深深野草的洼地，接着在树丛中蜿蜒前行，开进长着果树丛的一座座山岭之中。

and curved around through the trees into the small hills of orchard bush.

In the orchard bush they found a herd of impala[①], and leaving the car they stalked one old ram with long, wide-spread horns and Macomber killed it[②] with a very creditable shot that knocked the buck down at a good two hundred yards and sent the herd off bounding wildly and leaping over one another's backs in long, leg-drawn-up leaps as unbelievable and as floating as those one makes sometimes in dreams.

"That was a good shot," Wilson said. "They're a small target."

"Is it a worth-while head?" Macomber asked.

"It's excellent," Wilson told him. "You shoot like that and you'll have no trouble."

"Do you think we'll find buffalo tomorrow?"

"There's a good chance of it. They feed out early in the morning and with luck we may catch them in the open."

"I'd like to clear away that lion business," Macomber said. "It's not very pleasant to have your wife see you do something like that."

I should think it would be even more unpleasant to do it, Wilson thought, wife or no wife, or to talk about it having done it. But he said, "I wouldn't think about that any more. Any one could be upset by his first lion. That's all over."

But that night after dinner and a whisky and soda by the fire

① impala：非洲的黑斑羚，体态优美，中等身躯，雄性有成脊状的向上弯曲的角。这种羚羊跳跃能力极强，一跃可达10英尺高，30英尺远。
② it：海明威在描写黑斑羚的时候用的人称代词是"it"，描述狮子和野牛的时候用的是"he"或"him"，表明海明威认为狮子和野牛在智力和体力上是可与人匹敌的对手。

在果树丛里，他们发现了一群黑斑羚。于是，他们离开汽车，蹑手蹑脚地靠近一只老公羊。这只羊有着长长的、张得很开的羊角。相隔还足足有两百多码时，麦康伯开了非常值得表扬的一枪，把那公羊撂倒，杀死了它；也使得羚羊群飞也似的逃窜开去。它们的腿一收，一放，跳得很远，争相从其他羚羊的背上飞越过去，让人觉得难以置信，就像人们在梦中才能飘过去的那样。

"那一枪打得很漂亮，"威尔逊说，"它们是小演习。"

"羚羊头是否还有点价值？"麦康伯问道。

"非常棒，"威尔逊告诉他。"你枪法那样准的话，就根本不用担心了。"

"你认为我们明天能找到野牛吗？"

"大有机会。他们一大早会出来觅食的。如果运气好的话，我们可能在开阔地逮住他们。"

"我想要清除狮子那档子事的影响，"麦康伯说，"让自己的老婆看到自己做那样的事可有些不大光彩啊。"[①]

我倒是认为，不管有没有老婆，更不光彩的是居然干出了这样的事，或是干了这事还要提起，威尔逊想。但是他说的却是："我才不愿再想那事呢。任何人碰到他的第一头狮子都会惴惴不安的。这事就到此为止吧。"

但是那天夜里，麦康伯在篝火边吃过晚饭，喝了杯威士忌苏打才去睡觉；当他躺在罩着蚊帐的帆布床上，倾听着夜的喧嚣的

① "It's not very pleasant to have your wife see you do something like that." 从这句话中可以看出麦康伯非常想在他老婆心目中树立起阳刚的男子汉形象。他的懦弱成了玛格丽特屡次红杏出墙的借口。

before going to bed, as Francis Macomber lay on his cot with the mosquito bar over him and listened to the night noises it was not all over. It was neither all over nor was it beginning. It was there exactly as it happened with some parts of it indelibly emphasized and he was miserably ashamed at it. But more than shame he felt cold, hollow fear in him. The fear was still there like a cold slimy hollow in all the emptiness where once his confidence had been and it made him feel sick. It was still there with him now.

It had started the night before when he had wakened and heard the lion roaring somewhere up along the river. It was a deep sound and at the end there were sort of coughing grunts that made him seem just outside the tent, and when Francis Macomber woke in the night to hear it he was afraid. He could hear his wife breathing quietly, asleep. There was no one to tell he was afraid, nor to be afraid with him, and, lying alone, he did not know the Somali proverb that says a brave man is always frightened three times by a lion; when he first sees his track, when he first hears him roar and when he first confronts him. Then while they were eating breakfast by lantern light out in the dining tent, before the sun was up, the lion roared again and Francis thought he was just at the edge of camp.

"Sounds like an old-timer," Robert Wilson said, looking up from his kippers and coffee. "Listen to him cough."

"Is he very close?"

"A mile or so up the stream."

"Will we see him?"

时候，这事并没有结束。这事既不是已经结束也不是即将开始。这事就像正在发生的那当儿一样明摆着，有些情节欲盖弥彰，令他羞愧难当。比羞愧感更为严重的是，在他内心深处，他感到一股冷森森、黑洞洞的恐惧。这恐惧肆无忌惮地占在那儿，就像一个冷森森、黏糊糊的黑洞，把他的自信一扫而尽后留下的一无所有的空间全部据为己有。这让他难受至极。这件事对他来说仍然挥之不去。

这件事开始于头一天夜里。当时他醒来，听到那狮子的咆哮声，就在河的上游某处。吼音深沉，尾音处夹着咳嗽似的咕噜声，让人觉得他就在帐篷外似的。弗朗西斯·麦康伯夜里醒来听到这声音的时候感到害怕。他听得到妻子平静的呼吸，她睡得正酣。无从告诉任何人说他害怕，也没有任何人和他一起害怕。他独自躺在那儿，并不知道索马里有句谚语，说的是：一个勇士总会被狮子吓三次，即他第一次看到他的踪迹的时候，第一次听到他咆哮的时候以及第一次与他交锋的时候[①]。后来，当他们在太阳出来以前，就着帐篷外的灯光吃早餐的时候，狮子又咆哮起来，而弗朗西斯以为他就在营地边上。

"听起来像头老掉牙的家伙，"罗伯特·威尔逊说着，从他的几条鲱鱼和咖啡前抬起头来。"听听他的咳嗽。"

"他离这里很近吗？"

"在河上游约莫一英里处。"

"我们会见到他吗？"

① 这个故事的讲述者以第三人称的全知视角，在这里插入的这个"Somali proverb"证明前面威尔逊说的"You know in Africa no woman ever misses her lion and no white man ever bolts"并不是事实，只是为了羞辱麦康伯。故事的讲述者在此有同情麦康伯的意味。

"We'll have a look."

"Does his roaring carry that far? It sounds as though he were right in camp."

"Carries a hell of a long way," said Robert Wilson. "It's strange the way it carries. Hope he's a shootable cat. The boys said there was a very big one about here."

"If I get a shot, where should I hit him," Macomber asked, "to stop him?"

"In the shoulders," Wilson said. "In the neck if you can make it. Shoot for bone. Break him down."

"I hope I can place it properly," Macomber said.

"You shoot very well," Wilson told him. "Take your time. Make sure of him. The first one in is the one that counts."

"What range will it be?"

"Can't tell. Lion has something to say about that. Won't shoot unless it's close enough so you can make sure."

"At under a hundred yards?" Macomber asked.

Wilson looked at him quickly.

"Hundred's about right. Might have to take him a bit under. Shouldn't chance a shot at much over that. A hundred's a decent range. You can hit him wherever you want at that. Here comes the Memsahib."

"Good morning," she said. " Are we going after that lion?"

"As soon as you deal with your breakfast," Wilson said. "How are you feeling?"

"Marvellous," she said. "I'm very excited."

"I'll just go and see that everything is ready," Wilson went off.

“我们会去瞧一瞧。”

“他的吼声传得那么远吗？听起来好像他就在营地似的。”

“传得可不是一般的远，”罗伯特·威尔逊说，“声音传得这么远，是让人觉得奇怪。希望它是头适合猎杀的猫儿。那些杂役说这附近有头非常大的家伙呢。”

“如果我开枪的话，我该打他哪里，”麦康伯问道，“才能放倒他？”

“打中肩部，”威尔逊说，“如果办得到的话就打脖子。朝致命处开枪。把他撂倒。”

“我希望我能办得好，”麦康伯说。

“你的枪法很好，”威尔逊告诉他，“别着急。要把准。头一颗打中的子弹最起作用。”

“隔多远的射程呢？”

“说不清。距离多少得由狮子说了算。要隔得特别近，拿得十分准，否则就别开枪。”

“一百码都不到吗？”麦康伯问。

威尔逊飞快地看了他一眼。

“一百码差不多了。也许不得不在更近一点的距离搞定他。别妄想在远远大于一百码的距离就开枪。一百是个合适的距离。你想打它哪儿就能打到它哪儿。瞧，尊夫人大驾光临了。”

“早上好，”她说，“我们要去找那头狮子吗？”

“你解决掉你的早餐就立马动身，”威尔逊说，“你感觉怎样？”

“妙极了！”她说，“我兴奋得很呢。”

“我正要去看看东西是不是都准备好了，”威尔逊走开了。

As he left the lion roared again.

"Noisy beggar," Wilson said. "We'll put a stop to that."

"What's the matter, Francis?" his wife asked him.

"Nothing," Macomber said.

"Yes, there is," she said. "What are you upset about?"

"Nothing," he said.

"Tell me," she looked at him. "Don't you feel well?"

"It's that damned roaring," he said. "It's been going on all night, you know."

"Why didn't you wake me," she said. "I'd love to have heard it."

"I've got to kill the damned thing," Macomber said, miserably.

"Well, that's what you're out here for, isn't it?"

"Yes. But I'm nervous. Hearing the thing roar gets on my nerves."

"Well then, as Wilson said, kill him and stop his roaring."

"Yes, darling," said Francis Macomber. "It sounds easy, doesn't it?"

"You're not afraid, are you?"

"Of course not. But I'm nervous from hearing him roar all night."

"You'll kill him marvellously," she said. "I know you will. I'm awfully anxious to see it."

"Finish your breakfast and we'll be starting."

"It's not light yet," she said. "This is a ridiculous hour."

Just then the lion roared in a deep-chested moaning, suddenly

他一走，狮子又咆哮起来了。

“吵人的家伙，”威尔逊说，“我们会叫他吵不成的。”

“出什么事啦，弗朗西斯？”他的妻子问他。

“没什么，”麦康伯说。

“得了，别瞒我了，”她说，“你干吗心烦意乱？”

“没有啊，”他说。

“跟我说实话，”她望着他，“你是不是不舒服？”

“是那该死的吼声惹的，”他说，“你不知道，这吼声折腾了一宿呢。”

“你为什么不叫醒我呢？”她说，“我倒想听听呢！”

“我一定要干掉这该死的东西，”麦康伯说着，模样却可怜兮兮的。

“唔，你上这儿来，就是为了干这个的，对不？”

“嗯。可是我感到紧张。听这东西咆哮，让我神经过敏。”

“那么，就像威尔逊说的那样，干掉他，让他咆哮不成。”

“话是不错，亲爱的，”弗朗西斯·麦康伯说，“听起来很容易，是不是？”

“你不是害怕吧，你害怕吗？”

“当然不。但是听他咆哮了整整一夜，这会儿我有点紧张。”

“你会很漂亮地干掉他的，”她说，“我知道你会的。我巴不得马上看到。”

“你吃完早餐我们就出发。”

“天竟然还没亮呢，”她说，“时间可真是太不会成全人了。”

就在这时，狮子咆哮出一声发自胸腔深处的悲鸣，突然又变

guttural, ascending vibration that seemed to shake the air and ended in a sigh and a heavy, deep-chested grunt.

"He sounds almost here," Macomber's wife said.

"My God," said Macomber. "I hate that damned noise."

"It's very impressive."

"Impressive. It's frightful."

Robert Wilson came up then carrying his short, ugly, shockingly big-bored .505 Gibbs[①] and grinning.

"Come on," he said. "Your gun-bearer has your Springfield[②] and the big gun. Everything's in the car. Have you solids?"

"Yes."

"I'm ready," Mrs. Macomber said.

"Must make him stop that racket," Wilson said. "You get in front. The Memsahib can sit back here with me."

They climbed into the motor car and, in the gray first daylight, moved off up the river through the trees. Macomber opened the breech of his rifle and saw he had metal-cased bullets, shut the bolt and put the rifle on safety. He saw his hand was trembling. He felt in his pocket for more cartridges and moved his fingers over the cartridges in the loops of his tunic front. He turned back to where Wilson sat in the rear seat of the doorless, box-bodied motor car beside his wife, them both grinning with excitement, and Wilson leaned forward and whispered,

"See the birds dropping. Means the old boy has left his kill."

---

① .505 Gibbs：英国布里斯托的吉布斯枪械公司于 20 世纪初生产的一种子弹。这里指装有吉布斯 505 子弹的来复枪。

② Springfield：由美国马萨诸塞州的春田兵工厂生产的 M1903 春田式步枪，20 世纪上半叶在美国军队服役。

成发自喉部的越来越高的颤音，似乎空气都颤动了，最后，是叹息般的一声，以及一句沉沉的、发自胸腔深处的咕噜声。

“听起来好像他就在这儿，”麦康伯的妻子说道。

“天哪，”麦康伯说，“我恨那该死的叫声。”

“给人印象很深。”

“印象很深。让人心惊肉跳呢。”

罗伯特·威尔逊走过来了。他扛着他那支短短的、式样难看、口径大得吓人的吉布斯505，正咧嘴笑着呢。

“来吧，”他说，“给你扛枪的人扛着你的春田枪和那支大枪呢。东西都在车里了。你有实心弹吗？”

“有的。”

“我准备好了，”麦康伯太太说道。

“一定要叫他止住那吵人的嚷嚷，”威尔逊说，“你坐前面，尊夫人不妨和我一起坐后面。”

他们爬上了汽车，在破晓氤氲的晨光中，直驱而去，穿过树林，溯河而上。麦康伯拉开他的来复枪的枪栓，看到他的金属子弹在那儿安然无恙，随之推上枪栓，给来复枪上了保险。他发觉自己的手在哆嗦。他伸手摸摸口袋，摸到有更多的子弹。接着他把手指头移过来摸了摸短上衣胸前套子里的子弹。他回头向这没有车门的、车身像个盒子似的汽车的后座望去，看到威尔逊坐在他妻子旁边，双双兴奋得咧嘴在笑。这时威尔逊向前探过身子，悄声说道：

“看到鸟儿都落下去了吗？意味着那头老不死的已经离开了他的猎物了。”

On the far bank of the stream Macomber could see, above the trees, vultures circling and plummeting down.

"Chances are he'll come to drink along here," Wilson whispered. "Before he goes to lay up. Keep an eye out."

They were driving slowly along the high bank of the stream which here cut deeply to its boulder-filled bed, and they wound in and out through big trees as they drove. Macomber was watching the opposite bank when he felt Wilson take hold of his arm. The car stopped.

"There he is," he heard the whisper. "Ahead and to the right. Get out and take him. He's a marvellous lion."

Macomber saw the lion now. He was standing almost broadside, his great head up and turned toward them. The early morning breeze that blew toward them was just stirring his dark mane, and the lion looked huge, silhouetted on the rise of bank in the gray morning light, his shoulders heavy, his barrel of a body bulking smoothly.

"How far is he?" asked Macomber, raising his rifle.

"About seventy-five[①]. Get out and take him."

"Why not shoot from where I am?"

"You don't shoot them from cars," he heard Wilson saying in his ear. "Get out. He's not going to stay there all day."

Macomber stepped out of the curved opening at the side of the front seat, onto the step and down onto the ground. The lion still stood looking majestically and coolly toward this object that his eyes only showed in silhouette, bulking like some super-

① seventy-five：这里可能是指 75 码。1 码= 0.9144 米。

在河流远岸上，树林上空，麦康伯可以看到一只只秃鹫或盘旋飞翔，或俯冲而下。

“很有可能他会来这儿喝水。”威尔逊悄声说，“然后它就要去倒头睡觉了。瞅紧了。”

他们沿着高高的小河岸缓缓驱车前行。河水在这一带将布满卵石的河床冲刷得很深。他们在那些大树中间弯弯曲曲地绕进绕出。麦康伯正关注着对岸，这时，他感到威尔逊抓住了他的胳膊。汽车停了。

“他在那儿，”他听到耳语，“前面，右边。出去，搞定他。这头狮子真棒啊。”

现在，麦康伯看到狮子了，几乎看到他伫立时的全部侧面。他的硕大的头部上抬，向他们望过来。清晨的微风朝他们这个方向吹来，此刻正吹动着狮子深色的鬃毛；他看起来庞大无比，在氤氲的晨光中，在河岸的凸起处，现出一个剪影：他的双肩浑厚，圆桶状的身躯显得平稳流畅。

“他有多远？”麦康伯问，举起了来复枪。

“大约七十五。出来，搞定他。”

“为什么不能从我现在所在的地方开枪呢？”

“你不能在汽车上开枪打猎，”① 他听到威尔逊在他耳边说，“出去。他可不会整天都待在那儿。”

麦康伯从前排座位的弯型开口的地方跨出来，踩着踏板下到地面上。那狮子仍旧伫立着，威武而沉着地看着这个目标。他只能看到这个目标的剪影，其模样像一头硕大无比的犀牛。

① You don’t shoot them from cars：根据当时的狩猎法规，狩猎者开着车朝动物开枪为非法。现在仍有许多狩猎的地方有这样的法规，如美国的田纳西州、加利福尼亚州等。

rhino. There was no man smell carried toward him and he watched the object, moving his great head a little from side to side. Then watching the object, not afraid, but hesitating before going down the bank to drink with such a thing opposite him, he saw a man figure detach itself from it and he turned his heavy head and swung away toward the cover of the trees as he heard a cracking crash and felt the slam of a .30-06[①] 220-grain solid bullet that bit his flank and ripped in sudden hot scalding nausea through his stomach. He trotted, heavy, big-footed, swinging wounded full-bellied, through the trees toward the tall grass and cover, and the crash came again to go past him ripping the air apart. Then it crashed again and he felt the blow as it hit his lower ribs and ripped on through, blood sudden hot and frothy in his mouth, and he galloped toward the high grass where he could crouch and not be seen and make them bring the crashing thing close enough so he could make a rush and get the man that held it.

Macomber had not thought how the lion felt as he got out of the car. He only knew his hands were shaking and as he walked away from the car it was almost impossible for him to make his legs move. They were stiff in the thighs, but he could feel the muscles fluttering. He raised the rifle, sighted on the junction of the lion's head and shoulders and pulled the trigger. Nothing happened though he pulled until he thought his finger would break. Then he knew he had the safety on and as he lowered the rifle to move the safety over he moved another frozen pace forward, and the lion seeing his silhouette now clear of the silhouette of the car, turned

① .30-06 指美制三零步枪的规格为 7.62 × 63mm 的子弹。

风不能把人味儿吹到他那边去；他盯着这个目标，时不时地转动一下他的硕大脑袋。盯着这个目标，毫无惧意，但有这样一个东西站在对面，他拿不定主意是否要走下河岸去饮水。他看到一个像人模样的东西从那玩意中分离开来，就扭过他的巨头，跃向树丛；与此同时，他听到“砰”的一声巨响，接着感到春田枪的一颗30-06，220谷的实心弹猛地撕咬着他的胁腹，扯破他的胃部，引起一股突如其来的火烧火燎的感觉令人恶心。他小跑开去，尽管步幅很大却步履沉重，晃荡着圆鼓鼓的受了伤的肚子；他穿过树丛，蹿向长着高高的野草的地方，寻找掩蔽所。巨响又来了，从身边呼啸而过，将空气撕裂开来。接着又是一声巨响，他感觉被击中了：子弹击中了他的下肋骨，一直刺进去；他的嘴里猛然涌出了热乎乎冒着泡沫的血。他奔向那野草茂盛的地方，那样他就可以蹲下来，不被发现，好让他们把那发出巨响的东西带到近处，这样他就能够扑过去，把拿着能发出巨响东西的那个人逮住。

麦康伯走出汽车的时候，倒没想到过狮子会有什么样的感觉。他只知道，他的手在瑟瑟发抖。当他从汽车里走出来时，两条腿怎么都不听使唤，几乎挪不动步子。他的大腿僵直，可他却能感到肌肉在颤抖。他举起来复枪，瞄到狮子头部和肩部的连接处，扣动了扳机。尽管他扣动了扳机，却毫无动静，直到他感到手指头都要断时，才意识到他上了保险。他放低来复枪，拉开保险，向前直僵僵地又挪了一步。这时狮子看到他的剪影从汽

and started off at a trot, and, as Macomber fired, he heard a whunk that meant that the bullet was home; but the lion kept on going. Macomber shot again and everyone saw the bullet throw a spout of dirt beyond the trotting lion. He shot again, remembering to lower his aim, and they all heard the bullet hit, and the lion went into a gallop and was in the tall grass before he had the bolt pushed forward.

Macomber stood there feeling sick at his stomach, his hands that held the Springfield still cocked, shaking, and his wife and Robert Wilson were standing by him. Beside him too were the two gun-bearers chattering in Wakamba[①].

"I hit him," Macomber said. "I hit him twice."

"You gut-shot him and you hit him somewhere forward," Wilson said without enthusiasm. The gun-bearers looked very grave. They were silent now.

"You may have killed him," Wilson went on. "We'll have to wait a while before we go in to find out."

"What do you mean?"

"Let him get sick before we follow him up."

"Oh," said Macomber.

"He's a hell of a fine lion," Wilson said cheerfully. "He's gotten into a bad place though."

"Why is it bad?"

"Can't see him until you're on him."

"Oh," said Macomber.

"Come on," said Wilson. "The Memsahib can stay here in the

① Wakamba：瓦卡姆巴语，非洲肯尼亚和坦桑尼亚等国家的班图人所用的一种语言。

车的剪影中离开，转身小跑开去。麦康伯开火了，他听到“嘭”的一声，这表明子弹命中了；但狮子还在跑。麦康伯又开了一枪，人人都看到子弹在小跑着的狮子前面扬起了一堆灰尘。他又开了一枪，记得将准星放低，接着他们都听到子弹打中了。狮子纵身一跃，跃进了高高的草丛。这时他还没来得及推上枪栓。

麦康伯站在那里，胃里直觉着恶心。他握着春田枪的双手仍保持着射击的姿势，且瑟瑟发抖；他的妻子和罗伯特·威尔逊站在了他的身旁。在他的身边也站着那两个扛枪的人，正用瓦卡姆巴语嘀咕着什么。

“我打中他了，”麦康伯说，“我打中了他两枪。”

“你打中了他的肚子，还打中了他身子前面的什么地方，”威尔逊说着，声音里毫无兴奋可言。扛枪的人看起来表情阴郁。他俩这会儿一声不吭了。

“你要是把他打死就好了，”威尔逊继续说，“现在我们可要等一会，才能再进去把他找到。”

“你这么说是什么意思？”

“让他撑不住了，我们再去惹他。”

“噢！”麦康伯说。

“这是头挺棒的狮子，”威尔逊神采飞扬地说道，“不过这会儿，他却躲到一个糟糕的地方去了。”

“为什么说是糟糕的地方？”

“要到你近他身时才能看到他。”

“噢！”麦康伯说。

“来吧，”威尔逊说。“尊夫人可以坐在汽车里。我们去查看一下血迹。”

car. We'll go to have a look at the blood spoor."

"Stay here, Margot," Macomber said to his wife. His mouth was very dry and it was hard for him to talk.

"Why?" she asked.

"Wilson says to."

"We're going to have a look," Wilson said. "You stay here. You can see even better from here."

"All right."

Wilson spoke in Swahili to the driver. He nodded and said, "Yes, Bwana."

Then they went down the steep bank and across the stream, climbing over and around the boulders and up the other bank, pulling up by some projecting roots, and along it until they found where the lion had been trotting when Macomber first shot. There was dark blood on the short grass that the gun bearers pointed out with grass stems, and that ran away behind the river bank trees.

"What do we do?" asked Macomber.

"Not much choice," said Wilson. "We can't bring the car over. Bank's too steep. We'll let him stiffen up a bit and then you and I'll go in and have a look for him."

"Can't we set the grass on fire?" Macomber asked.

"Too green."

"Can't we send beaters?"

Wilson looked at him appraisingly. "Of course we can," he said. "But it's just a touch murderous. You see we know the lion's wounded. You can drive an unwounded lion—he'll move on ahead of a noise—but a wounded lion's going to charge. You can't see

“待在这儿，玛戈，”麦康伯对他妻子说道。他极度口干舌燥，开口说话都很费劲。

“为啥？”她问。

“威尔逊说的。”

“我们要去瞧瞧，”威尔逊说，“你待在这里。从这里你甚至可以看得更清楚呢。”

“好吧。”

威尔逊用斯瓦希里语对司机说了些什么。他点点头，说道：“是，先生。”

接着，他们走下陡峭的河岸，穿越小河，在卵石阵中攀爬而出，爬向河的对岸，抓住一些突起的根须，爬上岸，一直走，直到他们发现了麦康伯开第一枪时狮子小跑着离开的地方。扛枪的两个人用草茎指出低矮的野草上的深红色血印。血印逃逸开去，一直延伸到河岸树林的后面去了。

“我们怎么办呢？”麦康伯问。

“没有多少选择余地，”威尔逊说，“我们无法把汽车开到这里来。岸太陡了。我们等他变僵硬一点，然后我和你就进去找他。”

“我们可不可以放火烧草丛？”麦康伯问道。

“太青了。”

“我们可不可以派赶野兽的人去啊？”

威尔逊抬眼估量着他。“我们当然可以这样做，”他说，“但这几乎是叫人去送命。你瞧，我们知道这头狮子受伤了。你可以赶跑一头未受伤的狮子——一有风吹草动他就会跑开——但是，一头受了伤的狮子却会伏击。你要靠近他才会看到他。他

him until you're right on him. He'll make himself perfectly flat in cover you wouldn't think would hide a hare. You can't very well send boys in there to that sort of a show. Somebody bound to get mauled."

"What about the gun-bearers?"

"Oh, they'll go with us. It's their *shauri*. You see, they signed on for it. They don't look too happy though, do they?"

"I don't want to go in there," said Macomber. It was out before he knew he'd said it.

"Neither do I," said Wilson very cheerily. "Really no choice though." Then, as an afterthought, he glanced at Macomber and saw suddenly how he was trembling and the pitiful look on his face.

"You don't have to go in, of course," he said. "That's what I'm hired for, you know. That's why I'm so expensive."

"You mean you'd go in by yourself? Why not leave him there?"[①]

Robert Wilson, whose entire occupation had been with the lion and the problem he presented, and who had not been thinking about Macomber except to note that he was rather windy, suddenly felt as though he had opened the wrong door in a hotel and seen something shameful.

"What do you mean?"

"Why not just leave him?"

"You mean pretend to ourselves that he hasn't been hit?"

① "Why not leave him there?" 麦康伯是出于对狩猎狮子的常识无知才问的这句话，但威尔逊却认为麦康伯这么想是他德行上有问题。

会全身隐蔽，完全平摊在地，这样的地方你甚至会以为连一只兔子都藏不住呢。你不能把杂役们往那儿一派了之。准有人会受伤的。”

“扛枪的人呢？”

“哦，他们会和我们一块去的。这是他们分内的事。你清楚，他们在合同上还为此签字了。尽管他们看起来也不大乐意去，对不？”

“我不想进到那里面去，”麦康伯说道。他这话脱口而出，自己都还没意识到呢。

“我也不想啊！”威尔逊非常随和地说道，“确实是别无选择了！”接着，他似乎想起了什么，瞟了瞟麦康伯，忽然发现他颤抖得很厉害，满脸的可怜相。

“你不是非进去不可的，”他说，“你晓得的，我被雇来就是做这类事的。这也是我的报酬为什么这么高的原因。”

“你的意思是说你要一个人进到里面去吗？为什么不就让他待在那儿呢？”

罗伯特·威尔逊的整个心思都在狮子以及随狮子而来的问题上。在这之前，他除了注意到麦康伯受到了极度惊吓之外，并没有对他太在意。此刻，他忽然觉得好像是在旅店里开错了一扇门，撞见了一桩丑事似的。

“你是什么意思？”

“为什么不放他一马呢？”

“你是说我们自己蒙自己，说他没被打中？”

"No. Just drop it."

"It isn't done."

"Why not?"

"For one thing, he's certain to be suffering. For another, some one else might run onto him."

"I see."

"But you don't have to have anything to do with it."

"I'd like to," Macomber said. "I'm just scared, you know."

"I'll go ahead when we go in," Wilson said, "with Kongoni tracking. You keep behind me and a little to one side. Chances are we'll hear him growl. If we see him we'll both shoot. Don't worry about anything. I'll keep you backed up. As a matter of fact, you know, perhaps you'd better not go. It might be much better. Why don't you go over and join the Memsahib while I just get it over with?"

"No, I want to go."

"All right," said Wilson. "But don't go in if you don't want to. This is my *shauri* now, you know."

"I want to go," said Macomber.

They sat under a tree and smoked.

"Want to go back and speak to the Memsahib while we're waiting?" Wilson asked.

"No."

"I'll just step back and tell her to be patient."

"Good," said Macomber. He sat there, sweating under his arms, his mouth dry, his stomach hollow feeling, wanting to find courage to tell Wilson to go on and finish off the lion without him.

"不是啊。只是到此为止。"

"还没完呢！"

"怎么没完呢？"

"一方面，他肯定会一直疼下去；另一方面，可能会有人一不小心撞到他。"

"我明白了。"

"但是，你并不是一定要去染指这件事的。"

"我愿意去，"麦康伯说，"你明白的，我不过是有点受惊罢了。"

"我们进去的时候，我会走在前面的，"威尔逊说，"让康戈佬追寻踪迹。你跟在我的后面，靠边上一点儿。我们很有可能会听到他嚎。如果我们看到他，我俩都开枪。什么也不用担心。我会为你当挡箭牌的。你清楚的，事实上也许你最好不要去。这样也许要好些。你干吗不过去和尊夫人待在一起呢？让我去了结这事得了。"

"不，我要去。"

"那好吧，"威尔逊说，"但是，如果你不想去就不要勉强了。现在这是我的分内事，你知道的。"

"我要去，"麦康伯说道。

他们在一棵树下坐下来，抽着烟。

"我们在这里伺机而动的时候，想要回去和尊夫人谈谈吗？"

"不用。"

"我这就回去告诉她耐心点。"

"好的。"麦康伯说道。他坐在那里，腋下汗直流，极度口干舌燥，肚子里感觉空洞洞的。他想要积攒起足够的勇气告诉威尔逊，要他继续前行，把狮子的事了结算了，别算上他的份。他

He could not know that Wilson was furious because he had not noticed the state he was in earlier and sent him back to his wife. While he sat there Wilson came up. "I have your big gun," he said. "Take it. We've given him time, I think. Come on."

Macomber took the big gun and Wilson said:

"Keep behind me and about five yards to the right and do exactly as I tell you." Then he spoke in Swahili to the two gun-bearers who looked the picture of gloom. ①

"Let's go," he said.

"Could I have a drink of water?" Macomber asked. Wilson spoke to the older gun-bearer, who wore a canteen on his belt, and the man unbuckled it, unscrewed the top and handed it to Macomber, who took it noticing how heavy it seemed and how hairy and shoddy the felt covering was in his hand. He raised it to drink and looked ahead at the high grass with the flat-topped trees behind it. A breeze was blowing toward them and the grass rippled gently in the wind. He looked at the gun-bearer and he could see the gun-bearer was suffering too with fear.

Thirty-five yards into the grass the big lion lay flattened out along the ground. His ears were back and his only movement was a slight twitching up and down of his long, black-tufted tail. He had turned at bay as soon as he had reached this cover and he was sick with the wound through his full belly, and weakening with the wound through his lungs that brought a thin foamy red to his mouth each time he breathed. His flanks were wet and hot and flies

① "who looked the picture of gloom" means "who looked extraordinarily gloomy"。这句话说明两个扛枪的人都知道狮子躲进草丛后形势的严峻。

没注意到威尔逊刚才是怒火中烧来着。因为他没早点儿注意到他的处境，竟然还把他打发到他妻子那儿去。威尔逊现身的时候，他还坐在那儿。“我拿来了你的大枪，”他说，“拿着。我们已给了他足够的时间了，我想。来吧。”

麦康伯接过大枪后，威尔逊说：

“跟在我后面，在右边约五码远。我叫你怎么做你就怎么做。”然后，他又用斯瓦希里语同那两个扛枪的人说话，他俩看起来如死人般阴沉。

“我们走吧，”他说。

“我能来点水喝吗？”麦康伯问道。威尔逊对那个年长点的皮带上挂着水壶的人说了句啥，于是那人解下水壶，拧开盖子，将水壶递给麦康伯。后者接过水壶，注意到水壶似乎沉甸甸的，毡制的壶套在手里感觉毛乎乎的，做工粗糙。他举壶喝水，抬眼前望，看到高高的野草丛，以及草丛后一溜平的树丛。一阵微风向他们吹来，野草在风中起伏。他朝那个扛枪的人望去，可以看到这个扛枪的人也在遭受着恐惧的煎熬。

草丛里三十五码处，巨狮在地上平躺开来。他的两只耳朵紧贴脑后。他唯一的动作就是，他那长长的、长着簇黑毛的尾巴偶尔会轻微地上下摆动。他一到达这个掩蔽处便做好了做困兽斗的准备。洞穿他圆滚滚肚子的伤口让他很难受，打穿他肺部的伤口让他逐渐虚弱，每呼吸一次就会从嘴里冒出带着些泡沫状的液体。他的两胁湿漉漉、热乎乎的，苍蝇叮在实心弹在他的

were on the little openings the solid bullets had made in his tawny hide, and his big yellow eyes, narrowed with hate, looked straight ahead, only blinking when the pain came as he breathed, and his claws dug in the soft baked earth. All of him, pain, sickness, hatred and all of his remaining strength, was tightening into an absolute concentration for a rush. He could hear the men talking and he waited, gathering all of himself into this preparation for a charge as soon as the men would come into the grass. As he heard their voices his tail stiffened to twitch up and down, and, as they came into the edge of the grass, he made a coughing grunt and charged.

Kongoni, the old gun-bearer, in the lead watching the blood spoor, Wilson watching the grass for any movement, his big gun ready, the second gun-bearer looking ahead and listening, Macomber close to Wilson, his rifle cocked, they had just moved into the grass when Macomber heard the blood-choked coughing grunt, and saw the swishing rush in the grass. The next thing he knew he was running; running wildly, in panic in the open, running toward the stream.

He heard the *ca-ra-wong!* of Wilson's big rifle, and again in a second crashing *carawong!* and turning saw the lion, horrible-looking now, with half his head seeming to be gone, crawling toward Wilson in the edge of the tall grass while the red-faced man worked the bolt on the short ugly rifle and aimed carefully as another blasting *carawong!* came from the muzzle, and the crawling, heavy, yellow bulk of the lion stiffened and the huge, mutilated head slid forward and Macomber, standing by himself in the clearing where he had run, holding a loaded rifle, while two

褐色皮毛上打穿的一个个小窟窿上。他那硕大的黄色的眼睛，因仇恨而眯缝着，朝前径直凝望，只有呼吸时疼痛难忍才眨巴一下；他的爪子刨进松软的干土。他的所有一切：疼痛、难受、仇恨以及所有残存的力气，都凝缩成全神贯注，准备千钧一发时一袭。他能够听到这几个人在说话。他集聚起全身力量，等待着，等待着这些人走进草丛时发动猛然一袭。听到他们的声音，他的尾巴挺直了，抽上抽下。他们走到草丛边上来了！他发出一声咳嗽似的咕噜声，猛然一扑。

康戈佬，那个年长的扛枪人，此刻仍打头观察着血迹；威尔逊持大枪随时准备开枪，关注着任何一点点风吹草动；第二个扛枪者正向前张望，凝耳倾听；麦康伯紧靠着威尔逊，他的来复枪随时待发。他们刚一走进草丛，麦康伯就听到被血噎住喉咙似的咕噜声，看到草丛里有东西“呼”地扑了过来。他醒悟过来的时候发现自己正在飞奔，在空地上惊恐地、没命似的飞奔，朝小河方向奔去。

他听到威尔逊的大来复枪的一声“卡—啦—轰”！接着又是第二声巨响“卡啦轰”！他转过身来，看到了那头狮子，这会儿样子恐怖至极，半边脑袋几乎都没了，在高高的草丛边缘向威尔逊匍匐爬去。此刻那个红脸男人，推上那支又短又粗的来复枪的枪栓，仔细瞄准。随着枪口又一声震耳欲聋的“卡啦轰”，那头匍匐爬行的狮子沉重的、黄色的身躯僵直了，他那硕大的、残缺不全的脑袋向前栽了下去。麦康伯一个人孤零零地站在他跑进的空地上，握着上满子弹的来复枪。此时两个黑人和一个白人回头轻蔑地望着他，他知道狮子死了。他走向威尔逊，他的高

black men and a white man looked back at him in contempt, knew the lion was dead. He came toward Wilson, his tallness all seeming a naked reproach, and Wilson looked at him and said:

"Want to take pictures?"

"No," he said.

That was all any one had said until they reached the motor car. Then Wilson had said:

"Hell of a fine lion. Boys will skin him out. We might as well stay here in the shade."

Macomber's wife had not looked at him nor he at her and he had sat by her in the back seat with Wilson sitting in the front seat. Once he had reached over and taken his wife's hand without looking at her and she had removed her hand from his. Looking across the stream to where the gun-bearers were skinning out the lion he could see that she had been able to see the whole thing. While they sat there his wife had reached forward and put her hand on Wilson's shoulder. He turned and she had leaned forward over the low seat and kissed him on the mouth.

"Oh, I say," said Wilson, going redder than his natural baked color.

"Mr. Robert Wilson," she said. "The beautiful red-faced Mr. Robert Wilson."

Then she sat down beside Macomber again and looked away across the stream to where the lion lay, with uplifted, white-muscled, tendon-marked naked forearms, and white bloating belly, as the black men fleshed away the skin. Finally the gun-bearers brought the skin over, wet and heavy, and climbed in behind with

个头此刻也似乎成为一种明摆着的羞辱。威尔逊看着他，说道：

"想要照相吗？"[①]

"不要，"他说。

他们抵达汽车之前，所有的人统共就只说过这两句话。然后威尔逊说了句：

"顶棒的一头狮子。杂役们会把他的皮剥下来。我们不妨在荫凉的地方待会儿。"

麦康伯的妻子没有朝他看，他也没有朝她看。此刻，他已在后座上坐到她的旁边，威尔逊坐在前座上。有一次他把手伸过去，握住他妻子的手，眼睛却没有看她。她把手从他的手里抽出来。他朝河那边望过去，扛枪的人正在那儿剥狮子皮。于是他明白了，她是看得到事情的全部经过的。他们坐在那儿，他的老婆向前凑过去，把一只手搁在威尔逊的肩上。威尔逊扭过头来，她从低座位上向前倾过去，亲了亲他的嘴。

"嗨，别！"威尔逊说，天然晒红的脸变得更红了。

"罗伯特·威尔逊先生！"她说，"漂亮的红脸蛋儿罗伯特·威尔逊先生！"

接下来她坐回到麦康伯身旁，扭头向小河望去。狮子摊在那儿，两条光秃秃的前腿朝天伸着，肌肉雪白，腱子肉凸显；还有白乎乎、鼓嘟嘟的肚子。此时那些黑人在削皮上的肉。扛枪的人终于把皮带过来了，湿漉漉、沉甸甸的。他们把皮卷了起来，

① 狩猎者经常通过照相、剥下兽皮或牛角等做法来纪念自己曾打死过凶猛猎物。

it, rolling it up before they got in, and the motor car started. No one had said anything more until they were back in camp.

That was the story of the lion. Macomber did not know how the lion had felt before he started his rush, nor during it when the unbelievable smash of the .505 with a muzzle velocity of two tons had hit him in the mouth, nor what kept him coming after that, when the second ripping crash had smashed his hind quarters and he had come crawling on toward the crashing, blasting thing that had destroyed him. Wilson knew something about it and only expressed it by saying, "Damned fine lion," but Macomber did not know how Wilson felt about things either. He did not know how his wife felt except that she was through with him.

His wife had been through with him before but it never lasted. He was very wealthy, and would be much wealthier, and he knew she would not leave him ever now. That was one of the few things that he really knew. He knew about that, about motor cycles — that was earliest — about motor cars, about duck-shooting, about fishing, trout, salmon and big-sea, about sex in books, many books, too many books, about all court games, about dogs, not much about horses, about hanging on to his money, about most of the other things his world dealt in, and about his wife not leaving him. His wife had been a great beauty and she was still a great beauty in Africa, but she was not a great enough beauty any more at home to be able to leave him and better herself and she knew it and he knew it. She had missed the chance to leave him and he knew it. If he had been better with women she would probably have started to worry about him getting another new, beautiful wife; but she knew

带着皮从后面爬进车内。汽车发动了。在回营地前没有人再多说过一句话。

那就是狮子事件的来龙去脉。麦康伯既不知道狮子发动猛然袭击前狮子是什么样的感觉；也不知道在狮子发动猛然一袭的刹那，当时速高达200里的505子弹“轰”的一声击进狮子嘴巴的时候，狮子是什么样的感觉。后来，当第二声巨响撕裂了狮子的后腿，他继续朝摧毁了他的那个发出“啪啪”的爆炸声响的东西匍匐爬去的时候，麦康伯也不知道是什么力量支撑着他这么做。威尔逊倒是知道点什么，但他只轻描淡写地说了句:“棒极了的一头狮子。”可麦康伯也不知道威尔逊是如何感受的啊！对于他自己的妻子，他除了知道她要和他闹崩之外，他也是一无所知。

他妻子在这之前也和他闹崩过，但从未持久过。他极其有钱，并且可能会更加有钱。他清楚，即便是现在，她也不会离开他。那是在他所知不多的事情中他所真正知道的一点。他知道那一点，也知道诸如摩托车——那都是陈年旧事了——知道汽车；知道打野鸭，知道钓鱼、鳟鱼啦、鲑鱼啦、大海鱼等等；知道书本里的性爱知识(许多书本里面的，太多太多书本里面的)；知道所有的球场运动；知道狗，但对马所知不多；知道牢牢抓住他的钱；对他所交往的圈子里的其他事情他知道得八九不离十；他也知道他妻子不会离他而去。他妻子曾是个大美人儿，在非洲她仍是个大美人儿；但是如果回到家后，她想要离开他过更好的生活的话，这位美人儿却不够美了。对此，她心知肚明，他也心知肚明。她已经错过了离开他的机会，对此他很清楚。倘若他和女人相处稍微更加如鱼得水一点的话，她或许会开始担心，担心他会弄到一位漂亮的新欢来当妻子。但是，她对他了如指掌，根本不用为此担心。再说了，他一直是能那么的一忍再忍，

too much about him to worry about him either. Also, he had always had a great tolerance which seemed the nicest thing about him if it were not the most sinister.

All in all they were known as a comparatively happily married couple, one of those whose disruption is often rumored but never occurs, and as the society columnist put it, they were adding more than a spice of *adventure* to their much envied and ever-enduring *Romance* by a *Safari* in what was known as *Darkest Africa* until the Martin Johnsons ① lighted it on so many silver screens where they were pursuing *Old Simba* ② the lion, the buffalo, *Tembo* ③ the elephant and as well collecting specimens for the Museum of Natural History. This same columnist had reported them *on the verge* as least three times in the past and they had been. But they always made it up. They had a sound basis of union. Margot was too beautiful for Macomber to divorce her and Macomber had too much money for Margot ever to leave him.

It was now about three o'clock in the morning and Francis Macomber, who had been asleep a little while after he had stopped thinking about the lion, wakened and then slept again, woke suddenly, frightened in a dream of the bloody-headed lion standing over him, and listening while his heart pounded, he realized that his wife was not in the other cot in the tent. He lay awake with that

① the Martin Johnsons：约翰逊夫妇指马丁 · 约翰逊 (1884—1937) 及其妻子奥莎 · 约翰逊 (1894—1953)。他们是美国的电影摄制者、探险家、博物学家及作家。他们探索了当时还不大为人所知的东部非洲、中部非洲及南太平洋等地区的野生动物及风土人情并将它们搬上屏幕。

② Simba：1928 年马丁 · 约翰逊非洲探险公司拍制的电影中的主角，电影名为《百兽之王辛巴》(*Simbathe King of Beasts*)。

③ Tembo：斯瓦希里语对大象的称呼。见奥莎 · 约翰逊写于 1930 年的《托托 — 坦波非洲丛林小象的故事》(*Toto-TemboThe Baby Elephant of the African Jungle: His Story*)。

这点如果说不是他最致命的弱点的话，倒可算是他身上最大的优点呢。

总的说来，他们被认为是比较幸福的一对已婚夫妇，是那些老有谣传说要散伙但却从未兑现过的夫妇中的一对。正如社交生活专栏作者所说的那样，他们正进行的这次狩猎给他们那备受人艳羡的、永不磨蚀的罗曼史加上的不仅仅是冒险的风味——这次狩猎是在被称作是“最暗黑的非洲地带”进行的。这块最暗黑的非洲地带是由马丁·约翰森夫妇在如此之多的屏幕上点亮的：在这里，他们曾追逐老辛巴狮子、野牛、坦波象，同时也为自然历史博物馆收集标本。同一个专栏作家报道说他们在过去至少有三次濒于临界状态，这对他们来说也确实如此。但他们总能言归于好。他们结合的基础相当牢靠。玛戈太漂亮了，麦康伯舍不得和她离婚；而麦康伯太有钱了，玛戈也从来都舍不得离开他。

现在，大约凌晨三点钟了。弗朗西斯·麦康伯停止思量那狮子后，曾小睡过一会。他醒过来，然后又睡着了。这时他忽然醒了过来，梦中的情形让他心惧。在梦中，那头有着血淋淋脑袋的狮子跨在他身上聚耳凝听；而他呢，则心跳如鼓。他意识到他的老婆不在帐篷的另一张帆布床上。带着这种意识，他躺了两个小时，不曾合眼。

knowledge for two hours.

At the end of that time his wife came into the tent, lifted her mosquito bar and crawled cozily into bed.

"Where have you been?" Macomber asked in the darkness.

"Hello," she said. " Are you awake?"

"Where have you been?"

"I just went out to get a breath of air."

"You did, like hell."

"What do you want me to say, darling?"

"Where have you been?"

"Out to get a breath of air."

"That's a new name for it. You *are* a bitch."

"Well, you're a coward."

"All right," he said. "What of it?"

"Nothing as far as I'm concerned. But please let's not talk, darling, because I'm very sleepy."

"You think that I'll take anything."

"I know you will, sweet."

"Well, I won't."

"Please, darling, let's not talk. I'm so very sleepy."

"There wasn't going to be any of that. You promised there wouldn't be."

"Well, there is now," she said sweetly.

"You said if we made this trip that there would be none of that. You promised."[①]

① 从"you promised"和"you said"可以看出麦康伯对别人的承诺表现出一厢情愿的孩子气。

这样终于过了两个小时，他的老婆走进帐篷，撩起蚊帐，惬意地爬进床。

“你到哪去了？”麦康伯在黑暗中问道。

“嗨？”她说，“你醒着呢？”

“你到哪里去了？”

“我只不过是出去透透气罢了。”

“你做过了，贱货。”

“你要我说什么呢，亲爱的？”

“你到哪里去了？”

“出去透透气呗，”

“这倒是个新鲜的名词。你这个骚货。”

“切，你这个孬种。”

“得了，”他说，“那又怎么了？”

“对我而言，倒是不值得一提。但是，求求你，咱们别说话了好吗，亲爱的？我好瞌睡好瞌睡哦。”

“你倒以为我什么都能迁就呢！”

“我知道你会的，甜心。”

“呸，我不会的。”

“求你啦，亲爱的。咱们别说话了。我瞌睡死了。”

“说好了不会再有那档子事的。你答应过不会再有的。”

“唔，现在有啦。”她甜甜地说。

“你说过，如果我们这次旅行成功的话，将永远不会再有那档子事的。你答应过的。”

"Yes, darling. That's the way I meant it to be. But the trip was spoiled yesterday. We don't have to talk about it, do we?"

"You don't wait long when you have an advantage, do you?"

"Please let's not talk. I'm so sleepy, darling."

"I'm going to talk."

"Don't mind me then, because I'm going to sleep." And she did.

At breakfast they were all three at the table before daylight and Francis Macomber found that, of all the many men that he had hated, he hated Robert Wilson the most.

"Sleep well?" Wilson asked in his throaty voice, filling a pipe.

"Did you?"

"Topping," the white hunter told him.

You bastard, thought Macomber, you insolent bastard.

So she woke him when she came in, Wilson thought, looking at them both with his flat, cold eyes. Well, why doesn't he keep his wife where she belongs? What does he think I am, a bloody plaster saint① ? Let him keep her where she belongs. It's his own fault.

"Do you think we'll find buffalo?" Margot asked, pushing away a dish of apricots.

"Chance of it," Wilson said and smiled at her. "Why don't you stay in camp?"

"Not for anything," she told him.

"Why not order her to stay in camp?" Wilson said to

① a bloody plaster saint：十足的石膏像圣人，指像柳下惠一样坐怀不乱的圣人。

“不错，亲爱的。我本来是这样打算的。但这次旅行在昨天就泡汤啦。咱们没必要来探讨此事，对不？”

“你一有机可乘就如此迫不及待？”

“求你了，咱们别说话了。我瞌睡死了，亲爱的。”

“我有话要说。”

“那可就不要介意我说不说话了，因为我要睡了。”她说到做到。

天亮前吃早餐的时候，他们三个人都在桌子旁边；弗朗西斯·麦康伯感觉到，在他所仇视过的所有男人里面，他最仇视罗伯特·威尔逊。

“睡得好吗？”威尔逊一边装着烟袋，一边用沙哑的声音问道。

“你呢？”

“棒极了，”白人猎手告诉他。

你这个杂种，麦康伯想道，你这个目空一切的杂种。

那么她走进去的时候把他给弄醒了，威尔逊一边想着，一边用他那不动声色的、冷冷的眼神打量着他俩。真是的，他为什么不让他老婆待在她该待的地方呢？他认为我是什么人呢？我又不是个彻头彻尾的石膏圣人！他该让她待在她该待的地方。这是他自己的错。

“你认为我们找得到野牛吗？”玛戈问着，把一盘杏子推到一边。

“机会是有的，”威尔逊说着，向她笑了笑，“你为什么不待在营地呢？”

“说什么也不行，”她告诉他。

“为什么不命令她待在营地呢？”威尔逊对麦康伯说道。

Macomber.

"You order her," said Macomber coldly.

"Let's not have any ordering, nor," turning to Macomber, "any silliness, Francis," Margot said quite pleasantly.

"Are you ready to start? " Macomber asked.

"Any time," Wilson told him. "Do you want the Memsahib to go?"

"Does it make any difference whether I do or not?"

The hell with it, thought Robert Wilson. The utter complete hell with it. So this is what it's going to be like. Well, this is what it's going to be like, then.

"Makes no difference," he said.

"You're sure you wouldn't like to stay in camp with her yourself and let me go out and hunt the buffalo?" Macomber asked.

"Can't do that," said Wilson. "Wouldn't talk rot if I were you."

"I'm not talking rot. I'm disgusted."

"Bad word, disgusted."

"Francis, will you please try to speak sensibly ！ " his wife said.

"I speak too damned sensibly," Macomber said. "Did you ever eat such filthy food?"①

"Something wrong with the food?" asked Wilson quietly.

"No more than with everything else."

"I'd pull yourself together, laddybuck," Wilson said very

① "Did you ever eat such filthy food?" 麦康伯说的这句话表面上是指食物但暗示着问威尔逊"你总是穿这样的破鞋吗？"也暗示着"你和我妻子做的好事对我来说就像眼前的食物一样让我觉得恶心。"

“你命令她吧，”麦康伯冷冷地说。

“我们还是别命令来命令去了，”她转向麦康伯，“也别犯傻了，弗朗西斯。”她说这话时妩媚动人。

“你准备好出发了吗？”麦康伯问。

“随时都可以，”威尔逊告诉他，“你想要尊夫人去吗？”

“我想与不想，会有什么不同？”

见鬼！罗伯特·威尔逊想到，真他妈见鬼！那么事情会怎么样就只能任其怎么样了。也罢，事情会怎么样就任其怎么样吧。

“是没什么不同，”他说。

“你确信你不想和她单独待在营地吗？让我出去捕野牛得了？”麦康伯问。

“那像什么话，”威尔逊说，“如果我是你，就不会像你这样信口开河。”

“我不是在信口开河。我是觉得恶心。”

“说恶心可有点过重了。”

“弗朗西斯，拜托了，你说话能不能通情达理点？”他老婆说。

“我说得够他妈通情达理的了，”麦康伯说，“你总是吃这么龌龊的食物吗？”

“这食物有什么不对头吗？”威尔逊心平气和地问道。

“不会比别的一切更不对头。”

“你的话有人会听得懂的，黄毛小子，”威尔逊非常冷静地说，“伺候吃饭的杂役中有个懂一点英语的。”

quietly. "There's a boy waits at table that understands a little English."

"The hell with him."

Wilson stood up and puffing on his pipe strolled away, speaking a few words in Swahili to one of the gunbearers who was standing waiting for him. Macomber and his wife sat on at the table. He was staring at his coffee cup.

"If you make a scene I'll leave you, darling," Margot said quietly.

"No, you won't."

"You can try it and see."

"You won't leave me."

"No," she said. "I won't leave you and you'll behave yourself."

"Behave myself? That's a way to talk. Behave myself."

"Yes. Behave yourself."

"Why don't *you* try behaving?"

"I've tried it so long. So very long."

"I hate that red-faced swine," Macomber said. "I loathe the sight of him."

"He's really *very* nice."

"Oh, *shut up*," Macomber almost shouted. Just then the car came up and stopped in front of the dining tent and the driver and the two gun-bearers got out. Wilson walked over and looked at the husband and wife sitting there at the table.[①]

"Going shooting?" he asked.

---

① 此时 "the husband and wife" 在威尔逊眼中名义上是夫妻，实质上却是同床异梦。

“让他见鬼去吧。”

威尔逊站起身，吧嗒着烟袋，踱开了去，跟站在一边等他的一个扛枪的人用斯瓦希里语说了几句什么。麦康伯和他老婆坐在桌旁。他盯着他的咖啡杯。

“如果你出洋相我会离开你的，亲爱的，”玛戈语气平静地说。

“哼，你才不会呢！”

“你可以试试看。”

“你才不愿意离开我呢！”

“是可以不离开，”她说，“我不离开你，但你要放规矩点。”

“我放规矩点？说得可真好听。要我放规矩点！”

“是的，你要放规矩点。”

“你为什么不试试放规矩点呢？”

“我好久以来都是这样做的，太久太久啦。”

“我恨那头红脸猪，”麦康伯说，“看到他我就作呕。”

“他真的棒极了。”

“得了，住嘴！”麦康伯差点吼起来。就在这时，汽车开过来停在了就餐帐篷的前面，接着司机和两个扛枪的人走了过来。威尔逊走过来看着在桌子那儿坐着的这对夫妻。

“去打猎？”他问。

"Yes," said Macomber, standing up. "Yes."

"Better bring a woolly. It will be cool in the car," Wilson said.

"I'll get my leather jacket," Margot said.

"The boy has it," Wilson told her. He climbed into the front with the driver and Francis Macomber and his wife sat, not speaking, in the back seat.

Hope the silly beggar doesn't take a notion to blow the back of my head off, Wilson thought to himself. Women *are* a nuisance on safari.

The car was grinding down to cross the river at a pebbly ford in the gray daylight and then climbed, angling up the steep bank, where Wilson had ordered a way shovelled out the day before so they could reach the parklike wooded rolling country on the far side.

It was a good morning, Wilson thought. There was a heavy dew and as the wheels went through the grass and low bushes he could smell the odor of the crushed fronds. It was an odor like verbena and he liked this early morning smell of the dew, the crushed bracken and the look of the tree trunks showing black through the early morning mist, as the car made its way through the untracked, parklike country. He had put the two in the back seat out of his mind now and was thinking about buffalo. The buffalo that he was after stayed in the daytime in a thick swamp where it was impossible to get a shot, but in the night they fed out into an open stretch of country and if he could come between them and their swamp with the car, Macomber would have a good chance at them in the open. He did not want to hunt buff with Macomber

“去，”麦康伯说着，站起身，“去。”

“最好带件毛衣。车里有点冷，”威尔逊说。

“我拿我的皮夹克好了，”玛戈说。

“杂役已经拿了，”威尔逊告诉她。他和司机爬进前边，弗朗西斯·麦康伯和他老婆坐在后排，一言不发。

但愿这个蠢货没想过要把我的后脑勺敲开花，威尔逊暗自思忖道。狩猎的时候有女人在可真是麻烦。

灰蒙蒙的天光中，汽车嘎吱嘎吱地在一处布满鹅卵石的浅滩过了河。然后蜿蜒爬上陡峭的河岸。头一天威尔逊已叫人在这里铲出了一条路，通过这条路他们就可抵达远端那猎苑般的丛林密布、绵延起伏的原野。

今天早上不赖，威尔逊想到。露气很重，当车轮碾过野草和低矮的灌木时，他可嗅到被碾碎的蕨类植物的芳香。这是种像马鞭草一样的香气。当汽车在这人迹罕至的、猎苑般的原野上穿行的时候，他喜欢这清晨里露珠及碾碎的蕨草的清香，喜欢晨雾中的树干黑魆魆的模样。这会儿，他已经把坐在后排的这两个人忘诸脑后，一心只想着野牛。他要追猎的野牛白天待在一个很深的沼泽里，毫无可能中弹；但在夜间他们会到一处开阔的原野去觅食，如果能开车在他们返回沼泽之前截住他们，那么麦康伯在开阔地带打到他们的机会就很大了。他不愿在树荫稠密

in thick cover. He did not want to hunt buff or anything else with Macomber at all, but he was a professional hunter and he had hunted with some rare ones in his time. If they got buff today there would only be rhino to come and the poor man would have gone through his dangerous game and things might pick up. He'd have nothing more to do with the woman and Macomber would get over that too. He must have gone through plenty of that before by the look of things. Poor beggar. He must have a way of getting over it. Well, it was the poor sod's own bloody fault.

He, Robert Wilson, carried a double size cot on safari to accommodate any windfalls he might receive. He had hunted for a certain clientele, the international, fast, sporting set, where the women did not feel they were getting their money's worth unless they had shared that cot with the white hunter. He despised them when he was away from them although he liked some of them well enough at the time, but he made his living by them; and their standards were his standards as long as they were hiring him.

They were his standards in all except the shooting. He had his own standards about the killing and they could live up to them or get some one else to hunt them. He knew, too, that they all respected him for this. This Macomber was an odd one though. Damned if he wasn't. Now the wife. Well, the wife. Yes, the wife. Hm, the wife. Well he'd dropped all that. He looked around at them. Macomber sat grim and furious. Margot smiled at him. She looked younger today, more innocent and fresher and not so professionally beautiful. What's in her heart God knows, Wilson thought. She hadn't talked much last night. At that it was a pleasure

的隐蔽处和麦康伯一起猎牛。他根本不愿和麦康伯一起猎牛或猎别的任何东西；可他是个职业猎人，他的狩猎生涯中接待过不少稀奇古怪的雇主。如果他们今天打到野牛，那就只差犀牛要猎了，于是这个可怜虫的危险游戏也将结束，事情也可有个了结。他和那娘们不会再有什么瓜葛，麦康伯也会逐渐淡忘那档事儿。看样子，他以前一定遭遇过好多次那样的事。可怜的家伙。他一定有他的一套淡忘的本领。唉，都是这个可怜的孬种自个儿造的孽。

罗伯特·威尔逊狩猎时总带着一张双人帆布床[1]，对送上门来的艳遇是来者不拒。他为不少的顾客打过猎，这些顾客来自不同的国家，生活放荡，游戏人生。那些娘们只有同这个白人猎手共享过那张帆布床后，才觉得她们的钱终于有所值了。尽管在那当儿，他也曾相当享受其中的一些娘们，可当他不跟她们在一起了的时候，他对她们很是不屑；但是，他们是他的衣食来源，只要他们雇用他，他们的准则就是他的准则。

在所有方面，他们的准则就是他的准则，但射猎除外。在猎杀上，他有他自己的准则。他们可以要么奉行这些准则，要么另请高明。他也知道，他们都因此而对他敬重有加。这个麦康伯可是个稀奇。他不是个稀奇才怪呢！还有这个妻子。嗯，这个妻子。呵，这个妻子。唔，这个妻子。好啦，他把一切都抛开于心了。他扭头看看他们。麦康伯坐在那儿，面色阴沉，怒火中烧。玛戈向他投以微笑。她今天看起来更青春、更无辜、更鲜活，添了些许天生丽质。天知道她心里在鼓捣些什么，威尔逊思忖

① 威尔逊受雇当猎手的时候总是带着“a double size cot”(双人床)，说明他对前来狩猎的有钱女人的放荡行径已经司空见惯，并且对送上门的艳遇是来者不拒。

to see her.

The motor car climbed up a slight rise and went on through the trees and then out into a grassy prairie-like opening and kept in the shelter of the trees along the edge, the driver going slowly and Wilson looking carefully out across the prairie and all along its far side. He stopped the car and studied the opening with his field glasses. Then he motioned to the driver to go on and the car moved slowly along, the driver avoiding warthog holes and driving around the mud castles[①] ants had built. Then, looking across the opening, Wilson suddenly turned and said,

"By God, there they are."

And looking where he pointed, while the car jumped forward and Wilson spoke in rapid Swahili to the driver, Macomber saw three huge, black animals looking almost cylindrical in their long heaviness, like big black tank cars, moving at a gallop across the far edge of the open prairie. They moved at a stiff-necked, stiff bodied gallop and he could see the upswept wide black horns on their heads as they galloped heads out; the heads not moving.

"They're three old bulls," Wilson said. "We'll cut them off before they get to the swamp."

The car was going a wild forty-five miles an hour across the open and as Macomber watched, the buffalo got bigger and bigger until he could see the gray, hairless, scabby look of one huge bull and how his neck was a part of his shoulders and the shiny black of his horns as he galloped a little behind the others that were strung out in

① mud castles：白蚂蚁营造的蚂蚁城堡王国，多呈圆锥状，一般四五米高，甚至可高达十多米。

道。昨天夜里，她说话不多。就这点来说，看到她倒也还算愉快。

汽车爬上一个缓坡，继续穿越树丛；穿出树丛后，开到一块长着野草的、几乎像大草原一样的开阔地；接着沿着这块草地的边缘，在树荫下开着。司机缓缓地行进，威尔逊朝草原及其远远的另一端仔细地把望。他让车停下来，用双筒望远镜观察这片开阔地。接着他示意司机继续走；司机避开一个个疣猪洞，绕过一座座蚁山，汽车慢吞吞地前行。忽然，观察着原野的威尔逊转过身来，说道：

“天哪，他们在那儿呢！”

汽车向前一蹿，威尔逊用斯瓦希里语急促地说着什么；麦康伯朝他指的方向望去，看到三头黑色的庞然大物，其圆柱般的又长又壮的身体看起来像是黑黑的大油槽车：他们正在开阔草地远远的另一端飞奔。他们飞奔时，脖子直挺挺的，身体直挺挺的；当他们伸直了脑袋飞奔的时候，他看得到他们头顶向上戳着的展得很宽的黑色犄角；他们的头纹丝不动。

“这是三头老公牛，”威尔逊说，“我们要在他们到达沼泽前截断他们。”

汽车以四十五英里的时速疯也似的穿过开阔地；麦康伯注视着，野牛显得越来越巨大：他看到一头庞大的公牛的躯体，那公牛身上灰不拉叽、牛毛全无、结满疮痂；看到他的脖子竟然和他的肩部连成一片，犄角黑得发亮。这头牛飞奔着，稍稍落在另外两头的后面。这另外两头正并列向前猛冲。接着，随着汽车一晃，好像猛然跃过了一截路似的，他们逼近了！他看到：这头向前猛冲的公牛庞大无比，身上尚有几根稀稀拉拉的毛，落满灰

that steady plunging gait; and then, the car swaying as though it had just jumped a road, they drew up close and he could see the plunging hugeness of the bull, and the dust in his sparsely haired hide, the wide boss of horn and his outstretched, wide-nostrilled muzzle, and he was raising his rifle when Wilson shouted, "Not from the car, you fool！" and he had no fear, only hatred of Wilson, while the brakes clamped on and the car skidded, plowing sideways to an almost stop and Wilson was out on one side and he on the other, stumbling as his feet hit the still speeding — by of the earth, and then he was shooting at the bull as he moved away, hearing the bullets whunk into him, emptying his rifle at him as he moved steadily away, finally remembering to get his shots forward into the shoulder, and as he fumbled to re-load, he saw the bull was down. Down on his knees, his big head tossing, and seeing the other two still galloping he shot at the leader and hit him. He shot again and missed and he heard the *carawonging* roar as Wilson shot and saw the leading bull slide forward onto his nose.

"Get that other," Wilson said. "Now you're shooting！"

But the other bull was moving steadily at the same gallop and he missed, throwing a spout of dirt, and Wilson missed and the dust rose in a cloud and Wilson shouted, "Come on. He's too far！" and grabbed his arm and they were in the car again, Macomber and Wilson hanging on the sides and rocketing swayingly over the uneven ground, drawing up on the steady, plunging, heavy-necked, straight-moving gallop of the bull.

They were behind him and Macomber was filling his rifle, dropping shells onto the ground, jamming it, clearing the jam, then

土，宽宽的犄角向上翘起，长着大大的鼻孔的春嘴前凸。麦康伯举起了来复枪，威尔逊立马吼道:"别在车上，你这蠢货！"可他内心毫无惧色，只有对威尔逊的怨恨。这时刹车减速，车子一滑，向旁一甩，差点就戛然而停；威尔逊出来了，在车的一侧，他在另一侧。当他双脚触地时，地面似乎仍在飞速闪动，他不禁打了个趔趄。紧接着，他向正跑开去的野牛开枪了，听到子弹"噗噗"地打进他的身体；当他打光了来复枪里的子弹，公牛还在稳步地跑着；他最后总算想起来，子弹是要向前射到牛的肩部的！他抖抖索索地重新上子弹的时候，看到公牛倒了下去，前腿双膝着地，大大的脑袋摆来摆去；他看到另外两头还在飞奔，就射向领头的那头，打中了他。他再一次开枪，没打中；接着就听到"卡啦轰"的巨响，是威尔逊在开枪；接下来，他看到领头的公牛向前滑倒，鼻子触地。

"搞定剩下的那头！"威尔逊说，"嗨，你射得不错！"

但是另一头公牛不慌不忙地稳步飞奔着，他打偏了，掀起一撮灰尘；接着威尔逊打偏了，灰尘如云状升起。威尔逊高声叫道："快！他隔得太远了！"接着抓住他的胳膊，他们又回到汽车上了。麦康伯和威尔逊挂在汽车边上，跌跌撞撞地在崎岖的路面飞驰，一步步逼近了那头有着粗壮的脖子正径直稳步向前飞奔着的野牛。

他们就在他后面了！麦康伯把弹壳卸到地上，枪卡住了，他排除了故障，给来复枪装上子弹。接下来他们几乎撞到公牛了，

they were almost up with the bull when Wilson yelled "Stop," and the car skidded so that it almost swung over and Macomber fell forward onto his feet, slammed his bolt forward and fired as far forward as he could aim into the galloping, rounded black back, aimed and shot again, then again, then again, and the bullets, all of them hitting, had no effect on the buffalo that he could see. Then Wilson shot, the roar deafening him, and he could see the bull stagger. Macomber shot again, aiming carefully, and down he came, onto his knees.

"All right," Wilson said. "Nice work. That's the three."

Macomber felt a drunken elation.

"How many times did you shoot?" he asked.

"Just three," Wilson said. "You killed the first bull. The biggest one. I helped you finish the other two. Afraid they might have got into cover. You had them killed. I was just mopping up a little. You shot damn well."

"Let's go to the car," said Macomber. "I want a drink."

"Got to finish off that buff first," Wilson told him. The buffalo was on his knees and he jerked his head furiously and bellowed in pig-eyed, roaring rage as they came toward him.

"Watch he doesn't get up," Wilson said. Then, "Get a little broadside and take him in the neck just behind the ear."

Macomber aimed carefully at the center of the huge, jerking, rage-driven neck and shot. At the shot the head dropped forward.

"That does it," said Wilson. "Got the spine. They're a hell of a looking thing, aren't they?"

威尔逊叫道："停！"汽车猛一刹车，几乎翻了个跟头。麦康伯落到地上，站稳脚跟，"啪"的一推枪栓，最大限度地向前瞄准那飞奔着的浑圆的、黑黑的牛背，开火！瞄准！再开火！再来一次！再来一次！子弹颗颗都打中了！可在野牛身上却看不到任何成效。然后，威尔逊开枪了，他听到震耳欲聋的巨响，看到野牛在踉跄。麦康伯仔细瞄准，又开了一枪。他倒了下去，屈膝于地。

"很好！"威尔逊说，"干得漂亮。这是第三头了。"

麦康伯感觉得意扬扬，如痴如醉。

"你开了几枪？"他问道。

"就三枪，"威尔逊说，"你撂倒了第一头公牛，最大的那头。我帮你了结了另外两头[1]。是担心他们会找地方躲起来。是你搞定他们的，我只不过是收了下尾而已。你枪打得相当不错。"

"我们到汽车那儿去吧，"麦康伯说，"我要喝口酒。"

"得先把那头公牛结果了，"威尔逊告诉他。野牛屈膝在地，眼睛又小又凹；当他们走近他时，他狂怒地甩动脑袋，咆哮如雷。

"留神，小心他爬起来了，"威尔逊说道。接着又说："稍稍往旁边一点，打他耳朵后面的脖子。"

麦康伯仔细地瞄准那粗大的、因狂怒而抽搐着的脖子，开了一枪。随着一声枪响，脑袋向前耷拉下去。

"打得好，"威尔逊说，"打中了椎骨。他们样子很可观，对吧？"

① 威尔逊屡次清楚地说明自己开了几枪，打了几头猎物，他的目的是想告诉他的雇主他的钱没有白拿。

"Let's get the drink," said Macomber. In his life he had never felt so good.

In the car Macomber's wife sat very white faced. "You were marvelous, darling," she said to Macomber. "What a ride."

"Was it rough?" Wilson asked.

"It was frightful. I've never been more frightened in my life."

"Let's all have a drink," Macomber said.

"By all means," said Wilson. "Give it to the Memsahib." She drank the neat whisky from the flask and shuddered a little when she swallowed. She handed the flask to Macomber who handed it to Wilson.

"It was frightfully exciting," she said. "It's given me a dreadful headache. I didn't know you were allowed to shoot them from cars though."

"No one shot from cars," said Wilson coldly.

"I mean chase them from cars."

"Wouldn't ordinarily," Wilson said. "Seemed sporting enough to me though while we were doing it. Taking more chance driving that way across the plain full of holes and one thing and another than hunting on foot. Buffalo could have charged us each time we shot if he liked. Gave him every chance. Wouldn't mention it to anyone though. It's illegal if that's what you mean."

"It seemed very unfair to me," Margot said, "chasing those big helpless things in a motor car."

"Did it?" said Wilson.

"我们喝口酒吧,"麦康伯说道。他感觉有生以来还从来没像现在这样痛快过。

汽车里坐着麦康伯的妻子,脸色煞白。"你棒极了,亲爱的,"她对麦康伯说道,"车开成这个样子!"[1]

"很难受吧?"

"简直是恐怖啊。我有生以来还从来没受过这样的惊吓呢。"

"我们都来喝口酒,"麦康伯说。

"恭敬不如从命,"威尔逊说,"把它给尊夫人吧。"她喝着酒瓶里没勾兑过的威士忌,咽下去的时候,微微哆嗦了一下。她把酒瓶递给麦康伯,麦康伯又将它递给了威尔逊。

"这种刺激太恐怖了,"她说,"让我头痛得要命。我原来还不知道竟然可以允许你们从车上向他们开枪呢!"

"没人从车上开枪,"威尔逊冷冷地说。

"我是说开着车追他们。"

"权宜之计而已,"威尔逊说,"我们那么干对我来说是很光明正大的。与步行射猎比起来,要穿过那布满坑坑洼洼以及杂七杂八东西的原野,开车的机会就大多了。如果野牛乐意的话,我们每开一枪都给了他机会,他可以随时袭击我们。不过别跟人提起这事。正如你的意思一样,这样做是非法的。"

"我看这样做是非常不公平的,"玛戈说,"竟然在汽车里追猎那些大个儿手无寸铁的东西!"

"是吗?"威尔逊说。

---

① 玛格丽特一看到麦康伯今非昔比马上就对他使用上了献媚 (You were marvelous, darling) 和撒娇 (What a ride) 的伎俩。

"What would happen if they heard about it in Nairobi[1]?"

"I'd lose my license for one thing. Other unpleasantnesses," Wilson said, taking a drink from the flask. "I'd be out of business."

"Really?"

"Yes, really."

"Well," said Macomber, and he smiled for the first time all day. "Now she has something on you."

"You have such a pretty[2] way of putting things, Francis," Margot Macomber said. Wilson looked at them both. If a four-letter man marries a five-letter woman, he was thinking, what number of letters would their children be? What he said was, "We lost a gun-bearer. Did you notice it?"

"My God, no," Macomber said.

"Here he comes," Wilson said. "He's all right. He must have fallen off when we left the first bull."

Approaching them was the middle-aged gun-bearer, limping along in his knitted cap, khaki tunic, shorts and rubber sandals, gloomy-faced and disgusted looking. As he came up he called out to Wilson in Swahili and they all saw the change in the white hunter's face.

"What does he say?" asked Margot.

"He says the first bull got up and went into the bush," Wilson said with no expression in his voice.

"Oh," said Macomber blankly.

① Nairobi(内罗毕)是肯尼亚的首都。玛格丽特在这里说"What would happen if they heard about it in Nairobi?"是明知故问，有一点点威胁的意味。这就是为什么麦康伯说"Now she has something on you"的原因。

② 玛格丽特在这里用的"pretty"一词是说的反话(irony)。

"假如他们在内罗毕听到这事会如何反应？"

"一方面，我的执照会被吊销；还有诸多不愉快，"威尔逊说着，从酒瓶里灌下一口酒。"我也会没活揽了。"

"真的呀？"

"当然，是真的。"

"呵呵，"麦康伯说道，今天以来他第一次绽开笑容。"现在，你可有把柄落她手上咯！"

"你说话总是说得这么好听，弗朗西斯，"玛戈·麦康伯说。威尔逊瞧了瞧他俩。如果一个下流胚跟另一个更下流的女人结婚，他想到，他们的孩子们将会是几等下流呢？他开口说的则是："我们把一个扛枪的人弄丢了。你们注意到了吗？"

"天哪，没注意，"麦康伯说。

"他过来了，"威尔逊说，"他没事。我们离开那第一头牛的时候，他一定是摔下去了。"

向他们走近的是那个中年的扛枪的人：他戴着编织帽，穿着卡其短上衣、短裤及橡胶凉鞋；他脸色阴沉，样子难受，一瘸一拐地走过来。他一边走来，一边用斯瓦希里语向威尔逊叫喊着。他们看到，白人猎手的脸色变了。

"他说什么来着？"玛戈问。

"他说第一头公牛爬起来，进到灌木丛去了，"威尔逊不动声色地说。

"噢，"麦康伯木木地说。

"Then it's going to be just like the lion," said Margot, full of anticipation.

"It's not going to be a damned bit like the lion,"① Wilson told her. "Did you want another drink, Macomber?"

"Thanks, yes," Macomber said. He expected the feeling he had had about the lion to come back but it did not. For the first time in his life he really felt wholly without fear. Instead of fear he had a feeling of definite elation.

"We'll go and have a look at the second bull," Wilson said. "I'll tell the driver to put the car in the shade."

"What are you going to do?" asked Margaret Macomber.

"Take a look at the buff," Wilson said.

"I'll come."

"Come along."

The three of them walked over to where the second buffalo bulked blackly in the open, head forward on the grass, the massive horns swung wide.

"He's a very good head," Wilson said. "That's close to a fifty-inch spread."

Macomber was looking at him with delight.

"He's hateful looking," said Margot. "Can't we go into the shade?"

"Of course," Wilson said. "Look," he said to Macomber, and pointed. "See that patch of bush?"

"Yes."

---

① "It's not going to be a damned bit like the lion" 威尔逊说的这句话表面上是驳斥玛格丽特，实则是在给麦康伯打气。

"这回又像那头狮子一样啦,"玛戈望眼欲穿地说。

"跟狮子的事情一丁点儿也不像," 威尔逊告诉她,"再来口酒吗,麦康伯?"

"好的,谢谢,"麦康伯说。他原以为他对狮子的感觉会再回来,但是却没有发生。有生以来他第一次真真切切地体会不到任何恐惧。不但没有恐惧,相反,他是完完全全地兴致勃勃。

"我们去看看那第二头牛," 威尔逊说,"我会要司机把汽车开到阴凉地方去的。"

"你们干吗去?"玛格丽特·麦康伯问道。

"去瞧瞧牛,"威尔逊说。

"我也要去。"

"来吧。"

他们三人来到了第二头野牛身边。牛在开阔地上堆成黑黑的一大团,头朝前伸在草地上,坚固的犄角张得宽宽的。

"这头牛非常不错," 威尔逊说,"两只角中间最大距离有近五十英寸宽了。"

麦康伯望着他,面露喜色。

"他实在面目可憎,"玛戈说,"我们到树荫下去好吗?"

"当然好,"威尔逊说。"瞧,"他对麦康伯边说边指,"看到那片灌木了吗?"

"嗯。"

"That's where the first bull went in. The gun-bearer said when he fell off the bull was down. He was watching us helling along and the other two buff galloping. When he looked up there was the bull up and looking at him. Gun-bearer ran like hell and the bull went off slowly into that bush."

"Can we go in after him now?" asked Macomber eagerly.

Wilson looked at him[①] appraisingly. Damned if this isn't a strange one, he thought. Yesterday he's scared sick and today he's a ruddy fire eater.

"No, we'll give him a while."

"Let's please go into the shade," Margot said. Her face was white and she looked ill.

They made their way to the car where it stood under a single, wide-spreading tree and all climbed in.

"Chances are he's dead in there," Wilson remarked. "After a little we'll have a look."

Macomber felt a wild unreasonable happiness that he had never known before.

"By God, that was a chase," he said. "I've never felt any such feeling. Wasn't it marvelous, Margot?"

"I hated it."

"Why?"

"I hated it," she said bitterly. "I loathed it."

"You know I don't think I'd ever be afraid of anything again," Macomber said to Wilson. "Something happened in me after we

① him：海明威此处用"him"来指代野牛，是将野牛拟人化，以此说明麦康伯与公牛之间的较量是强者的对决。

"第一头牛就是进到那里面去了。扛枪的说他掉下车的时候公牛还倒在地上。他看到我们开着车在狂跑,另外两头牛在飞奔。他一抬眼,却看到公牛爬起来了,在盯着他。扛枪的人没命地跑开了,野牛则缓缓地进了灌木丛。"

"我们现在就进去找他?"麦康伯迫不及待地问。

威尔逊打量着他。这家伙如果不是个怪物,那才奇怪了呢!他想到。昨天他还吓得屁滚尿流,今天他却连老虎屁股都想摸。

"别。我们让他再待会。"

"求你们啦,到树荫下去吧,"玛戈说。她面色苍白,神情憔悴。

他们走到停在一棵孤零零的、枝繁叶茂的树下的汽车旁,全都爬进了车里。

"极有可能他会死在那儿,"威尔逊发话道,"待会儿我们去瞧瞧。"

麦康伯体验到一股他从未有过的难以理喻的狂喜。

"我说啊,这场追猎太精彩了,"他说,"我还从来没有过这样的感觉呢!是不是很精彩,玛戈?"

"我根本就不喜欢。"

"为什么?"

"不喜欢就是不喜欢,"她愤愤地说,"我觉得非常讨厌。"

"你瞧,我觉得从此以后我不会再畏首畏尾了,"麦康伯对威尔逊说,"那会儿我们刚刚看到牛,开始追他的时候,我就感到某种变化。就像大坝决堤一样。兴奋得无可遏制。"

first saw the buff and started after him. Like a dam bursting. It was pure excitement."

"Cleans out your liver," said Wilson. "Damn funny things happen to people."

Macomber's face was shining. "You know something did happen to me," he said. "I feel absolutely different."

His wife said nothing and eyed him strangely. She was sitting far back in the seat and Macomber was sitting forward talking to Wilson Who turned sideways talking over the back of the front seat.

"You know, I'd like to try another lion," Macomber said. "I'm really not afraid of them now. After all, what can they do to you?"

"That's it," said Wilson. "Worst one can do is kill you. How does it go? Shakespeare. Damned good. See if I can remember. Oh, damned good. Used to quote it to myself at one time. Let's see. 'By my troth, I care not; a man can die but once; we owe God a death and let it go which way it will, he that dies this year is quit for the next.'① Damned fine, eh?"

He was very embarrassed, having brought out this thing he had lived by, but he had seen men come of age before and it always moved him. It was not a matter of their twenty-first birthday.

It had taken a strange chance of hunting, a sudden precipitation into action without opportunity for worrying beforehand, to bring this about with Macomber, but regardless of how it had happened it had most certainly happened. Look at the beggar now, Wilson thought. It's that some of them stay little boys so long, Wilson

① 见《亨利四世》第二部第三幕第二场。

"换了你的胆啦,"威尔逊说,"什么奇妙的变化都有可能发生的。"

麦康伯的脸神采奕奕。"你瞧,我真的变了,"他说,"我觉得我截然不同了。"

他妻子一言不发,神情古怪地盯着他看。她紧靠着后座的椅背;麦康伯坐着,身体前倾,跟威尔逊说着话;威尔逊侧着身子,越过前排座位的椅背说着话。

"你知道吧,我想再试一头狮子,"麦康伯说,"现在我真的不会再怕他们了。说到底,他们又能把你怎么样呢?"

"说得对,"威尔逊说,"至多不过是要了你的命罢了。那话是怎么说的?莎士比亚的话。相当的好。不晓得我还能不能背出来。哦,相当的好。有那么一阵子我老对自己引用这几句呢。我背背看。'凭良心说,我倒不在乎。死了第一次就甭死第二次。我们谁都欠着上帝一条命。顺其自然,今年死了明年就不用再死了。'妙极了,嗯哼?"

说出了他赖以支撑生命的信仰,他不禁有点难为情。但他以前也曾看到过男子的成人礼,这总是叫他感动。成人礼并不是指他们的21岁生日。

这次狩猎中一次奇特的际遇,一次根本无暇事先担忧就贸然采取的仓促行动,铸就了麦康伯的成人礼。不管他是如何发生的,他却发生得令人毋庸置疑。现在再看看这个家伙吧,威尔逊想道。原因在于他们中有些人的奶腥期太长了,威尔逊想。

thought. Sometimes all their lives. Their figures stay boyish when they're fifty. The great American boymen. Damned strange people. But he liked this Macomber now. Damned strange fellow. Probably meant the end of cuckoldry too. Well, that would be a damned good thing. Damned good thing. Beggar had probably been afraid all his life. Don't know what started it. But over now. Hadn't had time to be afraid with the buff. That and being angry too. Motor car too. Motor cars made it familiar. Be a damn fire eater now. He'd seen it in the war work the same way. More of a change than any loss of virginity. Fear gone like an operation. Something else grew in its place. Main thing a man had. Made him into a man. Women knew it too. No bloody fear.

From the far corner of the seat Margaret Macomber looked at the two of them. There was no change in Wilson. She saw Wilson as she had seen him the day before when she had first realized what his great talent was. But she saw the change in Francis Macomber now.

"Do you have that feeling of happiness about what's going to happen?" Macomber asked, still exploring his new wealth.

"You're not supposed to mention it," Wilson said, looking in the other's face. "Much more fashionable to say you're scared. Mind you, you'll be scared too, plenty of times."

"But you *have* a feeling of happiness about action to come?"

"Yes," said Wilson. "There's that. Doesn't do to talk too much about all this. Talk the whole thing away. No pleasure in anything if you mouth it up too much."

"You're both talking rot," said Margot. "Just because you've chased some helpless animals in a motor car you talk like heroes."

有时甚至持续一辈子。即便他们已到了知天命的年纪，他们的表现仍旧是孩子气。了不起的美国老顽童哦。这些人太奇怪了。可是，他喜欢现在的麦康伯。这家伙真是个怪家伙。也许也意味着他老婆红杏出墙的终结吧。嗯，那样也不错。也不错。这家伙也许一辈子都在担惊受怕。不晓得是什么引起的。但现在结束了。无暇考虑是否要害怕牛。还有，是因为正在气头上。还有汽车。汽车使人大胆放开手脚。这会儿他可是个连老虎屁股都敢摸的人了。在战争作品中，他看到过类似的情形。这种变化比初夜的变化都来得大。恐惧就像被手术切割了一样。在原地长出了新的东西。长出了男人主要的东西，使他成为男子汉。女人对此也心知肚明。即不再有莫名的恐惧。

紧贴在座位的一角，玛格丽特·麦康伯打量着他俩。威尔逊一如既往。她看到的威尔逊还是她昨天看到的威尔逊——那时她第一次发现他伟大的天赋所在。但她现在看到弗朗西斯·麦康伯身上的变化了。

“对于即将发生的事情，你是否也感到乐不可支？”麦康伯问道。他还在探索着他的新财富呢。

“你可不要高兴得太早，”威尔逊说着，盯着另一个的脸，“用流行的话来说，你是感到心惊肉跳呢。留神，你还会心惊肉跳的。机会可多的是。”

“你对即将采取的行动到底有没有一种乐不可支的感觉呢？”

“有，”威尔逊说，“就是那种感觉。对此喋喋不休地唠叨可有点煞风景。把什么感觉都唠叨没了。什么事情如果你提个没完就都了无生趣了。”

“你俩说话有点不知天高地厚呢，”玛戈说，“只不过是在汽车里追猎了几头手无寸铁的畜生，你们说话就像是大英雄似的。”

"Sorry," said Wilson. "I have been gassing too much." She's worried about it already, he thought.

"If you don't know what we're talking about why not keep out of it?" Macomber asked his wife.

"You've gotten awfully brave, awfully suddenly," his wife said contemptuously, but her contempt was not secure. She was very afraid of something.

Macomber laughed, a very natural hearty laugh. "You know I *have*," he said. "I really have."

"Isn't it sort of late?" Margot said bitterly. Because she had done the best she could for many years back and the way they were together now was no one person's fault.

"Not for me," said Macomber.

Margot said nothing but sat back in the corner of the seat.

"Do you think we've given him time enough?" Macomber asked Wilson cheerfully.

"We might have a look," Wilson said. "Have you any solids left?"

"The gun-bearer has some."

Wilson called in Swahili and the older gun-bearer, who was skinning out one of the heads, straightened up, pulled a box of solids out of his pocket and brought them over to Macomber, who filled his magazine and put the remaining shells in his pocket.

"You might as well shoot the Springfield," Wilson said. "You're used to it. We'll leave the Mannlicher[①] in the car with the

① Mannlicher：这里指斐迪南·曼利切(1848 年生于德国 1904 年逝于奥地利）设计的 6.5 M-S 来复枪。

"不好意思啊,"威尔逊说,"我牛吹得太多了。"她已经在为此担心了,他想。

"我们说的话你如果一懂不懂,你干吗要来搅和?"麦康伯质问他的妻子。

"你倒是威风起来了,突然威风起来了,"他妻子不屑地说道。但这种不屑里却有着忐忑。她很为什么事情而惴惴不安。

麦康伯放声一笑,是非常自然地发自内心的一笑。"你看得出来我飙起来了,"他说。"我真的飙起来了。"

"是不是有点太迟了?"玛戈挖苦道。在过去的很多年,她可算是仁至义尽了。他们目前相处的格局可不能说是哪一个人单方面的错。

"对我可不迟,"麦康伯说。

玛戈一言不发,却往座位的角落靠紧。

"你觉得我们给他的时间是否够长了?"麦康伯跃跃欲试地问威尔逊。

"我们可以去瞧瞧,"威尔逊说,"你还剩有实心弹吗?"

"扛枪的人有几颗。"

威尔逊用斯瓦希里语喊起来;那个年长些的扛枪人这会儿正剥牛皮呢。他站起身,从口袋里掏出一盒实心弹,拿过来递给麦康伯。麦康伯给枪里的弹盒上满子弹,然后把剩下的子弹装进口袋。

"你还是用春田枪吧,"威尔逊说,"你也用习惯了。我们把曼利切留给汽车里的尊夫人。给你扛枪的人可以给你扛大枪。

Memsahib. Your gun-bearer can carry your heavy gun. I've this damned cannon. Now let me tell you about them." He had saved this until the last because he did not want to worry Macomber. "When a buff ② comes he comes with his head high and thrust straight out. The boss of the horns covers any sort of a brain shot. The only shot is straight into the nose. The only other shot is into his chest or, if you're to one side, into the neck or the shoulders. After they've been hit once they take a hell of a lot of killing. Don't try anything fancy. Take the easiest shot there is. They've finished skinning out that head now. Should we get started?"

He called to the gun-bearers, Who came up wiping their hands, and the older one got into the back.

"I'll only take Kongoni," Wilson said. "The other can watch to keep the birds away."

As the car moved slowly across the open space toward the island of brushy trees that ran in a tongue of foliage along a dry water course that cut the open swale, Macomber felt his heart pounding and his mouth was dry again, but it was excitement, not fear.

"Here's where he went in," Wilson said. Then to the gun-bearer in Swahili, "Take the blood spoor."

The car was parallel to the patch of bush. Macomber, Wilson and the gun-bearer got down. Macomber, looking back, saw his wife, with the rifle by her side, looking at him. He waved to her and she did not wave back.

The brush was very thick ahead and the ground was dry. The

② buff: 非洲野牛是比非洲狮子强壮高大得多的动物。狩猎野牛比狩猎狮子挑战性更大。

我拿这支火铳得了。现在我来跟你谈谈他们，”他把话一直憋到现在，因为他不想让麦康伯担忧。“牛冲过来时，他会高举着头，径直往前戳。他的翘起的两只犄角使得任何子弹都打不进他的脑袋。唯一能搞定他的是直接打进他的鼻子。另外一个能搞定他的是打中他的心脏，或者，如果你是在他侧面的话，则打进脖子或肩膀。他们中一次弹后，可就会大开杀戒了。千万别异想天开。哪儿容易就朝哪儿打。现在他们已经剥完那张牛皮了。我们可出发了吗？”

他朝扛枪的人喊话。他们一边擦手一边走过来。年长些的爬上了车尾。

“我只带康戈佬去，”威尔逊说，“还有一个不妨守着赶赶鸟。”

汽车慢慢地穿过开阔地带，驶向那片有着灌木林的岛状地域。这片长满簇叶的狭长地域沿着一条穿过洼地的干枯河道伸展开去。麦康伯听到自己的心在咚咚跳，嘴里又口干舌燥了。不过这是出于兴奋，而不是害怕。

“他就是从这里进去的，”威尔逊说道。然后用斯瓦希里语对扛枪的人说：“追踪血迹。”

汽车这会儿正对着灌木林。麦康伯、威尔逊和扛枪人下车了。麦康伯回头望去，看到他的妻子。她身边搁着来复枪，正朝他看呢。他朝她挥挥手，她没有挥手作答。

往前的灌木林变得稠密起来，地面干烘烘的。此刻，中年扛枪人汗流浃背，威尔逊把帽子拉下来遮在眼睑上。他的红脖子

middle-aged gun-bearer was sweating heavily and Wilson had his hat down over his eyes and his red neck showed just ahead of Macomber. Suddenly the gunbearer said something in Swahili to Wilson and ran forward.

"He's dead in there," Wilson said. "Good work," and he turned to grip Macomber's hand and as they shook hands, grinning at each other, the gun-bearer shouted wildly and they saw him coming out of the bush sideways, fast as a crab, and the bull coming, nose out, mouth tight closed, blood dripping, massive head straight out, coming in a charge, his little pig eyes bloodshot as he looked at them. Wilson, who was ahead was kneeling shooting, and Macomber, as he fired, unhearing his shot in the roaring of Wilson's gun, saw fragments like slate burst from the huge boss of the horns, and the head jerked, he shot again at the wide nostrils and saw the horns jolt again and fragments fly, and he did not see Wilson now and, aiming carefully, shot again with the buffalo's huge bulk almost on him and his rifle almost level with the on-coming head, nose out, and he could see the little wicked eyes and the head started to lower and he felt a sudden white-hot, blinding flash explode inside his head and that was all he ever felt.

Wilson had ducked to one side to get in a shoulder shot. Macomber had stood solid and shot for the nose, shooting a touch high each time and hitting the heavy horns, splintering and chipping them like hitting a slate roof, and Mrs. Macomber, in the car, had shot at the buffalo with the 6.5 Mannlicher as it seemed about to gore Macomber and had hit her husband about two inches

就在麦康伯眼前晃。突然，扛枪人用斯瓦希里语对威尔逊说了些什么，接着向前跑去。

“他死在那里了，”威尔逊说，“干得不错。”接着转过身来拉住了麦康伯的手。正当他们握着手相视咧嘴而笑的时候，扛枪的人狂喊起来。他们看到他侧着身子跑出灌木丛，像螃蟹一样飞快地横着跑。公牛过来了。他鼻子突出，嘴巴紧闭，鲜血直滴，巨大的脑袋笔直向前，猛袭过来；他看着他们，又小又凹的眼睛红得要喷血。前面的威尔逊屈膝开枪。麦康伯开枪了，却没听到自己的枪响，威尔逊枪的巨响盖住了他的枪响。他看到一块块碎片从翘起的大犄角上掉了下来；牛脑袋猛冲过来，他朝阔大的鼻孔又开了一枪。他看到犄角又一震，碎片飞散开来。这时他看不到威尔逊了。他仔细瞄准，再次开枪。此刻野牛庞大的身躯几乎快压到他身上来了，他的来复枪和鼻子突出的撞过来的牛头差点撞个正着。他看到了小小的怨毒的眼睛，看到牛头在开始下垂。他感到有道突如其来的、白热的、让人睁不开眼睛的亮光在自己脑子里爆裂开来。紧接着就什么感觉都没有了。

那一刻，威尔逊正在一侧弯着身子向牛的肩部开枪；麦康伯则稳稳地站立着朝牛鼻子开枪，每次都有点偏高，射到坚实的犄角上，像打中了石板屋顶似的，削下纷纷碎片。麦康伯太太待在汽车上，当野牛似乎快要用犄角抵伤麦康伯的时候，她用6.5曼利切射向野牛，却射中了她的丈夫，打在他的颅底骨上面大约两寸高、稍微偏向一侧的地方。

up and a little to one side of the base of his skull.

Francis Macomber lay now, face down, not two yards from where the buffalo lay on his side and his wife knelt over him with Wilson beside her.

"I wouldn't turn him over," Wilson said.

The woman was crying hysterically.

"I'd get back in the car," Wilson said. "Where's the rifle?"

She shook her head, her face contorted. The gun-bearer picked up the rifle.

"Leave it as it is," said Wilson. Then, "Go get Abdulla so that he may witness the manner of the accident."

He knelt down, took a handkerchief from his pocket, and spread it over Francis Macomber's crew-cropped head where it lay. The blood sank into the dry, loose earth.

Wilson stood up and saw the buffalo on his side, his legs out, his thinly-haired belly crawling with ticks. "Hell of a good bull," his brain registered automatically. "A good fifty inches, or better. Better." He called to the driver and told him to spread a blanket over the body and stay by it. Then he walked over to the motor car where the woman sat crying in the corner.

"That was a pretty thing to do," he said in a toneless voice. "He *would* have left you too."

"Stop it," she said.

"Of course it's an accident," he said. "I know that."

"Stop it," she said.

现在，弗朗西斯·麦康伯倒下了，脸朝下[1]，距离倒在他身边的野牛还不到两码远。他的妻子屈膝俯在他身上，威尔逊站在她的旁边。

“我不会将他翻过身来的，”威尔逊说。

这女人歇斯底里地哭喊着。

“我要回到汽车上去了，”威尔逊说，“来复枪在哪？”

她摇摇头，脸都走了样。扛枪人捡起来复枪。

“不要动现场，”威尔逊说道。接着又说：“去把阿卜杜拉叫来，好让他为怎么出事的作证。”

他屈下膝，从口袋里掏出一块手帕，将之覆盖到弗朗西斯·麦康伯剪着水手式头发的后脑勺上。鲜血渗进了干燥、松软的地面。

威尔逊站起身，看着在他身边的野牛：野牛四肢叉开，肚子上有着几根稀稀疏疏的毛，爬满了扁虱。“一头非常不错的公牛，”他脑子里不由自主地估量起来，“两角之间最大距离足足有五十英寸。也许还出点头。还出点头。”他喊来司机，要他用毯子盖住尸体，守在尸体旁边。接着他走到汽车那里。这个女人正坐在角落里哭呢。

“这么干实在是太漂亮了，”他用平板的声音说，“他迟早也会离开你的。”

“别说了，”她说。

“当然啦，这是场意外，”他说，“我明白的。”

“别说了，”她说。

① 狩猎者狩猎身亡时，若脸朝下，则表明死时并不是被猎物迎面所伤。这里表明麦康伯并不是被野牛夺去了生命。

"Don't worry," he said. "There will be a certain amount of unpleasantness but I will have some photographs taken that will be very useful at the inquest. There's the testimony of the gun-bearers and the driver too. You're perfectly all right."

"Stop it," she said.

"There's a hell of a lot to be done," he said. "And I'll have to send a truck off to the lake to wireless for a plane to take the three of us into Nairobi. Why didn't you poison him? That's what they do in England."

"Stop it. Stop it. Stop it," the woman cried.

Wilson looked at her with his flat blue eyes.

"I'm through now," he said. "I was a little angry. I'd begun to like your husband."

"Oh, please stop it," she said. "Please, please stop it."

"That's better," Wilson said. "Please is much better. Now I'll stop."

“不用担心，”他说。“虽说会有不少的不愉快，但我会让人照些相的。这些相片在审讯时会非常有用的。也还有两个扛枪的人和司机的证词呢。你一点事都不会有的。”

“别说了，”她说。

“接下来要做的事情太多了，”他说，“我必须派辆卡车到湖边去发电报，要架飞机来，好把我们三个人带到内罗毕去。你干吗不干脆毒死他呢？在英国这种做法可是很风行啊。”

“别说了，别说了，别说了，”这女人哭喊道。

威尔逊看着她，蓝眼睛里看不出任何神情。

“现在，我送佛送到西了，”他说，“刚才我有点生气。原来我已经开始喜欢你的丈夫了。”

“请你别说了，”她说，“拜托了，请你别说了。”

“这还像话，”威尔逊说，“请字听起来像话多了。现在，我不说了。”